REASON AND
RELIGION

REASON AND RELIGION

EDITED BY

STUART C. BROWN

Cornell University Press

ITHACA AND LONDON

Copyright © 1977 by The Royal Institute of Philosophy

All rights reserved. Except for brief quotations in a review, this book, or parts thereof, must not be reproduced in any form without permission in writing from the publisher. For information address Cornell University Press, 124 Roberts Place, Ithaca, New York 14850.

First published 1977 by Cornell University Press.
Published in the United Kingdom by Cornell University Press Ltd., 2–4 Brook Street, London W1Y 1AA.

First printing, Cornell Paperbacks, 1977

International Standard Book Number (cloth) 0-8014-1025-8
International Standard Book Number (paperback) 0-8014-9166-5
Library of Congress Catalog Card Number 77-3115
Printed in the United States of America by Vail-Ballou Press, Inc.
Librarians: Library of Congress cataloging information appears on the last page of the book.

Contents

Preface

These five symposia originated at a conference sponsored by the Royal Institute of Philosophy and held at the University of Lancaster in 1975. Most of the papers published here are substantially the same as those presented on that occasion. In some cases the authors have revised their contributions in the light of discussion. In other cases a postscript has been added by way of response to the comments of others. With one exception the remarks made by the chairmen are also included. As Peter Winch's paper contained remarks critical of a position adopted by Michael Durrant, it seemed right to vary the pattern in the case of the symposium on "Meaning and Religious Language". Accordingly Durrant has contributed a reply on his own account. Renford Bambrough, whose original remarks as chairman of that symposium are here supplanted by my own contribution, has written the Introduction to the volume. I am grateful to the authors for making these contributions. I should also like to record my gratitude to Georgina Coleman for her help in preparing the typescript.

S.C.B.

Milton Keynes, Buckinghamshire

Contributors

RENFORD BAMBROUGH is a Fellow of St. John's College, Cambridge.

STUART C. BROWN is Senior Lecturer in Philosophy at The Open University.

MICHAEL DURRANT is Senior Lecturer in Philosophy at University College, Cardiff.

RONALD HEPBURN is Professor of Moral Philosophy at the University of Edinburgh.

JOHN HICK is H. G. Wood Professor of Theology at the University of Birmingham.

HYWEL LEWIS is Professor of the History and Philosophy of Religion at the University of London.

COLIN LYAS is Lecturer in Philosophy at the University of Lancaster.

NORMAN MALCOLM is Susan Linn Sage Professor of Philosophy at Cornell University.

HUGO MEYNELL is Lecturer in Philosophy and Theology at the University of Leeds.

BASIL MITCHELL is Nolloth Professor of the Philosophy of the Christian Religion at the University of Oxford.

D. Z. PHILLIPS is Professor of Philosophy at University College, Swansea.

SYDNEY SHOEMAKER is Professor of Philosophy at Cornell University.

HARRY V. STOPES-ROE is Senior Lecturer in Science Studies at the University of Birmingham.

RICHARD SWINBURNE is Professor of Philosophy at the University of Keele.

9

GODFREY VESEY is Professor of Philosophy at The Open University.

PETER WINCH is Professor of Philosophy at the University of London.

REASON AND
RELIGION

Introduction

RENFORD BAMBROUGH

When Plato maintains in the *Republic* that the traditional Greek stories about the gods are not fit to be told to children or to be believed by grown-up people, his argument against the stories is *logical*. The beings described by Homer cannot be divine, since they are represented as having attributes that are fatal to such a description, or as lacking attributes that are necessary for divinity. A god could not be deceitful, or licentious, or vengeful, or quarrelsome.

Plato is here contributing to what Wittgenstein would have called a *grammatical* inquiry, to 'theology as grammar' in the sense in which 'grammar tells us what kind of object a thing is'. Such an inquiry naturally has a bearing on whether there are any objects of the kind that it helps to characterize, but it does not directly tell us whether or not there are any such objects. It tells us only indirectly, and with the aid of additional premises about whether there are any beings with the properties that would, according to the 'grammatical' account offered, deserve to be called, e.g., 'divine'.

In a similar manner, geometry contributes to our understanding of the 'grammar' of triangles, squares and circles, points, lines and planes. It does not tell us whether there *are* any triangles, but that if there are any triangles they will satisfy certain descriptions, and that if anything satisfies certain descriptions it will be a triangle.

In his paper in this collection Peter Winch makes this parallel between gods and triangles, and does so in connection with Wittgenstein's understanding of grammar. I take this parallel as my starting point for this introduction not only because my

13

own contribution to the Lancaster conference was in that same symposium, but also and chiefly because it raises in an acute form some central issues in philosophical theology which preoccupy most of the essayists in this volume, and hence make the volume representative of current controversies in the field. Again and again in these essays, and in the discussions that they provoked, there are disagreements about whether and in what sense the theologian or the religious believer is talking about *how things are*, about what *exists*, about the world or the universe or reality.

The topics of the symposia cover a wide range: Hugo Meynell and Harry Stopes-Roe discuss the intelligibility of the universe; Norman Malcolm and Colin Lyas speak of the grounds or groundlessness of religious belief; Peter Winch and Stuart Brown, like many recent thinkers, are concerned primarily with meaning rather than with truth or existence; D. Z. Phillips and Richard Swinburne treat the problem of evil; and Hywel Lewis and Sydney Shoemaker discuss the related notions of personal identity and immortality. But across this range there goes the main division between those who might be called the grammarians and those who still think of theology and religion as being concerned decisively, though not only, with the world or the universe or reality or how things are.

In my remarks as chairman of the symposium between Winch and Brown I made clear that I was of the latter party, and I cannot and do not wish to hide that allegiance. This disqualifies me from writing the judicious on-the-one-hand/on-the-other-hand type of introduction that some collections need and are given, but it leaves open to me an alternative and I think serviceable mode of introduction in which the issues are both separated out and related together. This may be done even by a partisan, especially if he is well watched by partisans.

Winch spoke at Lancaster of 'the standard conception' which he wished to undermine. I remain sufficiently attached to this conception to feel that, as Brown hints in his paper, Winch and Phillips and Malcolm owe us further and better particulars if we are not to speak of them in the same breath as of Matthew Arnold, who openly renounces belief in a God who is author and governor and sustainer of the world, or even as Richard Braithwaite, who treats all references to God as 'stories' whose only relevance to religion is that they serve as psychological stimuli to the formation and implementation of the resolutions or policies that are the essence of religion.

Phillips and Winch are not so clear. They continue to use the traditional language of religion, and to speak of it as expressing religious *beliefs*, religious *convictions*. Yet they reject both the idea that such beliefs and convictions are about the nature of this world and the idea that they are about the nature of another world. They do not seem to me to have made plain what they do think such beliefs are about.

Winch's attempt to answer this question by describing the primitive beginnings of a religious attitude and practice is soon involved in the use of the notions of *worship, reverence, devotion,* etc. As Brown points out (Chapter 12), these are all attitudes that require *objects*. Do they require merely 'grammatical' objects—internal accusatives—or is it envisaged that these emotions are directed at something external to and independent of human beings? That it is difficult to explain what these objects are or might be is true but not, at least for a philosopher, a justification for not making the attempt. The burden is all the more pressing on a *Christian* philosopher. Winch properly reminds us that there are religions, such as Buddhism, whose language involves no reference to gods. Christianity is not one of them. And there are further and equally central points that need to be remembered before we try to accommodate the God of Isaac and of Jesus and of Saint John the Evangelist and of Saint Paul within the limits of a Wittgensteinian grammar. Christianity is not only a theistic religion, it is also a historical religion. It speaks of the Incarnation of God in Jesus Christ at a particular time and place.

It is true that some who have called themselves Christians, and not only in recent times, have repudiated such beliefs, even when they have continued to use for other purposes the language that was designed to express them: but at least until recently they were set down as heretics. Are the modern reinterpreters, including those whose work is in this book, willing to face, as Arnold and Braithwaite were, the recognition that their understanding of the Christian religion is profoundly unorthodox? Do they cheerfully accept the consequence that all or nearly all Popes and Cardinals, and Luther and Milton and Donne and Saint Thomas Aquinas profoundly misunderstood their faith or faiths?

The remarks of Wittgenstein on which Winch relies are brief and not very explicit. Even so they are clear enough to rule out a requirement which Winch seems to be imposing on their interpretation. He seems to wish to construe the parenthesis 'Theology as grammar' in such a way as to confine theology to its role as a grammatical inquiry. But when we set these three words in their context we can see that there is no need for this restriction, and that the passage as a whole strongly suggests the contrary. Wittgenstein says that grammar tells us what kind of object anything is. 'Theology as grammar' therefore presumably tells us what kind of object God is, and what it is for God to will or to create or to answer men's prayers. But it may and must also be presumed that grammar will tell us what kind of object a number is, and a mind, and a virtue. Yet it would have been at best misleading of Wittgenstein, if he had repeated his remark in the context of discussion about any of these objects, to add in brackets 'Mathematics as grammar' or 'Psychology as grammar' or 'Morality as grammar'. In the relevant sense of 'grammar' we may speak of philosophy of mathematics, philosophy of mind, moral philosophy (or at least part of moral philosophy) as grammatical inquiries. But that would still 'leave everything as it is' within psychology, or mathématics or morals.

Wittgenstein did not after all say in his parenthesis '*Religion* as grammar'. I suggest that Winch and others are being most un-Wittgensteinian when they preach in Wittgenstein's name and on Wittgenstein's text a sermon whose upshot would be to allow all attempts at rendering religion articulate to be swallowed up in 'theology as grammar'.

In the list of philosophical inquiries which are grammatical in Wittgenstein's sense we may also include the philosophy of *matter*. We might describe Locke, Berkeley, Moore, Price, and Ayer as trying to tell us what kind of object a *material* thing is. This example helps us to make clear a point that nevertheless applies to this whole range of inquiries, the very point which allows Wittgenstein and those who accurately follow him to represent philosophy as 'leaving everything as it is'. To know what kind of object a thing is is to be equipped or partially equipped to determine whether there are any objects of the kind in question, and what properties and relations, among those that are recognized in our 'grammatical' understanding to be relevant, actually characterize any such objects of that kind as may actually exist. Physics and astronomy and chemistry and geography are not to be construed as parts of grammar.

In his contribution to the symposium on the intelligibility of the universe Meynell refers to an example that is often discussed in connection with these issues in the interpretation and assessment of Wittgenstein's work, and whose right understanding would be helpful for the wider questions about theology that concern us here: he wonders if 'the questions of whether chemistry, Islamic theology, astrology, or witchcraft constitute a form of knowledge, or rather of elaborately articulated ignorance, can be dealt with only on the basis of herd instinct, snobbery, or individual caprice'. It may be said of astrology, as of each of the activities in this list, that 'This game is played'. The game is a language-game and its characterization is a grammatical activity. For this reason its characterization must 'leave everything as it is' in the practice, if any, of astrology. This is often thought to mean that once we have noted that the game is played, we are debarred from either rejecting or endorsing any astrological judgments; we must simply note that there is such a practice, and pass on to the next game and its grammar. There is no warrant for this conclusion. A language-game is a means of asserting *and denying,* and in particular it is a means of denying anything that it is a means of asserting. This is why a grammatical investigation leaves the language-game as it is: the characterization of the grammar of a kind of assertion is also the characterization of the grammar of the corresponding kind of denial, and gives us no basis for preferring any proposition belonging to the game to the denial of that proposition. A grammatical remark about astrology, giving a rough indication of the scope of the game, might be that astrology is the study of the relations between the movements and positions of the heavenly bodies and the lives and circumstances of human beings. Such a characterization rightly leaves open the question of whether any given astrological observation or prediction is correct. In particular it leaves it open to us to say, as most of us would wish to say, that the only true astrological remarks are boring enough to be summed up in the general conclusion that there are *no* interesting correlations between the movements of the stars and planets and the changes and chances of this mortal life.

If we now return to theology, and apply the same lessons there, we can see that something remains to be done which Winch and Phillips and Malcolm might seem to suggest is at best unnecessary and at worst perverse: to discuss which religious beliefs are true and which are false. The grammar of any assertion to the effect that God or a god or gods exist will continue to need careful study (philosophical theology as grammar). But the study of the grammar of any such assertion will also be the study of the grammar of its denial and will 'leave everything as it is', i.e., will not make our religious affirmations or denials for us. The grammar of a language-game is among other things the grammar of the disagreements that may be expressed by those who play the game. The playing of 'the religious language-game' is no more limited to the endorsing of any one or more traditional forms of words than the playing of the physical language-game commits us for or against a flat earth or the evolution of species or the steady state theory.

But to leave the matter there will not do justice to what is true and important in their critique of the standard conception. They are objecting to positivistic restrictions on what is to count as making an assertion, offering an argument or reason, talking about reality. In this negative part of their task I have no difficulty in agreeing with them, and indeed in a work written from the point of view of the standard conception I have myself inveighed against such prohibitions and restrictions. But it still seems to me that Winch and Phillips and Malcolm could correct an important error in their positive characterization of religion if they were more loyal to the insights of Wittgenstein and less loyal to the exact phrasing of his expression of some of those insights. They are themselves clinging too closely to some assumptions that Wittgenstein was rightly opposed to, and in particular to the assumption that 'talking about reality' must be construed on the lines adopted alike by the positivist and by the traditional natural theologian of the type of William Paley.

To suppose that all theology—or philosophy or morals or sociology—must be a priori elucidation of internal properties ('grammar') if it is not to be understood as the devising and testing of *hypotheses,* is to play into the hands of positivism. Wittgenstein himself made no such mistake. He recognized that philosophy involves, if it does not consist in, the assembly of *reminders;* that one way of reasoning, and one that is central for the purposes of the philosopher, is the finding or inventing of *objects of comparison.* Even if the Christian religion were to abandon its traditional Platonism (something that it could not afford to do) there are still means by which it could continue to tell us about the world, to aspire after the enunciation of a truth as well as the pointing of a way and the renewal of a life.

PART ONE
THE INTELLIGIBILITY
OF THE UNIVERSE

1

The Intelligibility
of the Universe

HUGO MEYNELL

In what follows, I want to show what might be meant by the claim that the universe is intelligible; to suggest that it is intelligible; and to insinuate that this constitutes rather good reason for belief in the existence of something like what is usually called God. Evidently the topic is rather a large one; I must apologize straightaway for being unable, in the space of a paper of more or less manageable size, to give all the steps of the argument the attention that they deserve.

It will be convenient, in connection with what I have to say, to keep in mind these two arguments, which I will label A and B.

A. If the universe were not intelligible, science would not be possible.

But science is possible.

Therefore the universe is intelligible.

B. If there were not something analogous to the human mind in the constitution of the universe, the universe would not be intelligible.

But the universe is intelligible.

Therefore there is something analogous to the human mind in the constitution of the universe.[1]

1. It is important that this argument is not quite the same as that from design, arguing as it does not from alleged artifact to artificer, but rather from intelligible to something analogous to intelligence. A version of it is to be found in C. S. Lewis's paper "Is Theology Poetry?" in *They Asked for a Paper* (London, 1962). In criticizing what he calls 'the popular scientific picture', Lewis says: 'One absolutely central inconsistency ruins it. . . . . The whole picture professes to depend on inferences from observed facts. Unless inference is valid, the

In accounting for human knowledge, Karl Popper has distinguished between 'three worlds', which he maintains to be separate from yet related to each other.[2] The first is the world of physical objects; the second is that of minds and their contents; the third consists of the concepts, propositions, arguments, and so on, which constitute the means by which members of the second world can achieve genuine knowledge of both the first world and one another. In making this distinction, Popper has been particularly at pains to stress that the third world cannot be merely reducible to subjective mental activity. If arguments, propositions, and so on, were mere 'subjective' mental events and processes, as would be the case if they belonged to the second world, they would not be the means by which one might achieve objective knowledge of the other two worlds; and so science, conceived as such objective knowledge, would be impossible.

---

whole picture disappears. Unless we can be sure that reality in the remotest nebula . . . obeys the thought-laws of the human scientist here and now in his laboratory—in other words, unless Reason is an absolute—all is in ruins. Yet those who ask me to believe this world picture also ask me to believe that Reason is simply the unforeseen and unintended by-product of mindless matter at one stage of its endless and aimless becoming. . . . They ask me at the same moment to accept a conclusion and to discredit the only testimony on which that conclusion can be based' (p. 162). Richard Taylor writes to similar effect: '. . . It would be irrational for anyone to say *both* that the marks he found on a stone had a natural, non-purposeful origin and *also* that they reveal some truth with respect to something other than themselves, something that is not merely inferred from them. So also . . . it would be irrational for one to say both that his sensory and cognitive faculties had a natural, non-purposeful origin and *also* that they reveal some truth with respect to something other than themselves.' Short of supposing 'that they somehow embody and express the purposes of some creative being . . . we cannot say that they are . . . reliable guides to any truth whatever, save only what can be inferred from their own structure and arrangement' (*Metaphysics* [Englewood Cliffs, N.J., 1963], pp. 100–101). (In comparing these passages it is crucial to note that the term 'inference' is meant very differently by Taylor and Lewis.) In the course of what is perhaps the most thoroughly worked out of existing versions of the argument, Bernard Lonergan writes: '. . . In so far as one considers in man . . . his intelligent and rational consciousness, one cannot but deal with what is related intimately to the universe and its ultimate ground. For what is the universe and its ground but the objective of man's . . . unrestricted desire to know?' (*Insight: A Study of Human Understanding* ([London, 1957], p. 657).

2. Karl Popper, *Objective Knowledge: An Evolutionary Approach* (London, 1972), pp. 74, 106–128, etc.

Evidently Popper's 'third world' is something of a metaphysical embarrassment, consisting as it does of entities which cannot be seen or touched or felt; and may well be felt to involve a wanton multiplication of entities. The way to dispose of the third world, it has been suggested, is to recognize that propositions, concepts, arguments, and the rest of it are nothing but human and in particular social products.[3] After all, what are propositions, concepts, and arguments other than words or strings of words which are spoken or written by people? It may be objected that there is a crucial difference between an argument which is valid and one which is invalid, a concept which is instantiated and one which is not, a proposition which is true and one which is false. Surely that aspect of propositions by virtue of which they are true or false, that aspect of arguments by virtue of which they are valid or invalid, is not reducible to what is social? But if the third world is really to be reduced to the first and second, they must be and in fact are so reducible. The authority of truth and validity, which the individual subject may experience as a constraint upon him, will be nothing other than the authority of his society; a true proposition and a valid argument will be nothing over and above what one's society or those of high repute within it are disposed to accept or assent to.[4]

The refutations of such accounts of truth and validity are well known to philosophers; what is primarily at issue here, of course, is not how they can be refuted, but what conclusions are ultimately to be drawn from the fact that they can be so. If Betelgeuse has the qualities which constitute it as a red giant star, it would presumably have had them even if no astronomers had ever evolved upon earth to discover that it had them. And the truth of the proposition 'Betelgeuse is a red

3. Cf. in particular David Bloor, "Popper's Mystification of Objective Knowledge," *Science Studies* 4 (1974), 65–76.
4. 'To appraise an argument for validity is to apply the standards of a social group. It cannot be other, or more, than this because we have no access to other standards. . . . The objectivity of knowledge resides in its being the set of accepted beliefs of a social group. This is why and how it transcends the individual and constrains him. . . . The authority of truth is the authority of society' (ibid., pp. 75–76).

giant star' depends upon its possession of these qualities, not on the authority of those within the scientific community who say that it has. They did not confer upon Betelgeuse the qualities which constitute it as a red giant star in the process of claiming it to be such. If we accept the view that truth is entirely dependent on social fiat, either we have to reject the proposition that 'Betelgeuse is a red giant star' is true if and only if Betelgeuse is a red giant star, or we have to assert that the scientific community makes it to be the case in the process of coming to assert it. Both conclusions seem absurd.

But even if such singular consequences were to be accepted, there are worse objections to the view. Consider the proposition which articulates the view itself, 'A true proposition is what my community or its most respected members assert, a valid argument is the kind of argument of which they will take account'. Is this being claimed to be the case on the basis of arguments and evidence not reducible to social fiat? If it is, the proposition is inconsistent with itself, as its truth is supposed to be based on independent arguments and evidence. If on the other hand it is simply being asserted, 'My community asserts those propositions which my community asserts, approves those arguments of which it approves', the claim is at best tautological and trivial, at worst sinister. It is sinister insofar as any community insinuates, by using the impressive language of 'truth', that outsiders ought to assent to any proposition merely by virtue of the fact that the community does so. But if the thesis is defended by appeal to arguments and evidence addressed to individuals and communities who doubt it, one can only conclude that, in Germain Grisez's elegant phrase, it 'self-destructs'.[5]

Apparently Popper's third world, then, is irreducible to his first two; since the view that it is so reducible leads to absurdity. In a sense, indeed, the reduction might actually more plausibly be carried out in the opposite way. What else are the contents of the first two worlds, it might reasonably be asked, than what are to be known in true propositions framed in terms of instan-

5. Grisez uses this phrase in his recent book on metaphysics and the philosophy of religion, *Beyond the New Theism* (Notre Dame, 1975).

tiated concepts, and arrived at by valid arguments based on adequate evidence—in fact, to be known by means of constituents of the third world? It would seem that the third world is that by which the other two worlds are to be known. What metaphysical consequences are to be drawn from this? What sort of a universe, in the last analysis, is it, that can come to be known through the hypothetico-deductive method?

The argument which I have used against the reduction of Popper's third world is, of couse, similar to that often employed against the Verification Principle of the Logical Positivists; that it is inconsistent with itself, since there is no sense-experience by which one could conceivably tend to verify or falsify the meaningful contingent proposition that every meaningful contingent proposition must be verifiable or falsifiable in sense-experience. It is mainly as a consequence of the failure, as it is generally admitted to be, of the Logical Positivist program, that later philosophers have largely given up the search for any overall account of human knowledge and its justification. Each sort of knowledge, it is often held, has its own principles of justification, and there is no formula which will cover all cases.[6] Forms of knowledge are rather like Wittgenstein's games; there are no principles common to all, so it is necessarily fruitless to conduct a search for them.

A major difficulty with this last view, however, is that it seems to follow from it that there is no fully critical way in which *any* claimant, however disreputable at first sight, to the status of a form of knowledge can be assessed as inadequate. As a consequence, the questions of whether chemistry, Islamic theology, astrology, or witchcraft constitute a form of knowledge, or rather of elaborately articulated ignorance, can be dealt with only on the basis of herd instinct, snobbery, or individual caprice. The Logical Positivists, one may infer, had some right on their side in their insistence on the need for a comprehensively critical device for determining which knowledge-claims had a sufficient basis, which had not; even if the device which they in-

---

6. Cf., for example, P. H. Hirst, "Liberal Education and the Nature of Knowledge," in R. D. Archambault, ed., *Philosophical Analysis and Education* (New York, 1972), pp. 113–137.

vented was not capable of doing what was required of it. Short of some such device, one is forced in the long run to fall back, openly or implicitly, on that conception of truth and validity as entirely matters of social consensus which has already been rejected.[7]

So we seem to be left with an unpalatable alternative, either a criterion for the validity of knowledge-claims which is no sooner clarified than it 'self-destructs', or no basis whatever, other than individual or group prejudice, for assessing whether or not claimants to the proud title of knowledge are actually worthy of it. We would not be confronted with so bleak a dilemma if there could be found a coherent and convincing principle or set of principles for this purpose. Is there such a principle or set of principles? It seems to me that there is. It was first set out by Aristotle in the *Posterior Analytics,* and was further developed by his medieval followers.[8] Of well-known contemporary philosophers, it seems to me that Karl Popper comes closest to expounding and applying it;[9] but its most comprehensive and convincing exposition is due to Bernard Lonergan,[10] to whose writings I am indebted for the general drift of the argument of this paper. As far as one can set out the theory of knowledge involved in a single sentence, it amounts to this: The world, or reality, is nothing other than what conscious subjects may come to know by putting questions to their experience.

The questions to be put are of two kinds, which may conveniently be labeled questions for intelligence and questions for reflection. It is characteristic of questions of the first kind that

7. This question becomes particularly acute when one considers the implications of Peter Winch's well-known paper, "Understanding a Primitive Society," in D. Z. Phillips, ed., *Religion and Understanding* (Oxford, 1967).

8. *Posterior Analytics,* II, 1–2. For the vicissitudes of this conception of knowing in medieval and later thought, cf. Bernard Lonergan, *Verbum: Word and Idea in Aquinas* (London, 1968), chaps. I and II.

9. This comes out both in Popper's determined epistemological realism, and in his sharp distinction between the two activities of concocting explanatory theories on the one hand, and determining whether they are probably or certainly true or false on the other.

10. *Insight,* especially chaps. I, XI–XV, and XIX.

they ask, with respect to any thing or state of affairs, *what* it may be or *why* it may occur. It is this kind of question which the scientist asks when he adverts to a puzzling phenomenon in his laboratory, or that the historian asks when he comes across an unexpected statement in one of his sources. The question for intelligence is answered by a possibility or a range of possibilities. Once the question for intelligence has been asked and answered, there comes the question for reflection; when one asks with respect to each of the possibilities arrived at by the questions for intelligence, 'Is it so?'; and one affirms as certainly or probably true the one which appears best supported by the evidence. (It is characteristic of questions for reflection, as opposed to questions for intelligence, that it makes sense to answer them 'Yes' or 'No'.) The real world comes to be known, that is, justified true judgments about it come to be made, by a reiterated asking of questions of these two kinds.

It is of importance to take note of the fact that when human inquiry into any aspect of the world reaches a certain stage of development, the things and properties whose existence and occurrence are postulated and verified are not and cannot be direct objects of experience, though their existence and occurrence are certainly more or less verified in experience. This is clear if one considers such concepts as mass, electrical charge, and valency; or indeed 'oxygen' or 'gold' as defined in terms of the intelligible scheme of relationships set out in the periodic table of the elements. It is, of course, notorious in the case of the wave/particles of contemporary nuclear physics. Now by this advance from description of things in terms of sensible properties to explanation of them in terms of intelligible properties and relations, we progress ipso facto from knowledge of things as related to us, to our senses, to knowledge of things as related to one another; to 'objective knowledge' in Popper's sense, knowledge of things as they really are. What other coherent conception could we have of the reality of things than what serves as the term of intelligent and reasonable inquiry in the manner described?

Such, in outline, is the fully critical theory of knowledge. Experience provides data [11] by inquiry into which we may come to know the real world; but understanding (which asks and answers the first type of question distinguished above) and judgment (in which one affirms an answer to the second) have to be taken into account as well. Contrasted with this fully critical account of knowledge is the naive but persistent assumption that knowledge is to be conceived on the analogy of taking a look. On this assumption, one cannot know what one cannot take a look at, and to come to know a thing or a state of affairs is to take a look at it. This erroneous notion, which seems to be at the base of behaviorism in psychology and operationalism in physical science, as well as of the social reductions of truth and validity discussed earlier, does appear to be confirmed by a few examples of what it is to come to know in the affairs of ordinary life. I may merely believe on the basis of hints which he has dropped that my neighbor has acquired a bidet, and only come to know that he has when I have visited his bathroom and taken a look. But in the case of scientific or mathematical inquiry, or investigation of other minds or of the historical past, what is to be known, and what is or could conceivably be available to be looked at, are very different from one another.

The history of philosophy may be understood as a series of stages of compromise between the naive and the fully critical theory of knowledge. The first stage of the compromise is represented in the philosophy of Locke, and in a vulgar version of the scientific world-view which is widely prevalent; indeed, it has recently been revived in the philosophy of J. J. C. Smart and David M. Armstrong.[12] This adverts to the fact that the sensible properties of objects as we actually perceive them are due to the effects of these objects upon our sense-organs; and concludes that real things (substances and their primary qualities) are what confront us, as it were to be looked at, when these sensible appearances (secondary qualities) are stripped

11. Reference to 'data' does not necessarily imply that there are or can be 'sense-data'. It is quite sufficient, for the thesis advanced here, if the 'data' for knowledge are the ordinary things and events acknowledged by common sense.

12. Cf. J. J. C. Smart, *Philosophy and Scientific Realism* (London, 1963); David M. Armstrong, *A Materialist Theory of the Mind* (London, 1968).

away. What is wrong with this view, of course, is shown by Kant and, more completely and effectively, I believe, by Hegel. Kant shows us that the world of theoretical understanding is a mental construction; [13] but his 'things utterly unknown as to what they are in themselves' remain as the ghosts of the things quite independent of our knowledge assumed by naive realism.

'What Hegel invites us finally to see is that if we penetrate behind the curtain of sensible appearances by understanding them, we shall find nothing there but ourselves.'[14] Hegel admits with Locke that the immediate objects of sensation are mere appearance; but what can be thought to be beyond sensation turns out to be nothing other than a product of thought. 'The naive consciousness feels certain that it is directly acquainted through sense-apprehension with a particular thing. But when we try to say what it is that we know, that is, to describe the object with which we claim to be acquainted, we find that we can describe it only in universal terms which are applicable to other things as well'.[15] So we proceed to an expla-

---

13. There is no space here to consider Kant's philosophy at length; but it seems proper to summarize what appears to be the bearing of the argument of this paper on his philosophy. The crucial question is how one interprets his view that the intelligible structure which apparently belongs to the universe itself is in fact imposed upon it by the human mind. If one takes this seriously, Kant becomes a phenomenalist; the sensory manifold is what is given, and we impose the scheme of our 'logical constructions' upon it. But if one reflects that certain intelligible possibilities are verified by human inquiry as in fact characteristic of the universe, then Kant's view becomes in effect identical with the one suggested here; in which case it is by no means clear that his arguments against natural theology will have a sufficient basis. Crucial to Kant's argument on this matter is that we cannot have knowledge of those things of which we cannot have experience. But this, of course, makes just as many difficulties for belief in the reality of the entities postulated by modern science as it does for belief in God. That we cannot know anything of whose nature and existence we cannot have *evidence* in experience is a much more defensible thesis, and is consistent with our knowledge of the sorts of entities that are postulated by modern physics; but on this view it is by no means obvious that knowledge of God is ruled out. According to many theists at least, we can and do have knowledge of God through reflection on the existence and overall nature of the world. I have argued these points at greater length in "Kant's Anaesthetic," *Philosophical Forum* 2 (1974), 340–354.

14. David Murray, "Hegel: Force and Understanding," in Godfrey Vesey, ed., *Reason and Reality* (London, 1972), p. 171.

15. Frederick C. Copleston, *A History of Philosophy*, VII (London, 1963), 182.

nation of the sensible world in terms of natural laws. But 'in the end the mind sees that the whole realm of the me-taphenomenal which has been invoked to explain sense-phenomena is the product of the understanding itself'.[16]

What is ascribed by Hegel to 'Spirit' is seen by many contemporary sociologists and philosophers in terms of 'society' or 'language'. According to them, what there is is only *for* or *in relation to* some particular society or group of language-users. Thus any 'real world' supposed to exist independently, or even any independently existing raw material *out of which* societies or groups of language-users construct each their own world, turns out in the last analysis to be sheer illusion.[17]

It is, of course, much easier to brush aside Hegel or the social relativists than to show just where it is that they go wrong. The question is whether a fully critical theory of knowledge is possible, which meets the difficulties these thinkers have raised, while preserving those very basic assumptions of common sense and of science that there *is* a real world to be thought about and ultimately to be known, which exists independently of and prior to the human process of thinking about it. It seems to me that we have such a theory of knowledge in the account to which I have already alluded. It will be remembered that two kinds of question were involved, for intelligence and for reflection. If the naive realist and the empiricist neglect the role of understanding in knowledge, the idealist neglects that of reflective judgment. In ordinary inquiry and in scientific investigation we not only have notions and propound hypotheses; we also verify or falsify them. It might be supposed that this concession throws us back on empiricism or naive realism; but this is *not* the case. Whatever may appear from some accounts of verification and falsification, to have a sense-experience or a series of such experience is one thing; to judge that it provides grounds for assessing a hypothesis as true or false is quite another. The difference may be brought out with special clarity, I

16. Ibid., pp. 182–183.
17. Among contemporary philosophers, this way of thought is represented particularly by Peter Winch and D. Z. Phillips. For the sociologists, cf. Peter L. Berger and Thomas Luckmann, *The Social Construction of Reality* (London, 1971), especially the Introduction.

think, in relation to three kinds of investigation; scientific, historical, and into the thoughts and intentions of other conscious subjects. It is one thing to see a tiny disk in one's visual field while looking through a telescope at the night sky; it is another to judge that here is a previously unknown planet. It is one thing to see one's friend suddenly narrowing his eyes; it is another to judge on the basis of this and other hints he has just become suspicious. It is one thing to see a pattern of marks on paper; it is another to see in these evidence that Queen Hatshepsut of Egypt lived in a manner or at a time different from that usually supposed by Egyptologists.

These examples bring out the difference, crucial for my argument here, between having an experience on the one hand, and on the other applying understanding and reflection to judge on the basis of the experience that something, often very different from what can on the very widest interpretation be held to be the object of that experience itself, exists or is the case. It seems characteristic of empiricism not to advert sufficiently to this difference. Yet if what I have described as the fully critical theory of knowledge is correct, one can at least see the point of empiricism and idealism, and admit that each of them emphasizes an aspect of the truth. A strict empiricism insists that knowledge can go no further than experience; but since the link between cause and effect, the theoretical entities postulated by scientists, ordinary events and objects when no one is there to perceive them, and (as we have seen) such things as 'truth' and 'validity', are none of them objects of experience, they have to be dismissed as fictions, 'logical constructions', concise ways of referring to highly complex human behavior, or whatever. The idealist goes further; the stream of sensations, or whatever it is that really exists according to the strict empiricist, has no more claim to reality than the ordinary world which the strict empiricist has destroyed by his criticism. But the critical realist acknowledges, in the process of knowing, not only having experiences; not only theorizing to account for this experience; but a culmination of the process in which the subject apprehends that there is reason to believe his theory or supposition to be true, and thus comes (if later stages of the process do not and would not show the reasons after all to be inadequate) to know the real world. His experience presents him not so much with the world itself, as with clues to the world; [18] to get at the real world, he needs to ask questions, frame hypotheses, and make judgments.

The real world is not merely what we experience; it is what we come to understand and affirm on the basis of our experience. It is nothing other than an intelligible complex of intelligible things, events, and states of affairs, which we affirm to exist and to be the case as the result of intelligent and reasonable inquiry. It is important that, pace Kant and Hegel, the intelligibility of the world does not come about simply with the human understanding of it; for hypotheses, which suggest that a particular aspect of the world is to be understood in such and such a way, are not only propounded, but verified as being probably or certainly true or false. The intelligible state of affairs which is the world *can* have existed and indeed, as we have excellent grounds for believing, *did* exist, prior to and independently of our human understanding of it.

I have already mentioned that the theory of knowledge which I have sketched is quite similar to Popper's view. In common with Popper, it stresses the objectivity of the theoretical knowledge achieved by scientists, and sharply distinguishes the business of propounding hypotheses on the one hand, and that of determining their truth and falsity on the other. It is not, however, or at least not very obviously, vulnerable to those arguments which have been leveled against Popper's account of knowledge by Thomas Kuhn; arguments which, in Kuhn's own view, render at least highly problematic the doctrine that scientists aim or ought to aim at knowledge of the truth about the world.[19] I think that Kuhn has effectively shown that, if Popper's account of the role of falsification in science were correct as it stands, few important scientific theories would ever have been able to establish themselves. Every such theory has given

18. This is in effect the starting point of Richard Taylor's argument mentioned in note 1 above.

19. Cf. Thomas S. Kuhn, *The Structure of Scientific Revolutions* (Chicago, 1962), pp. 169–171.

rise to prima facie anomalies, and so ought on Popper's account to have been rejected by scientists, rather than, as has actually been the case, being refined and elaborated until the
anomalies could be accommodated.[20] But there seems to me no
good reason why one should not retain Popper's view that
science really does make progress toward knowledge of objective truth, by the propounding of theories and the testing of
them in experience, while conceding to Kuhn that such testing
is apt to be gradual and cumulative rather than an immediate
and knock-down affair.

Is science possible, short of the kind of intelligibility that I
have attributed to the universe? Someone might say that, even
if the universe were not intelligible, the speech and activity
characteristic of scientists would still be possible. I admit that
persons might go on uttering the strings of phonemes and
making the sets of marks on paper which go by the name of scientific speech and writing; and cause the visual patterns on
screens, the clicks, the smells, and the explosions, which go by
the name of scientific experiments. But, in my view at least,
these activities are scientific only in virtue of the fact that they
are part of an ongoing and cumulative business of propounding and testing hypotheses; and this, as I have argued, both
presupposes and vindicates the overall hypothesis that the
world is intelligible. At least, short of this intelligibility, science
in the sense of knowledge of what is probably the case about
the world, and would have been the case even if there had
evolved no scientists to find out about it, *is* rendered impossible.

It might be asked whether the theory of knowledge which I
have sketched does not 'self-destruct' in the same way as those
which I have rejected. Is it consistent with itself? It is consistent
with itself, as far as it is an intelligent and reasonable assessment of the relevant evidence to hold that one comes in general to know the truth by an intelligent and reasonable assessment of evidence. It seems to me that it certainly is so; and
therefore that the proposed theory of knowledge does not 'self-
destruct', and thus is not subject to the defects imputable both

20. Ibid., pp. 145–146.

to the Verification Principle, and to the account of validity and truth which makes them entirely dependent on social fiat.

It might further be questioned whether the universe might not be only partially or incompletely intelligible. The hope that it might be completely so, it might be urged, is a very proper one for scientists; but this does nothing to show that the hope will in fact be fulfilled.[21] It is perhaps worth pointing out that even if the universe were only partly intelligible, the fact of its partial intelligibility, given the validity of the main argument advanced in the rest of this paper, would still have to be admitted and accounted for. (Alfred North Whitehead seems to have postulated his nonomnipotent God partly in order to account for a universe of such incomplete intelligibility.) [22] There are reasons for thinking that this supposition is not really a coherent one, however. What it amounts to is that there are perhaps some things, facts, or states of affairs in the universe which are in principle impossible to understand. But what could 'things', 'facts', or 'states of affairs' be, other than what would answer to certain conceivable descriptions; and how could such descriptions be framed except in terms of our own or some other kind of being's intelligent conception and reasonable judgment? What seems to underlie the supposition we are considering is the view attributable to Kant, which we suggested above was less than fully critical, to the effect that things or facts as they really are in themselves might be somehow other than what are to be conceived intelligently and affirmed reasonably. But, on the fully critical view, that aspect of the world that we know can only be that which we can intelligently conceive and reasonably affirm; and that aspect of the world that we do not know that which remains to be intelligently conceived and reasonably affirmed. If this is so, is not the suggestion that the world might be ultimately or partly unintelligible at bottom as incoherent as the suggestion that it might be contradictory? Is not the maker of such a suggestion perhaps rather like the lady who said to

21. Cf. Ronald W. Hepburn, "Method and Insight," *Philosophy* 48 (1973), 158–159.
22. Cf. chap. XI of *Science and the Modern World*.

her husband at a cocktail party, 'Oh, Edgar, do stop drinking; you're getting blurry round the edges'?

It may be argued that it cannot in principle be known why the world in general has the kind of intelligibility that it has, rather than any other. Later I shall suggest myself that such an argument is valid; but it has no bearing on the present question, which is *whether* the world is intelligible, not how, if at all, we could know exactly why it has the kind of intelligibility that it has.

So much for Argument A, its meaning and justification. The world is intelligible, and science, which seeks to understand and explain the world, both presupposes and confirms the fact of its intelligibility. Now we turn to Argument B. Given that the world is intelligible, what explanation are we to give of this? I shall consider three possibilities: (1) that the intelligibility of the world must be taken as a mere matter of fact, without explanation; (2) that the intelligibility of the world is imposed upon it in the human process of coming to understand it; (3) that the intelligibility of the world is to be accounted for by something in its constitution which is analogous to the human mind.

(1) 'The intelligibility of the world must be taken as a mere given matter of fact, without explanation.' I do not see why the search for explanations of matters of fact which is the hallmark of the comprehensively critical attitude should stop short just at this point; or, to put the same thing in a more pointed manner, why *this* kind of obscurantism should be preferable to obscurantism of any other kind. If it is objected that the question is of a transcendental rather than an empirical kind, the justification for refusing to ask such 'transcendental' questions has still to be given. If the reply is given, 'Because such questions are inconsistent with empiricism', it may be pointed out that we have already suggested that empiricism cannot be true. It may be doubted whether any strict formulation of it can be given which does not 'self-destruct' in the manner of the Verification Principle.

'But if the existence of an intelligible world has to be explained, does not the existence of whatever is invoked to explain it itself demand explanation?' This objection, forcibly expressed by Hume and others,[23] will be considered later.

(2) 'The intelligibility which may be ascribed to the world is not really attributable to the world itself, but is imposed on it in the course of man's coming to understand it.' This assumes that while the question of why the world is intelligible is, at least in a sense, legitimate, the answer to the question is different from what might at first be supposed. But the question then arises of the nature of the world prior to the imposition of intelligibility upon it. To recapitulate briefly what was argued earlier, the more critical a theory of knowledge becomes, the less sense can be made of the notion that the universe might somehow be other than what is to be clearly and distinctly understood and affirmed as a result of putting questions to data. And such a universe is intelligible.

(3) 'The intelligibility of the universe is to be accounted for by something in its constitution which is analogous to human intelligence.' Do we have, it might be asked, any model for the explanation of an intelligible state of affairs which *is* the case, but does not *have* to be the case? Of course we do, in human agency. The typical product of a human agent is conceived by him as one among a range of possibilities, and executed as a result of a decision among them. The intelligible but not necessary state of affairs which is the universe may similarly be explained as due to an intelligent agent who understands all possibilities whatever, and decides to execute the one which actually obtains. And such an agent would be what is generally meant by the term 'God'. 'Not *how* the world is, but *that* it is, is the mystical', said Wittgenstein.[24] On the view suggested here, both how the world is and that it is are ultimately the theological. The divine wisdom accounts for the intelligibility of the universe, the divine will for which all of the intelligible possibilities are in fact realized in it.[25] If the account of knowledge

23. David Hume, *Dialogues Concerning Natural Religion,* ed. N. Kemp Smith (London, 1935), Part IV, pp. 161–162.

24. Ludwig Wittgenstein, *Tractatus Logico-Philosophicus,* 6.44.

25. This point is clearly made by Michael B. Foster, "The Christian Doctrine of Creation and the Rise of Modern Natural Science," reprinted in C. A. Russell, ed., *Science and Religious Belief* (London, 1973), pp. 294–315. Cf. especially

briefly expounded above is recalled, it will be noted that one of
the two components of this conception of God in his relationship with the world corresponds to questions for intelligence, the other to questions for reflection.[26]

Evidently such an argument from the existence and nature
of the universe to the existence of God is not by any means 'scientific' in the usual sense. It does, however, seem in accordance
in some respects at least with the comprehensively critical attitude which gives rise to science. In science, the investigator is
confronted by a phenomenon or range of phenomena; he
thinks up a range of explanations; he rejects those among them
which seem inadequate, and retains provisionally the one which
appears to do the job. In this case, what is to be explained is the
existence of an intelligible universe. It has seemed unsatisfactory to say that this is to be taken as a mere given, without explanation. It has seemed equally unsatisfactory to deny that the
world is really intelligible at all, or to hold that its intelligibility
is not, as it were, intrinsic, but imposed by human intelligence
in the act of coming to understand it. Thus the remaining possibility, that it is to be explained as due to the existence in the
constitution of the universe of something analogous to human
intelligence, would appear to be the one to be preferred.

pp. 311ff. In case it should be thought that the association of belief in God on
the one hand, with belief in a truth which is such as to transcend the fiat of any
community on the other, is merely a crotchet of theistic apologists, it is worth
pointing out that it has been admitted by those to whom no such apologetic
motive could plausibly be attributed. In attacking Popper's conception of a
'third world', David Bloor has written that this, and the notions of truth and validity as transcending social context which go along with it, are redolent of a
theistic mythology ("Popper's Mystification," p. 69). Similarly, Kuhn has hinted
that there are theological overtones to the view that science is concerned with
truth, and to the view that scientific theories approach ever nearer and nearer
to the truth as opposed to merely getting increasingly sophisticated and complicated with the passage of time (*Scientific Revolutions*, pp. 169–171). It is of interest that both of these writers appear to hold a belief at least approximate to the
major premise of our argument B; and so can maintain the plausibility of atheism in effect only at the cost of denying the minor premise. Most upholders of
the scientific world-view who are atheists would rather, I think, assert the
minor premise and deny the major; that is, they would assert as a matter of
course the intelligibility of the world while claiming that this was at best irrelevant to, at worst inimical to, the claim that there is a God.

26. Cf. Bernard Lonergan, *Method in Theology* (London, 1972), pp. 101–102.

A being such as we have described, who understands all possibilities and wills those which actually obtain, could not depend
on the existence of anything else; the existence of any other entity, on the contrary, would depend on its will. Of its nature, to
employ a useful term of James Ross, it could not be 'hetero-
explicable.' [27] On the other hand, it is not a being such that it
must exist simply by virtue of its definition—such as could be
proved to exist by some form of the Ontological Argument.
The claim is only that *given* the existence of an intelligible
world, such a being cannot but exist if the existence and intelligibility of such a world are to be fully explained.[28]

'But should it not be maintained that it is the world as a
whole, and not some being supposed somehow to transcend or
to be other than the world, which is not hetero-explicable?' [29] If
what is meant by the world is 'the totality of what exists', plainly
one cannot coherently state that the totality of what exists depends on something supposed to exist which is quite other than

27. James F. Ross, *Philosophical Theology* (Indianapolis and New York, 1969),
pp. 124, 135, 173, 294.
28. 'Why does God exist?' is an ambiguous question. It may mean (a) 'What
are the adequate reasons, if any, for stating that God exists?'; or (b) 'What is it
that brings it about or at least makes concretely possible the state of affairs that
God exists?' It seems to me that there is a tendency to confuse these questions,
even in some of the most interesting of recent writers on natural theology.
Question (a) would be answered, according to the argument outlined here, by
showing that a being with some at least of the divine attributes would have to
exist in order to account for the existence of the world as we know it, without
itself having to be accounted for in the same kind of way. It seems to me that if
a being were such as to understand every possible state of affairs, and willed
those which actually obtain, it would meet this last requirement; if it existed at
all, its existence could not be accounted for by some further state of affairs, and
it would thus have the divine attribute of aseity. However, both Ross and A. C.
Ewing feel that the argument must be taken further; and both their attempts to
do so, it seems to me, confuse questions (a) and (b). Ross argues that God's existence, given that it is logically possible but not hetero-explicable, must be logically necessary (*Philosophical Theology*, pp. 121–139); Ewing that God must exist
because it is supremely good for him to do so (*Value and Reality* [London, 1973],
pp. 156–163). In my opinion, Ross's argument ultimately founders on the objection that necessity of *this* kind at least cannot be attributed to any thing that
may exist or state of affairs that may obtain; Ewing's on the fact that, though
value provides a reason for the existence of anything given the prior existence
of a conscious agent capable of envisaging and realizing the value, it does not
do so when this condition is not fulfilled.
29. Cf., e.g., Antony Flew, *God and Philosophy* (London, 1966), 3.15–3.16.

it. But if what is meant by the world is 'the totality of what exists, excluding God (assuming that he exists)', then it is quite in order to ask whether the totality of what exists and is hetero-explicable must not depend on the existence of something else which is not hetero-explicable. Let us distinguish between 'World A' and 'World B', as meaning respectively 'the totality of everything that exists and is the case', and 'the totality of everything that exists and is the case, excluding God (if he exists)'. Then the question whether the world does not depend for its existence on something other than itself, while admittedly incoherent as applied to World A, seems perfectly proper when it is World B which is in question. Doubts on this matter appear to me to be largely due to a confusion between the two senses of 'world' which I have distinguished.

In *Chance and Necessity*, Jacques Monod invokes a 'Postulate of Objectivity', which he states as follows: 'The systematic confrontation of logic and experience is the sole source of true knowledge'. [30] That this postulate, if it were itself elevated to the status of putative knowledge, would 'self-destruct' (how would you derive it from 'the systematic confrontation of logic and experience'?), is not immediately at issue. More significant for our present purposes is its ambiguity. If 'logic' is understood in a narrow sense, as the study of deductive systems and the principles of formally valid inference, science would never have advanced a single step if 'the postulate of objectivity' as stated above had been rigorously adhered to. If it is taken in a broader sense, sufficient to accommodate scientific method, it would seem to include the whole business of propounding and testing hypotheses, a process which notoriously has never been reduced to logic in the narrower sense. In mature sciences at least, hypotheses quite systematically go beyond the data to be explained, in that they treat of entities which are defined in theoretical terms, whose existence has admittedly to be provisionally *verified in observation,* but which themselves cannot and could not conceivably be *observed.* A theory is scientifically acceptable, as Popper has always argued, as far as while it *might have been* falsified, it has *in fact* not been so; and as far as rival

30. Jacques Monod, *Chance and Necessity* (London, 1972), p. 154.

theories *have* been falsified. The same in a sense applies, as I have tried to show, to the postulation of something like what has always been known as God in explanation of the existence of the intelligible world.

It may be objected that the notion of God involved in this argument is very 'anthropomorphic'. So, in a sense, it is. The claim is that the intelligence and will of the human subject provide the best model available for human understanding of God. I do not think that this falls foul of anthropomorphism in the sense in which theologians and philosophers of the central Christian tradition have objected to it. What they have attacked as 'anthropomorphism' is the conception of God as having either a bodily shape or the sensations, feelings, and desires which go with embodiment. But even granted that the view we have advanced does involve 'anthropomorphism' of a kind, what other analogy than human consciousness can we find among creatures in our attempt to conceive God? And if we can find no such analogy, had we not better abandon all talk about God? As Hume's Cleanthes tellingly argues, if a theist who denies, on grounds perhaps of reverence, that any conception applicable to creatures has any real bearing on the nature of God, he might just as well join the atheists.[31]

Kai Nielsen is notable among the many contemporary philosophers who have faced theists with the dilemma, that they must either embrace a crudely anthropomorphic doctrine of God which is obviously at odds with the whole contemporary scientific and philosophical outlook; or they must retreat to a view of God so qualified and etiolated as effectively to make no sense at all.[32] The answer to this dilemma for theists is simply to state clearly and distinctly those aspects of human conscious activity which provide the model for their conception of God. God is

31. Hume, *Dialogues*, Part IV, pp. 158–159. Cf. the very similar point made by Leibniz: '. . . our notions of the justice and the goodness of God . . . are spoken of sometimes as if we had neither any idea nor any definition of their nature. But in that case we should have no ground for ascribing these attributes to him, or lauding him for them' (Gottfried W. Leibniz, *Theodicy*, trans. by E. M. Huggard [Don Mills, Ontario, 1966], p. 11).

32. Kai Nielsen, "Language and the Concept of God," *Question* 2 (1969), 34–52.

deemed by them to be that which understands all possibilities whatever, and wills those states of affairs which actually obtain; rather as men characteristically act and produce by conceiving a comparatively restricted range of possibilities, and choosing to implement one among them. If talk of God in terms of understanding and will is necessarily anthropomorphic, then any theism which is not incoherent is anthropomorphic. But this does not entail that theists cannot and ought not to reject anthropomorphism in the traditional sense of the term.

It is commonly argued, and even more commonly assumed, that belief in the existence of God on the one hand, and acceptance of the world-view characteristic of contemporary science and philosophy on the other, are at odds with each other.[33] Such a view is not just characteristic of atheists. It is hinted at at least in the claim by many theologians and religious philosophers that religious belief is basically 'paradoxical', or that it is completely sui generis; and in the consequent dismissal of traditional attempts to show that belief in God is an intelligent and reasonable response to the theoretical problems set by the universe and the practical problems set by human life within it. Certainly there is a widely accepted world-view which is both inconsistent with theism, and often supposed to be part and parcel of the scientific attitude. But if my arguments in this paper have been on the right lines, this world view is not only neither a presupposition nor a consequence of the pursuit of scientific method, but is not even consistent with it. On the contrary, that the world is susceptible to the kind of investigation exemplified by scientific method provides some reason for believing in the existence of a being with many of the attributes traditionally ascribed to God.

33. Of the many recent defences of this view, Kai Nielsen's *Scepticism* (London, 1973) seems to me among the most forceful and readable.

2

The Intelligibility
of the Universe

HARRY V. STOPES-ROE

1. Introduction

The concept of the "intelligibility" of the world is difficult; the concept of God being "in the constitution of" the world is difficult; the idea of explaining the former by the latter introduces new difficulties; the idea of constructing an argument for the existence of God on this basis boggles the mind—or at least, it boggles my mind. One of the things I must do, therefore, is to try to de-boggle my mind.

But first some encouraging points. Hugo Meynell and I agree on many things. Our ideas of "reality" or "the world", as such, are basically compatible: "there *is* a real world to be thought about and ultimately to be known, which exists independently of and prior to the human process of thinking about it" (p. 32).[1] We agree in rejecting the relativism of Bloor, Kuhn, Winch and so on. Our idea of the construction of scientific knowledge is hypothetico-deductive, with Popper's comment that the process works by falsification, not verification. There are differences here, but I think they need not be bones of contention between us. Meynell sets up his account of the way theories are constructed in terms of two kinds of activity, of "intelligence" and of "reflection" (which seem to me unfortunate words for the distinction in question), and he looks upon himself as following Lonergan. I would accept—and for that matter, so would very many other philosophers—that the overall process of science (and of life) involves what philoso-

1. Simple page references, without other explanation of source, are to Meynell's paper.

phers pompously call formulating hypotheses and testing them; and that there is a distinction between having experience and judging that it provides grounds for assessing a hypothesis as true or false.

Our elements of agreement concentrate around the starting point, and the finishing point, of the scientific process: we tend to agree about the world and experience on the one hand, and about our construction of theories on the other; but how does one tie together the one and the other? What is it to describe, or talk about, the world? to experience it? to know, understand it? More generally, what is it for us (intelligent human beings) to be in any intensional relation to it? The answer to this complex of questions obviously would illuminate our problem very profoundly. Perhaps it *is* our problem! Here, I think, Meynell and I will see things differently. But I will leave these questions to the end. My own ideas are extremely tentative.

This paper will run its course along roughly these lines. I will first, in Section 2, try to understand what Meynell means when he claims that the universe is "intelligible". I do not resolve the matter unambiguously. But this is not disastrous, for the main discussion turns on the explanation of "intelligibility," not on the detail of what the term means. In Section 3, therefore, I examine "explanation," and in particular the distinctive kind of "explanation" that can (as Meynell claims) be used as the basis for an argument that God exists. Here one has an ideal of "explanation" which is such that one is not satisfied with scientific explanation, but presses the request for explanation until it meets a terminus; I therefore call it a "terminal quest." The full examination of terminal quests, and the arguments based on them, would require answers to two groups of questions: those concerning the validity of such concepts as "necessary being", and those concerning the possibility of a scientific explanation of "intelligibility" which makes no reference to God. I leave over the former group of questions entirely; but I add two short final Sections 4 and 5 which outline some of the points concerning the existence of intelligent beings, and the use of intelligence. These are really no more than abstracts of what should be full-length papers—or books.

2. Intelligibility

When someone asks: "How is the world intelligible?" he may be presenting either of two problems. In part, one can distinguish the questions by replacing the word "intelligible" by either "understood" or "meaningful"; but this does not bring out the full difference. In the first interpretation, the questioner may be accepting that we do understand the world, or some parts or features of it, and asking how that is possible. In the second, he may be asking how the world as a whole (or particular parts of it) can be said to be meaningful. In the first use, the intelligibility (understandability) of the world is accepted as a fact, and one asks for an explanation. (This itself can be taken in various ways, as an explanation of how we do it, or how the world came to be such that we can do it.) In the second use, intelligibility (meaningfulness) is the goal; we are asked to make it meaningful. The confusing question, "How can we make it intelligible that the world is intelligible?" may be used to bring both uses together—in this sense it could be restated: "How can we make it meaningful to us that the world can be understood?"

For the convenience of future reference I will call the question concerning meaningfulness "the supreme question". It sets the "supreme problem". It is often asked of evil; it is often asked of the world as such; it can be asked of the understandability of the world. I will not discuss it. I do not think Meynell discusses it.

I suppose Meynell is operating in the area of the first problem: he is concerned with the explanation of the understandability of the world. This seems to be clear from such remarks as "[the] ongoing and cumulative business of propounding and testing hypotheses . . . both presupposes and vindicates the overall hypothesis that the world is intelligible" (p. 35). But this does not fully explain what Meynell has in mind; and I do not find sufficient clarification elsewhere. There are two difficulties in understanding Meynell: what does he mean by "intelligible" and "intelligibility"? and how can the thesis that "the world is intelligible" support the conclusion "God exists"? Meynell's first batch of uses of the word "intelligible" is on p. 29 (on p. 23 he is merely stating his position). He has just expounded Lonergan's account of the activity of knowing the real world, which uses intelligence as a key element, and he then applies this analysis to the processes of a developed science. He says that the principal concepts used therein are defined in terms of "intelligible properties and relations" rather than in terms of sensible properties; and that thereby we achieve "knowledge of things as they really are". As we pass from sensible to intelligible, we pass from things and properties which are "direct objects of experience" to ones which cannot be such.

I find in these passages two difficulties which are of philosophical importance; but I do not think these contribute to my difficulty in understanding Meynell. First, though of course I recognize that properties are more or less "sensible" or "inferential", I cannot accept an absolute contrast between what is, and what cannot be, the "direct object of experience". In fact, I cannot myelf justify anything as the former; even "experience" itself does not qualify as an object of experience. Second, I cannot accept that there is any absolute contrast between inquiry after it "reaches a certain stage of development" (p. 29) and before—nor that there is a sharp contrast between science and common sense. Summing up these two points, I would say that there is an interpretive element in *all* human knowledge of the world. But Meynell's case clearly depends on the fact that there is an interpretive element in developed science, not on any contrast between developed science and anything else; so these reservations strengthen his case rather than weaken it. If this is what he is pointing to by "intelligible", however, how does he draw his conclusion?

On the face of it, to say that the world is intelligible is straightforward. "What other coherent conception could we have of the reality of things than what serves as the term of intelligent and reasonable inquiry in the manner described?" (p. 29). With reservations set out above, this is true! But I do not see that "intelligible properties and relations" are anything other than just properties and relations; or, if you like, they are properties and relations considered as objects of knowledge. And "intelligibility" is just the world being "there", interacting with us, and the subject of our scientific "propounding and testing hypotheses". If the word "this" were deleted, I would be quite happy to say with Meynell that "short of *this* intelligibility, science in the sense of knowledge of what is probably the case about the world . . . *is* rendered impossible" (p. 35: first, but not second, italics added). But this word "this" makes me fear that he has done something I have missed. Again, I am made uneasy by various negative statements he makes, as "The real world is not merely what we experience. . . . It is nothing other than an intelligible complex of intelligible things, events . . . which we affirm . . . to be the case" (p. 34). Does the discussion really turn on some difficulty about our intensional relation to the world? Certainly the world *is* not experience, but do we not experience it? We stand in experiential relation to it; it is what we experience. If further we understand it (in some degree), it is intelligible; does this not derive from our having stood in this relation with it, and having thought "about" it? All that Meynell says about intelligibility in his discussion of Argument A seems to me to be compatible with an entirely naturalistic account of intelligibility.

Why does Meynell think that "intelligibility" requires God for its explanation? At first one thinks that the problem lies in the nature of "intelligibility". Do Meynell and I have different ideas about it? Do I accept explanations of it which he would reject? Would our disagreements be resolved if we had a careful analysis of how we *do* understand the world? There certainly are difficulties here, and I have hinted at a few in the two previous paragraphs. But I do not think that these are at the heart of our fundamental difference. I think our difficulties turn on "explanation", not "intelligibility". I therefore turn to the second part of Meynell's paper, his Argument B, and examine the way he argues about "intelligibility" for the purpose of proving God's existence. If the mainspring of his argument to God lies

in his particular concept of "explanation", then this should become clear.

Argument B opens with the question: "Given that the world
is intelligible, what explanation are we to give of this?" (p. 37).
Argument A having established that the world is intelligible (a
fact which I accept), Argument B derives the existence of God
from this fact. It proceeds by the elimination of alternatives.
Three possible responses to the fact of "intelligibility" are considered. It seems to me that, without stretching words too
much, all three are true. I will consider his third alternative
first: " 'The intelligibility of the universe is to be accounted for
by something in its constitution which is analogous to human
intelligence' " (p. 38). I can accept this, on the ground that
human intelligence is implicit in the very constitution of our
universe: it had at the beginning and always had, that required
for the evolution of human beings. (I do not take this to mean
that our "human beings" would necessarily have evolved.) Now,
certainly, I am not here taking quite seriously what Meynell
meant by "analogous to" and "in the constitution of" (this is
clear from the overall drive of his argument); but I am taking
them as they stand in the passage quoted. I am taking "analogy" in the mathematician's sense which includes the nul case
which is identity; I am taking "in the constitution" not in the
sense of "bringing together (by God)," but in the sense "the way
it is together"—and the "in" is for me the "in" of "implicitly in".
Finally, Meynell has shifted slightly (but significantly) from the
formulation he used for the question, to that he used for the
answer: the question was "what explanation are we to give for
. . . ?" the answer is ". . . is to be accounted for by . . ." The
latter form imports the suggestion of something extraneous to
the universe, which the former avoids. That about the universe
which produced human intelligence is (I would say) internal to
it. Thus, I would make my acceptance of Meynell's third alternative more explicit if I reframed it:

(3) The explanation of the intelligibility of the universe lies
    in that which, in its constitution, led to the evolution of

human intelligence (which understands the universe in some degree).

I hope I make it clear that I am not saying that the universe *becomes* intelligible with the advent of human intelligence—it is so, by virtue of what it is at all times. The claim I am accepting in (3) above is that the universe is such that human beings developed naturally, in a way that science is beginning to unfold.

But this leaves three important questions:

(a) Is it true that there is something in the universe, by virtue of which, and by virtue of it alone, human intelligence evolved entirely "naturally", without reference to a God?

(b) The scientific answer hinted at in (a) still leaves unanswered the question: Granted that this "intelligibility" is fully within the universe, in the scientific sense, what is the explanation of *that*?

(c) My answer assumed that the universe is such that human intelligence *can* arise; what if the universe were not such?

The first of these questions is really the validity of the natural view of man. To substantiate a positive answer, I would have to explain what I mean by "natural", and also to substantiate (what I conceive to be) the contemporary scientific view of man as natural. A positive answer is fundamental to my further discussion of our topic; but its adequate treatment would be too long, and therefore I do no more than summarize the basic points in Section 4 below. On this basis, we can proceed to question (b). This I see as the principal topic of my paper: how does one pass from a scientific question to a terminal quest? How can one terminate a quest for explanation? I continue these discussions in Section 3. Question (c) is, I suspect, in a sense a side issue, but it may illuminate certain aspects of intelligibility, and I take it up now.

The statement (3) above presupposes that the universe is such that human intelligence can evolve. I think Meynell makes this presupposition. The point of course, is not whether "intelligence" is human or Martian. The question is: what if the universe were such that intelligent beings were impossible

(even Martians)? Would such a universe be intelligible? Counterfactual conditionals are always notoriously difficult; and if
one starts considering a universe with totally different structure
and laws one does not know where to begin. We just do not
know enough about the inner structure and workings of our
world to be able to contemplate any meaningful alternatives, at
this level of generality. The actual question before us, however,
is so abstract that we can say something: suppose there were
some sort of very simple universe (I suspect that a sufficiently
complex one would of necessity allow "intelligent beings"),
would that be intelligible? Say there were fifty mutually repell-
ing particles in a finite but unbounded space, set in equilibrium
positions. Is this a coherent idea? Or could there be an absolutely random universe? These questions take us back to the essentially unanswerable counterfactual question—and the question, What causal laws and particular facts are possible? But
suppose some sort of intelligence-free universe is possible: is it
intelligible?

   We, in the reality we know, can contemplate (in some sense)
a "reality" that is radically without us. I mean, this hypothetical
alternative "reality" is not merely such that we are not in it (as
we were not in our actual reality one hundred million years
ago); it is such that intelligent beings cannot arise in it, or even
cannot exist in it. How do we explain the intelligibility of such a
universe? The answer cannot refer to anything about that universe which allows intelligent beings, inmates of it, to form scientific theories about it—for there are no such beings. If Meynell's question is intended to make sense when asked of such a
universe as this, it must amount to: How can such a universe
(without intelligences, that is) be thought, who thinks about it?
The straightforward answer is: No one would be thinking
about this universe—ex hypothesi it has no thinking beings associated with it.

   Such strange thoughts as I have just been contemplating easily confuse us. We think of ourselves, and we are here thinking.
But why suppose there is any thinking associated with this hypothetical "world", when the point of the example was to exclude it? Any *possible* universe *is in fact* "intelligible" only be-

cause *there are* (actual) "intelligences"—if there were not any, there would not be any intelligibility. The actual intelligibility of a possible universe depends on *our* intelligences, not on there being any "intelligences" in the other (possible) universe. We cannot make suprahuman intelligence necessary by thinking of a universe which by definition cannot contain men.

I turn now to Meynell's answer (2): " 'The intelligibility which may be ascribed to the world (is not really attributable to the world itself, but) is imposed on it in the course of man's coming to understand it' " (p. 38, parentheses added). The question, "What is the explanation of the intelligibility of the world?" looks in a number of directions. As we saw above, one element of the explanation is the fact that there are intelligences which understand the world. *We* are the intelligences in question; and (as I suggest in Section 4) we evolved naturally without dependence on a God. Thus far, "intelligibility" does lie in us. But I want to use Meynell's answer (2) to bring out another aspect of the explanation of the intelligibility of the world, namely an account of how we do come to understand the real world as it is. For this purpose, I have inserted parentheses to distinguish the positive and the negative parts of this statement, which are, I suggest, unrelated. It is the positive part that has the core of truth which I want to develop. Further, the element of "imposition" is out of place: in this aspect of the explanation of intelligibility, the intelligibility of the world consists in the way we come to understand it, and is not an imposition on the world. Therefore I would rephrase Meynell's statement:

(2) The intelligibility which may be ascribed to the world is that about the world whereby men come to understand it. (Therefore it really is attributable to the world itself.)

We can give a perfectly "natural" account of the world as it is, whereby we come to understand it; there is no need for a God. I sketch such an understanding of "intelligibility" in this sense in Section 5 below.

Have I faced Meynell's request for an explanation? No: he will not be satisfied with any of these "internal" answers, or all of them together. He will continue pressing his question against any answer, till he finds an answer that will terminate his quest. This brings us to the first answer he considers. He rejects it, but I accept it.

(1) " 'The intelligibility of the world must be taken as a mere given matter of fact, without explanation' " (p. 37).

I accept this wording as it stands, but it requires detailed exposition, which I will develop in the next section. What is at issue here is not, I suggest, the explanation of some particular feature of the world, but something much wider. When one has pushed to the limits one's quest for an explanation, and the choice is between "God" and "It just is like that", then the starting point is no longer of any consequence; it does not really matter what "intelligibility" *means*. Thus we have come to the end of this section, and we can move on to consider Meynell's explanations of intelligibility, and his arguments.

3. Explaining "Intelligibility"

The main topic of this section is the peculiar features of "terminal" explanations and "terminal" arguments. But I will introduce this with a few wider considerations concerning "explanation".

When one is presented with something, some state of affairs or phenomenon, it is a fundamental human tendency to seek an "explanation" of it. Explanation may consist in simply describing how the thing works, or how it came about; or setting it in some broader context; or giving an account of it in some more fundamental terms. In mentioning these alternatives my intention is not to be restrictive: as far as I am concerned in this paper, just about anything goes when you are seeking an explanation. I know that such claims to openness can be slyly deceptive; I hope and believe this one is not. I hope that I am right in supposing that my final conclusions follow from the very nature of what it is to talk and argue reasonably. There is a difference between merely entertaining an idea, and accepting it (as true). To be an "explanation", a statement must satisfy the criteria of the latter. For a belief to be *reasonable* there must be *reasons* for it; at the very least, it must do some work.

When one seeks to explain how things came about in the course of time, or what they really are, one may or may not be successful. (I attempt to outline some such explanations in subsequent sections.) When one asks of the universe as a whole how it is that it has some very general characteristic or feature, the situation seems more difficult. But I do *not* claim that it is impossible. One might say that such an attempt is of its nature self-contradictory, for one is, at this point, looking for something 'outside' the universe to explain how the Universe is as it is; and one might claim that the universe is, by definition, everything. But this, like all purely logical points, is a mere verbal quibble, of value just insofar as it makes one think more clearly. Here one is, implicitly, thinking of the universe as delimited in some sense (as the created universe, for example), and it is legitimate to look for the explanation of this "outside" it. One may look to God, for example. Some people use the word "cosmos" for universe when they allow some restricted sense. The context of any particular discussion should make clear the kind of "limitation" that is contemplated, for it is the basis of the distinction between "cosmos" and "the beyond". It will turn on some such concept as "created" or "contingent". In essence, the cosmos is the universe insofar as we all agree about it. The function of the word is to hold the balance between presupposing that there is something "beyond", and presupposing that there is not. By definition, it presupposes nothing either way, and leaves all questions open. It would be valueless to define questions out of existence by a mere verbal quibble.

When one first takes some particular feature of the world and seeks to explain it, one will normally find an explanation which is of the same "order" as the thing to be explained; it will be "internal" to the world; it will be a "scientific" explanation. I will not attempt now to examine what these adjectives mean. I will merely remark that, as I see it, they do not as such, exclude God as such. To say that science necessarily does not admit God as a scientific hypothesis is a mere prejudice, engendered by the particular way scientific discovery happens to have gone in the last three to four hundred years. Really, it is (as I would put it) the expression of the scientific discovery that God makes no difference to the world (if there is a God). But this, of course, is merely my view of the situation. To build it into the definition of science causes much confusion, in particular by

destroying the framework for discussing whether it is true that
God makes no difference. This does not mean, however, that
science encompasses everything. One leaves the domain of
science, and calls upon God in a rather special way, when one
presses back these "internal" answers.

Let us take the "intelligibility of the world" as an example.
This is "a particular feature of the world", though a rather
broad one. Prima facie, the world might have not been like
that; one can point to particular features which mark the intelligibility of the world—Meynell points to aspects of scientific
activity, for example. These clearly require explanation. I gave
in the last section a couple of factors that contribute to this explanation. But any explanation developed along these lines can
be looked upon as inadequate: how do these factors work? why
are they like that? These may be normal 'scientific' questions—
such questions are the lifeblood of major scientific advance. But
if one's dissatisfaction is of a special kind, if one seeks something that will terminate this series of questionings, then one
embarks upon what I call a "terminal" quest.

It is perhaps preferable to use the word "cosmos" when one
discusses the fundamental structure of terminal quests, for this
makes explicit that one is not prejudicing the question of God.
(I will usually follow Meynell in using the words "world" and
"universe".) One must, of course, be careful not to prejudice
the question in either way. The point of a terminal quest is that
in the end it questions "everything"—while allowing that this
may be "everything" in some delimited sense. On this basis, I
will set out the general form of a terminal quest:

> In a *terminal quest* one contemplates the cosmos as possessing
> some specific feature; and one asks Why or How it is that
> this is the case—*where* one seeks an answer which cannot be
> capped with the request: "And now explain that".

One still asks the question even in the face of a scientific answer. Scientific answers do not terminate a quest for explanation. "Questions" as such are not "terminal", unless one includes the context and the manner of asking as part of a
"question". One may ask, "How is it that the world (the cosmos)
is intelligible?" and show that one is not interested in the scientific answers; but normally this becomes unambiguous only as

the quest for an answer proceeds. I will refer to "terminal questions", however, as a shorthand for questions asked in this terminal way. It is, in fact, rather difficult to be unambiguous in
one's asking of terminal questions.

It might seem that terminal quests, thus characterized, are
obviously doomed to failure. But I think this is wrong. I think
one must have in mind some basis of distinction between "the
cosmos" and "the beyond" if one is to have an adequate launch-
ing pad. The terminal question then seeks an answer from
beyond the cosmos. And, if Meynell is right, the consideration
of terminal questions, and their possible answers, allows us to
develop an argument for God's existence. Such an argument
shows that God is the only entity that can provide a terminus
for a terminal quest.

Before going on to analyze terminal arguments, I want to
show briefly that the crucial part of Meynell's argument,
namely Argument B, should be taken as terminal. As I have
said (p. 49), I accept the conclusion of Argument A—we are,
therefore, concerned with explaining intelligibility. Meynell's
initial modes of expression leave open whether he is concerned
to *terminate* the quest for explanation, or whether he is concerned merely to *further* the quest:

Question: "The world is intelligible, what explanation are we
to give of this?"

Answer: "The intelligibility of the world is to be accounted
for by something in its constitution which is analogous to
the human mind" (p. 38).

The special quality of the argument comes out clearly, however, as it develops. First, Meynell rejects the response "the intelligibility of the world must be taken as a mere matter of fact,
without explanation" (p. 37), without questioning the existence
of scientific-type explanations. He is not concerned with the
possibility. He insists on there being an explanation; but it must
be of a kind science cannot offer. It must, it seems, terminate
the quest for explanation. He then goes on to argue that God is
self-dependent (p. 40); this is what would be required to terminate the quest. Finally, his offered proof of God's existence proceeds by examining what he considers to be all the putative an-

swers to his question; and showing that the other explanations, which do not refer to God, are "unsatisfactory" (p. 39). The alternatives are just the ones one might think to be terminal, and "satisfaction" clearly amounts to the termination of the quest for explanation.

But it must be acknowledged that, particularly in Argument A, Meynell seems to suppose that there is no possibility of *any* explanation of intelligibility without God, not that there is no possibility of a *terminal* explanation without God. Thus, again, Sections 4 and 5 of this paper have a part to play in replying to Meynell's paper.

I suggest that we will understand terminal questions and arguments better if we have in front of us a number of examples. A classic example is:

The world contains a multiplicity of efficient causes: what is the efficient cause of all these?

Answer: a first efficient cause of the totality, which all men call God. If one considers the formal structure of these questions, one may let "existence" be an example of the "characteristic" considered:

The world exists: why is this?

Answer: God created it.

One might suppose, from the above examples, that there is a remarkable uniformity in the answers that are given to terminal questions. As a statistical summary of the state of the literature, this would probably be true. Those who set out on a terminal quest, for an explanation of some feature of the universe, usually explain the feature in question by reference to God. He is represented as the natural terminus to the terminal quest. What other explanation is possible for any characteristic of the world, if one looks at it in this "terminal" way? Clearly nothing short of God will do. The real alternative is just that: Nothing. This alternative may be put less epigramatically as the claim that the world's having this characteristic just is a brute fact—the world just *is* like that.

So far we have considered terminal quests in terms of a simple linear pattern of question and answer. Further thought suggests that this is not adequate. It is fundamental to the "comprehensively critical attitude which gives rise to science" (p. 39) that it generalizes, and that it critically presses for possible counterexamples. Therefore if we ask of some characteristic the question, "How does the world have this characteristic?" (I will call this the first-place question), we must also press the same question, or a related one, of God: "How does God have this characteristic?" This is the second-place question. The "characteristic" in question is not necessarily the same in both questions. The answer to this question is: "He just does". The passage from the first-place to the second-place question is really Hume's point, and Meynell notes it at p. 38. But the answer, "It/he just does" could, prima facie, have been given to the first-place question. A fair presentation of a terminal quest shows it to have a forked structure:

A: How is it that the world should exist?

It just does.   God created it.

How is it that
God should exist?

He just does.

The answer "It/he just does" may arise either to the first-place or to the second-place question. A necessary condition for the successful development of an *argument* for the existence of God depends on this answer having a different status in the one place and in the other. What are the relative values of "God" and "the universe" as termini to a terminal quest? Can one say that God *just has* the characteristic, and no explanation is required, whereas this is not so of the universe? Or is there some other resolution of the problem?

The above remarks are entirely general. The terminal quest in its purest form is the quest for the explanation of existence. Here the first-place question, and the second-place question, differ in just this: the one refers to the world, and the other refers to God. In other terminal quests one may move on somewhat when one shifts from the first-place to the second-place question. Each example requires individual examination.

Different interpretations of the characteristic "intelligibility" give different diagrams; and the quest in each case can be detailed in many different ways. I give the following as representative examples:

B: How is it that the world is such that intelligent beings can (in some degree) understand it?

It just is.   God made it so.

How is it that God is such that he makes a world such that intelligent beings can (in some degree) understand it?

He just is.

C: How is it that there are intelligent beings?

There just are.   Something in the contribution of the universe which is analogous to human intelligence made it so (cf. pp. 38, 39).

How is it that there is something in the constitution of the universe which is analogous to human intelligence?

There just is.

Diagrams A and C are closely analogous; the difference is merely the feature of the universe taken as the starting point of the quest. In both cases the first-place question is the same as the second-place.

What is the significance of the variety of initiating questions for terminal quests? As demands for explanations of special features of the world, each is subject to a specific scientific answer. One may accept that there is or could be a successful scientific answer in each case; or one might not. But this is not to the present point. It is part of the definition of a "terminal quest" that the existence, or the possible existence, of a scientific answer is not what is being discussed. If one rejected the possibility of a scientific answer, then one might develop an argument for God's existence on the ground that he is the only possible explanation of this feature. This is a well-used type of argument: for example, Newton argued thus in relation to the formation of the solar system, and Paley argued thus in relation to certain significant features of the world. But these arguments are of a different kind. In a "terminal question", the special feature is merely the point of departure. It is a general feature of metaphysical questions that they may be asked of particulars, but to take them at their face value is to show that one has missed the point. As John Wisdom used to say: When a philosopher asks "Does that chair really exist?" he is not mad, he is asking a metaphysical question! There is nothing special about chairs, for his purposes. On the other hand, we would not reach the metaphysical question if there really were doubt, in common sense, of the existence of chairs; similarly, we are set on to the terminal quest only because we are not doubting the scientific answer. Thus the existence of the scientific answer has some significance.

Given that there is a scientific explanation of something, what can one be asking if one goes on asking for an explanation? It can only be an explanation of that in terms of which the scientific explanation is (or would be) given. And if one supposes that there is, or could be, a scientific explanation of *that*? When *all* scientific answers are irrelevant, one must have shed all reference to the particularity of the world; one can only be asking for an explanation of the world as such—of its very existence, in fact. When one is really pursuing a terminal question, one is really only interested in the terminus of the quest, not its initiation. The particularity from which one starts is only the occasion of one's quest; all terminal quests are really quest A taken in different guises or instantiations.

Though I suggest that terminal argument for God's existence has in fact detached itself from the particularity of the different terminal quests, the particularity would contribute to our understanding of God's nature, *if* it were allowed that the argument established that there is something 'beyond' to have a nature. Meynell passes on to this, in fact, at p. 41, for example, and in his final sentence (p. 43). But this is running ahead.

Meynell says that his argument is not "scientific" in the usual sense, but that it accords with the scientific pursuit of explanation (p. 39). The argument proceeds by considering alternative possible explanations; and showing that only one is effective (pp. 39–42). I first consider this kind of argument. As a general form, it is effective. But it requires that the alternatives shall genuinely have explanatory power. In general, an explanation may either use an already established entity, or it may itself establish an entity. We are concerned with the latter type of case, for Meynell is presenting an argument for God's existence. We must be careful here. There may be many arguments—or persuasions—for accepting the existence of something; but the reasonableness of the final belief is a function of the reasonableness of the different persuasions considered individually. So our analysis of Meynell's argument takes it as if it stood alone. It must endow God with some status.

What is required to give an entity some status as a hypothesis? This is a subject of dispute among philosophers. If a criterion is applied which is artificially stringent, then it may be rejected as ad hoc and (probably) in some sense "self-destructing". Turning to the other limit, the basic requirement in itself is merely a statement of what is obviously necessary: if something has no status, then "it" cannot support an explanation. In the limit, the mere fact of formulating a hypothesis which involves a certain supposed entity gives that entity some status—as long as the words which pick out the entity have meaning. Thus to say that an explicans must have some status as a hypothesis if it is to have any explanatory power is to be looked upon as platitudinous rather than as controversial: the point lies in deciding whether any given entity has or has not the necessary status.

As in so much scientific-type thinking, it is a delicate matter to draw the line between profligacy and niggardliness in the acceptance of hypotheses. The line is not drawn on the basis of some metaphysical principle, discerned or assumed. To accept or to reject an entity is to make a claim about the way the world is: is there such an entity? As long as the words used have meaning, the claim and its rejection both have meaning. But this broad liberalism must be qualified in two respects: first, one must remember that some claims are, *on given evidence,* just plain silly; second, if one seeks to go beyond "there *might be* such an entity" to "*I think* that *there is* such an entity" (in other words, if one looks upon one's deliberations as having, in any degree, some value as *reasoning*), some greater stringency is required. That a given claim may seem, in given circumstances, to be just plain silly does not mean that it is not true; the atomic hypothesis in 1828 is such an example.[2] But the requirements of "reasoning" are not entirely vacuous.

I accept the general form of argument that Meynell is using. The difficulty lies in actually establishing the reasons for the particular claim in question. Here we must look at the special features of terminal argument. Again, my first move is to accept basic features of Meynell's argument. Whatever defects terminal questions have, it is not that they fall foul of some semantic criterion. No doubt Meynell is right (p. 37) that any such formulation would "self-destruct", that is, the criterion itself would fall foul of its own standards. The questions are fair questions. Yet I suggest that terminal questions do fail, from their very nature. This is a "logical" comment in that it turns on the meaning of the questions (what they are trying to say), not

2. Gerd Buchdahl, "Sources of Scepticism in Atomic Theory," *British Journal of the Philosophy of Science* 9 (1959), 120–134.

on the way the world is. They are so set up that they cut themselves off from any answer that moves one forward. They are
"meaningless", not in the sense that they lack semantic content,
but in the sense that they are pointless. The only possible answer is the unsatisfying "It just is".

I now come to the crucial feature of terminal argument: such
argument is concerned with explanations which terminate terminal quests. Ex hypothesi we have, or allow, scientific explanations of the matters to be explained. We press on with our
quest for explanation; and this is "meaningful" only if we can
add further content in our explanation, or if we can terminate
the quest. In what ways can a terminal quest for explanation
terminate? I think the principal passages in Meynell's paper
that bear on this are on p. 39, with introductory remarks p. 37.
But these passages seem very inadequate when stood beside the
work to be done.

A terminal quest either stops before it gets started with the
answer "It just does" referring to the world; or it stops with the
answer "He just does" referring to God. The quest is produc-
tive only if the God explanation does have some status as an explanatory hypothesis, and if it is an effective terminus for the
quest. But these two points are interlocked. We are conceiving
this as a free-standing argument (or persuasion) for God's existence. Therefore, it gets started only if the God-answer does
have some explanatory status. But the only explanatory power
that the God-answer would have would be dependent upon this
terminating quality: therefore everything turns on the power
of an appeal to God to terminate a terminal quest, *more significantly* than an appeal to the cosmos does.

Prima facie, the second-place question about God follows on
immediately, just as the first-place question arises in reference
to the world. How can God be better placed to terminate the
quest than the world was? The general difficulty may be put
with respect to diagram A: if one is puzzled by the existence of
"everything", one should also be puzzled by the existence of
God. As Schopenhauer said, "We cannot use the causal law as if
it were a sort of cab, to be dismissed when we have reached our

destination".[3] The same goes for all other terminal explanatory demands. The core of any terminal argument must be the demonstration that the drive of the question, "How is it that God . . .?" is significantly less than the drive of the question, "How is it that the world . . .?"

It will be observed that the position I am taking up is more liberal than that of Russell in his debate with Copleston: [4] I do not deny the reality of the problem; I do not deny the rationality (as a flight of fancy) of the answer; I just deny the rationality of the argument. I do not think anyone has given the necessary basis from which the argument can get started— namely the ability of an appeal to God to transform the quest for explanation.

In the good old high days of theology, people thought that concepts like "necessary being", "uncaused cause", "self-existent", had some meaning. And further, they thought that these concepts applied to God in a way they did not apply to the world. If both these conditions were satisfied, then certainly the God-answer would be significantly different from the world-answers: "God just is" would have a necessity that "The world just is" lacks. But things have changed. Now (it seems clear to me) we see that these words have no meanings which bear upon reality; at best they are part of a self-contained and unattached system of interconnected definitions. Thus this foundation for terminal questions collapses. These claims I have just made may, of course, be looked upon as controversial, even today, by some. But their discussion would take us too far from our present topic, and I therefore leave them.

John Hick has tried another account of how it is that God is "self-explanatory" but the physical universe is not; he calls this claim the "cosmological principle".[5] "This explanatory ultimacy of mind for minds, or inevitable prejudice of mind in its own favour as an intrinsically intelligible kind of entity, may be said

3. Arthur Schopenhauer, *On the Fourfold Root of the Principle of Sufficient Reason,* 1st ed., 1813; (London, 1888), Section 20; I take this quote from Antony Flew, *God and Philosophy* (London, 1966), Section 4.41.

4. Bertrand Russell and F. C. Copleston, *The Existence of God,* in Russell, *Why I Am Not a Christian* (London, 1957).

5. John H. Hick, *Arguments for the Existence of God* (London, 1970), p. 46.

to place the cosmological principle among the 'natural beliefs'
to which humanity tends spontaneously to assent. As conscious
minds we can accept the existence of purposive intelligence as
an ultimate fact, neither requiring nor permitting explanation
in terms of anything more ultimate than itself".[6] Hick is concerned, in these pages, mainly with what I have called (above p.
46) "the supreme question", not with terminal questions. But if
his approach worked, it would contribute to the latter also, for
it would give grounds for saying that one had made a genuine
advance on passing from the first-place question to the second-
place question.

We may perhaps accept that the "cosmological principle"
would cover all these terminal arguments, if it were valid at
all—except, if it is thus supported, we might find that C is destroyed, in that this argument starts by questioning the existence of (finite) purposive intelligence. But really this is no basis
for a rational argument at all; it is just another example of self-
deceptive religious wishful thinking. Hick demonstrates the na-
ivity of this view: "Although no one is logically obliged to accept it, yet the principle is so entirely natural an expression of
man's own self-awareness that to adopt it cannot be regarded as
in any way irrational".[7] Perhaps not—until one stops to think!
But the *point* of being a reasoning human being (other aspects
of humanity have other points) is that one tries to open one's
mind to reasoning about fresh thoughts; certainly, once a difficulty has been noticed, one does not sink into obscurantism!
Unfortunately Hick seems to cherish, at the end of this chapter, the belief that we do have some sort of "ground" for belief
in God on this basis, though short of "demonstration".

It is a pity that Russell claimed too much, for by doing so he
obscured the basic issue, namely whether the argument is reasonable. Hicks leads up to his conclusion by quoting Copleston
on Russell, "one has to deny the reality of the problem . . .
and if one refuses even to sit down at the chess-board and
make a move one cannot, of course, be checkmated"; [8] on this
basis he claims that the cosmological argument "points very
clearly to the possibility of God as the ground of the ultimate

6. Ibid., p. 50.   7. Ibid.   8. Ibid., p. 51.

intelligibility of the universe. . . ." It does nothing of the sort: it contributes nothing to the bare possibility of God in the sense that the concept is *meaningful*. Why should one deny the concept, as a coherent figment? Does not the arguement *assume* this at least before it starts? And it contributes nothing to the *reasonableness* of the belief, for an unattached implication gives no support to anything: if pigs could fly they would need wings—does that "point to the possibility of" pigs having wings? This is the form of the question to be answered. Why should we suppose that pigs can fly, or that the universe is "intelligible" or "explainable" in the rather special sense in question? The dichotomy "unintelligible/explained by God's creativity" inclines one to accept the latter term only if one is predisposed to believe what one finds to be comforting.

It seems to me that Meynell never really comes to terms with the inherent difficulty of terminal arguments. My point is not that the problem is a pseudoproblem,[9] but that the theistic answer is a pseudoanswer. A terminal quest may have its uses; but these do not include being the foundation for an argument toward God's existence. Meynell refers to the basic point at p. 37, mentioning Hume's classic statement of it; and passes it forward for consideration later. But at p. 40 he does no more than throw down the claim, "A being such as we have described, who understands all possibilities and wills those which actually obtain, *could not* depend on the existence of anything else" (italics added). He says that this is true of this being "of its nature"—but yet not "simply by virtue of its definition". Whence this "could not"? This is crucial, for he is here touching the heart of the problem. If he could establish this he would be well on the way to showing that the answer "It just does" has an entirely different force when given to the second-place question "How is it that there is a God?", and when given to the first-place question "How is it that there is a cosmos?" "Could not" appears also in note 28 attached to this paragraph; but again there is no adequate explanation.

One objection he does take up at p. 40, namely that " 'the totality of what exists' " cannot depend on something other than

9. Russell and Copleston, *Existence of God*.

itself. His response turns upon segmenting "the totality of what exists" into "The totality of what exists, excluding God (assuming he exists)" and "God". This, I think, corresponds to the distinction 'cosmos'/'universe' which I introduced above (p. 54). But, as I pointed out there, this issue concerns words, not a real problem. Logic [10] does not forbid the idea of a God creating the world—this has at least the consistency of a fairy tale. I grant, before we start, that the idea is *meaningful:* the question I ask is—is there any *reason* to suppose it *true?*

4. The Origin of Intelligence

In this section I present by title and abstract (as it were) another entire paper. If we grant the nonliving world as we know it, is it reasonable to suppose that the intelligent being Man evolved by entirely "natural" processes? This is a scientific question, though philosophical-type difficulties are sometimes raised. If the answer is yes, then terminal quest C of the previous section, based on the search for an explanation of the existence of intelligent beings, does reduce to quest A, which starts from the mere existence of the world; and "intelligibility" would cease to be a problem, in this context.

The two basic problems of natural evolution are the origination of living from nonliving matter, and the evolution of biological man from this primitive origin. Both are under active scientific investigation. The key to the former is chemistry, and to the latter is random change in hereditary content, combined with natural selection. There is no question of "proof" on either point, but the hypothesis now stands as plausible.

But man is significantly different from even the higher primates. Primatology is showing that these differences are prop-

---

10. Really there is very little (if anything?) that logic prevents one from doing. As Russell pointed out, perhaps the world was created, including him and his memories, five minutes before. Perhaps this was done by "God". "God" is so flexible a notion that He can be set up to do this without inconsistency. Theists only run into trouble when they try to make their ideas *sensible* and not merely *logical;* and when they make claims about infinities and perfections and so on. OK, cut the universe in half and let one half create the other half—why not?

erly to be seen as of degree and not of kind; but they must be attended to. Moral sense and intelligence are the two principal factors, if we think in broad terms oriented to our present interests. Cultural evolution enters to complement genetic evolution, and analyses of moral sense and intelligence (which I here take to include all intelligence-based activities) in these terms are actively being developed. It may seem curious, but there are just two ways in which intelligent beings can arise: as creations of an Intelligent Being; or by *chance* processes combined with natural selection.

There is one respect, however, in which "man" really is unique: *we* are men. Man's introspective and philosophical tendencies introduce new problems. The full corporeality of man, though not strictly entailed by evolutionary theory, follows naturally from it. This idea, sometimes called the "mind-brain identity theory", seems to generate strong—often curiously irrational—opposition. Its fundamental strength seems to be insufficiently appreciated, even by its proponents. If men, with their ability to think, just *are* bodies functionally operating (including brains and the rest of the nervous system) then this is true of *every* element of our activities, and the significance of this truth must be carried through consistently. Objections of the form "my neurons don't appreciate Beethoven" are merely puerile.

"Consciousness" is an essential factor of man as himself a consciously intelligent being. Here it is fundamental that all our awareness is either of our own conscious (psychological) states, or of things and persons as the intensional objects of our thought. "Introspection" does *not* reveal our brains nor any element thereof. Properly understood this, I think, yields the answer to all the so-called "philosophical" objections to the "identity theory". Our testing of the theory can only be indirect, or structural. But I will not now take this discussion any further.

There is something within the universe by virtue of which, and by virtue of it alone, human intelligence evolved—namely inanimate matter, and the natural laws under which it operates.

5. Understanding the World

If the intelligibility of the world is founded on the fact that intelligent men (who are themselves the products of natural processes) understand it by processes which are entirely natural, then there can be no argument for God's existence which turns upon the possibility of science. I hope I made it sufficiently clear in p. 47 above that taking this as the core of the problem does not imply that the world came to be intelligible with the advent of intelligent men.

The first and most basic problem in understanding the world is to understand that there are other people, who are like oneself, and of parity with oneself. I pass over this, and assume a community of persons. I also pass over the next problem, namely the establishment of the idea of language, and of the basic syncategorematic words and devices which enable one to structure propositions. I restrict myself to the assertive use of language, and its use to give information and express theories and so on; I will ignore the expression of emotion, commands and so on. These restrictions are appropriate in the context of a discussion of Meynell's paper, which takes advanced scientific theories as its point of departure. I will remark in passing, however, that the existence of innate linguistic ideas or propensities is not inconsistent with empiricism. Here the understanding of evolution is fundamental; the founders of British empiricism were, of course, ignorant of this theory.[11]

The heart of the intelligibility of the world lies in statements and concepts which refer to the world. How are they built up, and from what? What is necessary for this to be possible? The basic problem is the establishment of a basic vocabulary, for the use of logic and mathematics to extend a given vocabulary is relatively unproblematic. It is a commonplace that dictionaries either send one round in a circle—or land one on a word or words for which no truly effective definitions are given. If one does communicate to other people statements about the way

11. As Meynell refers (in his note 1) to Richard Taylor as a philosopher who has developed a version of his argument, it may be worth pointing out that Taylor also (but less excusably) fails to understand evolution.

the world is, then the circle of giving meaning to words by the use of other words, and nothing other than words, must be broken somehow.

The point in Meynell's paper where it seems that he seeks to relate "intelligibility" to "science" is the central paragraph of p. 29. He says that 'oxygen' (for example) is "defined in terms of the intelligible scheme of relationships set out in the periodic table of the elements"; and he goes on to refer to such properties as "intelligible". I suggest that the so-called definition which he has in mind is spurious—it does not *express* the meaning of 'oxygen' but *indicates* it. I mean, the truth values of uses of the word defined do not follow from the applicability, in the relevant situations, of the words used in the "definition"; it is necessary to make further reference to the world, to perform other experiments. (The point I am making here is a logical one, quite independent of the feasibility of the investigations which would be required to establish the applicability of the definiens words.) There is a sharp contrast here with "a bachelor is an unmarried male".

The important point about a definition which is to count as "basic" is not that no words are used, but that something more than words is used—there is a reference to the world. The former condition might distinguish the definition of 'oxygen' from that of 'red', which might be ostensively defined; the latter condition will be satisfied by classic definitions of both words. 'Oxygen' is a basic word, in the sense pursued above. The propounding of the theory is, as it were, a set of clues that one gives to the novice in his treasure hunt for the significant natural property [12] that one thinks oneself to have discovered.

The intrusion of "theory" seems to be the foundation of Meynell's point—he refers to the periodic table as an "intelligible scheme of relationships". Does this introduce a "mentalistic" element? But the theory is no more than a device for pointing to the intended property, for making it obvious. The periodic theory fitted the facts fairly well; Lavoisier's theory, which was

12. I am here thinking, for the sake of simplicity, particularly of natural science; extension beyond this involves further developments. In general, the discussion of this section has been very much simplified.

the basis of the first "definition" of 'oxygen', was profoundly wrong. These truths and falsities of theories matter surprisingly little. Two things are important: that everyone is talking about, and interacting with, the real world; and that the real world does have properties which do affect us. We give meanings to our words, and come to understand the meanings other people give, by using them—asserting, modifying, withdrawing—in relation to the world with which we all interact. Thus the universe is intelligible.

3

Remarks

RONALD HEPBURN

Part of the complexity of this topic (as the symposiasts are fully aware) is that there are many, interconnected but distinguishable, arguments to the existence of God from the intelligibility of the universe. There are also various different senses of 'intelligible'. Here are a few variants that seem important to keep in mind: some but not all are distinguished in the papers.

(1) In one very strong sense of 'intelligible' (indeed, the limiting case), 'The universe is intelligible' would mean something like this: The structure of the universe has the unity and coherence of a logical or mathematical calculus; and there are, in principle and ultimately, no states of affairs that must elude all explanation and remain matters of sheer brute fact; nor is even the existence of the universe an ultimately contingent circumstance: it exists necessarily. The *theist* will not, of course, wish to argue for this view. For him, the universe as a whole is not, in this sense, a necessary being; though he may wish so to describe the God from whose creative will the universe flows, and on which it depends.

(2) Some theists urge that *being as such* is intelligible, and that what is inexplicably brute-factual at one level of explanation must therefore be explicable (able to have the bruteness taken out of it) at some other level. The natural sciences impressively show this progressive reduction of the contingent, of what we have merely passively to accept as happening to be the way it is; but only a metaphysical extrapolation beyond the world of experience to God removes the final barrier to intelligibility, namely the sheer factual being-there of the world. The really

crucial claims are obviously (a) that being indeed is intelligible in this thoroughgoing way; and (b) that as far as the world of our experience is concerned, it is the *in*completely intelligible nature of that world which affords the jumping-off point to God's existence.

One serious question here—as Stopes-Roe reminds us—is whether in fact appeal to God does make completely intelligible what lacked full intelligibility without him. And here we appeal to God not only to supply a mind to think the processes and laws of nature and to will their instantiation, but also to mitigate the contingency of the world. Can this appeal succeed? Only if God himself does not just 'happen-to-be', and might not have been. Stopes-Roe sees this too, and mentions, though only to dismiss, the concept (once again) of 'necessary being'. Such words, he says, "have no meanings which bear upon reality" and "at best . . . are part of a self-contained and unattached system of interconnected definitions" (p. 64). Some theists would claim they *are* attached, particularly to their experience of worship: as well attached as are some of the more sophisticated interpretative concepts of natural science to experience of nature. But though I am inclined to be more patient with them than is Stopes-Roe, my own reflection on necessary being takes a direction unhelpful to its theistic employment. For those cases, other than God, in which it is most plausible to acknowledge necessary existence seem to me to have an essentially abstract or formal status: a status that in the case of God would be incompatible with much else a theist needs that concept to do for him. For he has to speak of God also as agent, creator, etc. If we mean by 'necessary being' a being that is uncreated and independent of all other beings, or whose existence is utterly secure and unthreatened, then this criticism is avoided; but God is not rescued from the class of beings which happen to exist.

In one other way too I doubt whether the extrapolation to God confers the intelligibility sought by this version of the argument. To advance our explanatory needs, an explanation of the cosmos in terms of God must have a greater intelligibility than do alternative explanations. This is an initially plausible claim, provided that we consider in isolation the aspect of God as supreme intelligence, an aspect that (by itself) seems coherent enough. It is quite different, however, when we consider the *total* concept of God: for in that concept theists themselves readily acknowledge abysses of mystery and incomprehensibility. It is hard to see how crowning intelligibility could be imparted to our knowledge of the world by way of the 'total' concept of God. But it is surely equally hard to justify the ad hoc abstracting of one aspect of God's nature, God as intelligence, in an argument which seeks to show that the world calls out for the existence of the God of Christian theism—in his whole being.

(3) In another version of the argument, no comprehensive metaphysical claim is made that being is thoroughly intelligible. It is argued, rather, that the more the sciences succeed in unifying explanations, the more they display of intelligibility in the world's fundamental processes, far more than could be held to be epistemologically ('transcendentally') necessary for our finding our way around the world or for acquiring such concepts as cause and effect. This apologist would try to work up to a surmise or reasonable conjecture that the world is the work of a single, vastly intelligent being. But we must press the question: How real is the explanatory gain in accounting for the extent of the world's intelligibility by postulating God? Suppose we fail to construct a coherent account of God as necessary being, then (to follow a familiar argument) if intelligibility in the world's processes prompts a restlessness to go beyond the world for a source of its intelligibility, that restlessness may not cease with the postulating of God. Is there, in fact, any more difficulty in saying that the systematic unity in explanation toward which the sciences seek to move reflects the intelligibility, as far as it goes, of *nature itself*? To move, in thought, beyond the universe does not resolve but only reiterates the enigma. (Compare Hume, *Dialogues Concerning Natural Religion*, Part IV.)

(4) A person sympathetic to theism may be impressed by the combination of two contrasted characteristics in the world as science explores it: (a) the high degree of intelligibility we discover in certain of the processes of nature when we progres-

sively unify our theories; and (b) the equally real and perhaps uneliminable contingencies of our empirical experience. (Compare Michael Foster's 1934 article, alluded to by Hugo Meynell.) Do not these characteristics beautifully match what one might (a priori) expect in a universe which is the work of Intelligence, but also the work of creative *Will*? This way of looking at the matter may well have some apologetic force, not indeed as a demonstration of God's existence, but as one of the more serious 'persuasions'.

(5) Hugo Meynell claims that for the universe to be intelligible it is enough for it to be amenable to our "propounding and testing hypotheses" (see p. 35 above); and that some of these activities and interactings with the world yield correct explanations of how things occur. To be intelligible is to be the object of intelligent conceiving and reasonable affirmation (p. 36). Science both "presupposes and confirms" that the universe is intelligible in this sense (p. 37).

One might imagine that those exploratory and cognitive activities could be carried on even if the universe were less than *wholly* intelligible. Of course I can understand that an admission that the actual extent of the intelligibility of the universe is impossible to know would be an embarrassment to certain apologists for the infinitely wise, powerful and good God of Christian theism, though not to all. Hugo Meynell rebuts a suggestion of mine (made in a Kantian spirit) that we might interpret claims about intelligibility as heuristic or regulative rather than constitutive. What would it mean, he asks, to affirm that the universe is incompletely intelligible?—that there are "things, facts, or states of affairs in the universe which are in principle impossible to understand"? But what could these be "other than what would answer to certain conceivable descriptions"? They would remain to be "intelligently conceived and reasonably affirmed" (p. 36). And, it is implied, to be thus is to be intelligible.

Now I think one could argue that this use of 'intelligible' is so weak as not really to be of much help to the argument to the existence of God. Might there not be certain problematic elements in the world, whose *existence* we might indeed be able to acknowledge intellectually, but which we were quite unable to integrate rationally with other and well-understood elements of our knowledge of nature? There is no way, in principle and a priori, of ruling out the possibility of anomalies and mysteries. Nothing prevents us stipulating, if we want to, that even a minimal description of such mysterious elements is to count as giving them intelligibility: but if we do that, we lose the right to *contrast* the intelligible with the anomalous and mysterious. And surely we cannot even take for granted the possibility of coherently describing everything we can acknowledge. We may have to describe some things or states of affairs in terms of mutually incompatible models and metaphors, or hint at rather than describe them in any logically smooth-running way.

That would not show that the universe is *un*intelligible: for it might be that in every case the failure is ours; we have simply not yet succeeded in finding a trouble-free mode of description, nor apprehended the lawful relationships that (if only we grasped them) would take the anomaly out of what perplexes us at present. But it does mean that we are not in a position to affirm a priori that the universe is intelligible, in a sense of 'intelligible' that allows a contrast with what is intellectually opaque or defies systematic rational grasp.

A final point. The symposiasts are concerned with a group of arguments which I am sure deserve particularly serious appraisal, and do not receive it often enough. The basic claim is this: the possibility of our gaining any knowledge of the world, of our having any reliable cognitive activity whatever, presupposes the thoroughgoing intelligibility of being. To deny such intelligibility is self-contradictory. One's very denial is an intellectual act, a judgment intended to be true: but only if being is intelligible can this or any other judgment be justified.

Now there are indeed metaphysical problems about the conditions necessary for reliable intellectual operations to occur. Chief among these conditions is the need for spontaneity or freedom from any 'alien determination' of those operations. It is not nearly so evident, however, that, over and above that requirement of freedom, freedom for the intellect to appraise what is before it, we need demand that the universe must be a thoroughly intelligible object of knowledge: 'intelligible' in the stronger senses. We might deny that 'ultimate explanations' are possible, deny that ideals of rational system are fully satisfiable by the universe, deny that brute-factuality can be eliminated from explanation. What would *not* have been shown is why any of this contingency should necessarily prevent the emergence of structures in one or more regions of the universe, structures that are capable of so interacting with their environment, and having such measure of control over it, as to engage in rational inquiry and achieve understanding. (In this I am in general agreement with Stopes-Roe in the later part of his paper.) The presumption of the argument under review is that to grant only limited intelligibility to the universe—or to some aspect of its operations—must somehow bring the threat of what I might call a 'transmission of unintelligibility' to *any* part of the universe, or to any other aspect of its operations. But the onus is on the person who uses that argument to show, more convincingly than has so far been done, why that transmission should necessarily occur.

To Hugo Meynell, if the universe is not intelligible, the "speech and activity" of scientists would be possible only as meaningless and pointless noises and manipulatings. To be meaningfully scientific, the activities are "part of an ongoing and cumulative business of propounding and testing hypotheses". What has not really been eliminated is the possibility that the activities of science can be carried on in an entirely meaningful way within a universe that may have only a limited intelligibility; and that part of the scientific activity itself is to help determine where these limits lie: to find what theories can be unified with what: which explanatory regress has some fully intelligible terminus, and which regresses seem to continue without discernible end.

PART TWO

THE PROBLEM

OF EVIL

4

The Problem of Evil

RICHARD SWINBURNE

God is, by definition, omniscient, omnipotent, and perfectly good. By "omniscient" I understand "one who knows all true propositions". By "omnipotent" I understand "able to do anything logically possible".[1] By "perfectly good" I understand "one who does no morally bad action", and I include among actions omissions to perform some action. The problem of evil is then often stated as the problem whether the existence of God is compatible with the existence of evil. Against the suggestion of compatibility, an atheist often suggests that the existence of evil entails the nonexistence of God. For, he argues, if God exists, then being omniscient, he knows under what circumstances evil will occur, if he does not act; and being omnipotent, he is able to prevent its occurrence. Hence, being perfectly good, he will prevent its occurrence and so evil will not exist. Hence the existence of God entails the nonexistence of evil. Theists have usually attacked this argument by denying the claim that necessarily a perfectly good being, foreseeing the occurrence of evil and able to prevent it, will prevent it. And indeed, if evil is understood in the very wide way in which it normally is understood in this context, to include physical pain of however slight a degree, the cited claim is somewhat implausible. For it implies that if through my neglecting frequent warnings to go to the dentist, I find myself one morning with a slight toothache, then necessarily, there does not exist a perfectly good being who

---

1. This account of omnipotence will do for present purposes. But a much more careful account is needed to deal with other well-known difficulties. I have attempted to provide such an account in my "Omnipotence," *American Philosophical Quarterly*, 10 (1973), 231–237.

foresaw the evil and was able to have prevented it. Yet it seems fairly obvious that such a being might well choose to allow me to suffer some mild consequences of my folly—as a lesson for the future which would do me no real harm.

The threat to theism seems to come, not from the existence of evil as such, but rather from the existence of evil of certain kinds and degrees—severe undeserved physical pain or mental anguish, for example. I shall therefore list briefly the kinds of evil which are evident in our world, and ask whether their existence in the degrees in which we find them is compatible with the existence of God. I shall call the man who argues for compatibility the theodicist, and his opponent the antitheodicist. The theodicist will claim that it is not morally wrong for God to create or permit the various evils, normally on the grounds that doing so is providing the logically necessary conditions of greater goods. The antitheodicist denies these claims by putting forward moral principles which have as consequences that a good God would not under any circumstances create or permit the evils in question. I shall argue that these moral principles are not, when carefully examined, at all obvious, and indeed that there is a lot to be said for their negations. Hence I shall conclude that it is plausible to suppose that the existence of these evils is compatible with the existence of God.[2]

Since I am discussing only the compatibility of various evils with the existence of God, I am perfectly entitled to make occasionally some (nonself-contradictory) assumption, and argue that if it was true, the compatibility would hold. For if p is compatible with q, given r (where r is not self-contradictory), then p is compatible with q simpliciter. It is irrelevant to the issue of compatibility whether these assumptions are true. If, however, the assumptions which I make are clearly false, and if also it looks as if the existence of God is compatible with the existence of evil *only* given those assumptions, the formal proof of compatibility will lose much of interest. To avoid this danger, I shall make only such assumptions as are not clearly false—and

2. Some of what I have to say will not be especially original. The extensive writing on this subject has of course been well described in John Hick, *Evil and the God of Love* (London, 1966).

also in fact the ones which I shall make will be ones to which many theists are already committed for entirely different reasons.

What then is wrong with the world? First, there are painful sensations, felt both by men, and, to a lesser extent, by animals. Second, there are painful emotions, which do not involve pain in the literal sense of this word—for example, feelings of loss and failure and frustration. Such suffering exists mainly among men, but also, I suppose, to some small extent among animals too. Third, there are evil and undesirable states of affairs, mainly states of men's minds, which do not involve suffering. For example, there are the states of mind of hatred and envy; and such states of the world as rubbish tipped over a beauty spot. And fourth, there are the evil actions of men, mainly actions having as foreseeable consequences evils of the first three types, but perhaps other actions as well—such as lying and promise breaking with no such foreseeable consequences. As before, I include among actions, omissions to perform some actions. If there are rational agents other than men and God (if he exists), such as angels or devils or strange beings on distant planets, who suffer and perform evil actions, then their evil feelings, states, and actions must be added to the list of evils.

I propose to call evil of the first type physical evil, evil of the second type mental evil, evil of the third type state evil, and evil of the fourth type moral evil. Since there is a clear contrast between evils of the first three types, which are evils that happen to men or animals or the world, and evils of the fourth type which are evils that men do, there is an advantage in having one name for evils of any of the first three types—I shall call these passive evils.[3] I distinguish evil from mere absence of good. Pain is not simply the absence of pleasure. A headache is a pain, whereas not having the sensation of drinking whiskey is, for many people, mere absence of pleasure. Likewise, the feeling of loss in bereavement is an evil involving suffering, to be

---

3. In discussion of the problem of evil, terminology has not always been very clear or consistent. See Gerald Wallace, "The Problems of Moral and Physical Evil," *Philosophy*, 46 (1971), 349–351.

contrasted with the mere absence of the pleasure of companionship. Some thinkers have, of course, claimed that a good God would create a "best of all (logically) possible worlds" [4] (i.e., a world than which no better is logically possible), and for them the mere absence of good creates a problem since it looks as if a world would be a better world if it had that good. For most of us, however, the mere absence of good seems less of a threat to theism than the presence of evil, partly because it is not at all clear whether any sense can be given to the concept of a best of all possible worlds (and if it cannot then of logical necessity there will be a better world than any creatable world) and partly because even if sense can be given to this concept it is not at all obvious that God has an obligation to create such a world [5]—to whom would he be doing an injustice if he did not? My concern is with the threat to theism posed by the existence of evil.

Now much of the evil in the world consists of the evil actions of men and the passive evils brought about by those actions. (These include the evils brought about intentionally by men, and also the evils which result from long years of slackness by many generations of men. Many of the evils of 1975 are in the latter category, and among them many state evils. The hatred and jealousy which many men and groups feel today result from an upbringing consequent on generations of neglected opportunities for reconciliations.) The antitheodicist suggests as a moral principle (P1) that a creator able to do so ought to create only creatures such that necessarily they do not do evil actions. From this it follows that God would not have made men who do evil actions. Against this suggestion the theodicist naturally deploys the free-will defense, elegantly expounded in recent years by Alvin Plantinga.[6] This runs roughly as follows:

4. Indeed they have often made the even stronger claim that a good God would create *the* best of all (logically) possible worlds—implying that necessarily there was just one possible world better than all others. There seem to me no grounds at all for adopting this claim.

5. That he has no such obligation is very well argued by Robert Merrihew Adams, "Must God Create the Best?" *Philosophical Review,* 81 (1972), 317–332.

6. See Alvin Plantinga, "The Free Will Defence," in Max Black, ed., *Philosophy in America* (London, 1965); *God and Other Minds* (Ithaca, N.Y., and London, 1967), chaps. 5 and 6; and *The Nature of Necessity* (Oxford, 1974), chap. 9.

it is not logically possible for an agent to make another agent such that necessarily he freely does only good actions. Hence if a being G creates a free agent, he gives to the agent power of choice between alternative actions, and how he will exercise that power is something which G cannot control while the agent remains free. It is a good thing that there exist free agents, but a logically necessary consequence of their existence is that their power to choose to do evil actions may sometimes be realized. The price is worth paying, however, for the existence of agents performing free actions remains a good thing even if they sometimes do evil. Hence it is not logically possible that a creator create free creatures "such that necessarily they do not do evil actions". But it is not a morally bad thing that he create free creatures, even with the possibility of their doing evil. Hence the cited moral principle is implausible.

The free-will defense as stated needs a little filling out. For surely there could be free agents who did not have the power of moral choice, agents whose only opportunities for choice were between morally indifferent alternatives—between jam and marmalade for breakfast, between watching the news on BBC 1 or the news on ITV. They might lack this power either because they lacked the power of making moral judgments (i.e., lacked moral discrimination); or because all their actions which were morally assessable were caused by factors outside their control; or because they saw with complete clarity what was right and wrong and had no temptation to do anything except the right.[7] The free-will defense must claim, however, that it is a good thing that there exist free agents with the power and opportunity of choosing between morally good and morally evil actions, agents with sufficient moral discrimination to have some idea of the difference and some (though not overwhelming) temptation to do other than the morally good. Let us call such agents humanly free agents. The defense must then go on to claim that it is not logically possible to create humanly free agents such that necessarily they do not do mor-

7. In the latter case they would have, in Kant's terminology, holy wills. I argue that God must be such an agent in my "Duty and the Will of God," *Canadian Journal of Philosophy*, 4 (1974), 213–227.

ally evil actions. Unfortunately, this latter claim is highly debatable, and I have no space to debate it.[8] I propose therefore to circumvent this issue as follows. I shall add to the definition of humanly free agents, that they are agents whose choices do not have fully deterministic precedent causes. Clearly then it will not be logically possible to create humanly free agents whose choices go one way rather than another, and so not logically possible to create humanly free agents such that necessarily they do not do evil actions. Then the free-will defense claims that (P1) is not universally true; it is not morally wrong to create humanly free agents—despite the real possibility that they will do evil. Like many others who have discussed this issue, I find this a highly plausible suggestion. Surely as parents we regard it as a good thing that our children have power to do free actions of moral significance—even if the consequence is that they sometimes do evil actions. This conviction is likely to be stronger, not weaker, if we hold that the free actions with which we are concerned are ones which do not have fully deterministic precedent causes. In this way we show the existence of God to be compatible with the existence of moral evil—but only subject to a very big assumption—that men are humanly free agents. If they are not, the compatibility shown by the free-will defense is of little interest. For the agreed exception to (P1) would not then justify a creator making men who did evil actions; we should need a different exception to avoid incompatibility. The assumption seems to me not clearly false, and is also one which most theists affirm for quite other reasons. Needless to say, there is no space to discuss the assumption here.

All that the free-will defense has shown so far, however (and all that Plantinga seems to show) is grounds for supposing that the existence of moral evil is compatible with the existance of God. It has not given grounds for supposing that the existence of evil consequences of moral evils is compatible with the existence of God. In an attempt to show an incompatibility, the an-

---

8. For the debate see Antony Flew, "Divine Omnipotence and Human Freedom," in Antony Flew and Alasdair MacIntyre, eds., *New Essays in Philosophical Theology;* John L. Mackie, "Evil and Omnipotence," *Mind,* 64 (1955), 200–212; and Plantinga, "Free Will Defence."

titheodicist may suggest instead of (P1), (P2)—that a creator able to do so ought always to ensure that any creature whom he creates does not cause passive evils, or at any rate passive evils which hurt creatures other than himself. For could not God have made a world where there are humanly free creatures, men with the power to do evil actions, but where those actions do not have evil consequences, or at any rate evil consequences which affect others—e.g., a world where men cannot cause pain and distress to other men? Men might well do actions which are evil either because they were actions which they believed would have evil consequences or because they were evil for some other reason (e.g., actions which involved promise breaking) without them in fact having any passive evils as consequences. Agents in such a world would be like men in a simulator training to be pilots. They can make mistakes, but no one suffers through those mistakes. Or men might do evil actions which did have the evil consequences which were foreseen but which damaged only themselves. Some philosophers might hold that an action would not be evil if its foreseen consequences were ones damaging only to the agent, since, they might hold, no one has any duties to himself. For those who do not hold this position, however, there are some plausible candidates for actions evil solely because of their foreseeable consequences for the agent—e.g., men brooding on their misfortunes in such a way as foreseeably to become suicidal or misanthropic.

I do not find (P2) a very plausible moral principle. A world in which no one except the agent was affected by his evil actions might be a world in which men had freedom but it would not be a world in which men had responsibility. The theodicist claims that it would not be wrong for God to create interdependent humanly free agents, a society of such agents responsible for each other's well-being, able to make or mar each other.

Fair enough, the antitheodicist may again say. It is not wrong to create a world where creatures have responsibilities for each other. But might not those responsibilities simply be that creatures had the opportunity to benefit or to withhold benefit from each other, not a world in which they had also the opportunity to cause each other pain? One answer to this is that if creatures have only the power to benefit and not the power to hurt each other, they obviously lack any very strong responsibility for each other. To bring out the point by a caricature—a world in which I could choose whether or not to give you sweets, but not whether or not to break your leg or make you unpopular, is not a world in which I have a very strong influence on your destiny, and so not a world in which I have a very full responsibility for you. Further, however, there is a point which will depend on an argument which I will give further on. In the actual world very often a man's withholding benefits from another is correlated with the latter's suffering some passive evil, either physical or mental. Thus if I withhold from you certain vitamins, you will suffer disease. Or if I deprive you of your wife by persuading her to live with me instead, you will suffer grief at the loss. Now it seems to me that a world in which such correlations did not hold would not necessarily be a better world than the world in which they do. The appropriateness of pain to bodily disease or deprivation, and of mental evils to various losses or lacks of a more spiritual kind, is something for which I shall argue in detail a little later.

So then the theodicist objects to (P2) on the grounds that the price of possible passive evils for other creatures is a price worth paying for agents to have great responsibilities for each other. It is a price which (logically) must be paid if they are to have those responsibilities. Here again a reasonable antitheodicist may see the point. In bringing up our own children, in order to give them responsibility, we try not to interfere too quickly in their quarrels—even at the price, sometimes, of younger children getting hurt physically. We try not to interfere, first, in order to train our children for responsibility in later life and second because responsibility here and now is a good thing in itself. True, with respect to the first reason, whatever the effects on character produced by training, God could produce without training. But if he did so by imposing a full character on a humanly free creature, this would be giving him a character which he had not in any way chosen or adopted for himself. Yet it would seem a good thing that a creator should allow humanly free creatures to influence by their own choices the sort of creatures they are to be, the kind of character they are to have. That means that the creator must create them immature, and allow them gradually to make decisions which affect the sort of beings they will be. And one of the greatest privileges which a creator can give to a creature is to allow him to help in the process of education, in putting alternatives before his fellows.

Yet though the antitheodicist may see the point, in theory, he may well react to it rather like this. "Certainly some independence is a good thing. But surely a father ought to interfere if his younger son is really getting badly hurt. The ideal of making men free and responsible is a good one, but there are limits to the amount of responsibility which it is good that men should have, and in our world men have too much responsibility. A good God would certainly have intervened long ago to stop some of the things which happen in our world." Here, I believe, lies the crux—it is simply a matter of quantity. The theodicist says that a good God could allow men to do to each other the hurt they do, in order to allow them to be free and responsible. But against him the antitheodicist puts forward as a moral principle (P3) that a creator able to do so ought to ensure that any creature whom he creates does not cause passive evils as many and as evil as those in our world. He says that in our world freedom and responsibility have gone too far— produced too much physical and mental hurt. God might well tolerate a boy hitting his younger brother, but not Belsen.

The theodicist is in no way committed to saying that a good God will not stop things getting too bad. Indeed, if God made our world, he has clearly done so. There are limits to the amount and degree of evil which are possible in our world. Thus there are limits to the amount of pain which a person can suffer—persons live in our world only so many years and the amount which they can suffer at any given time (if mental goings-on are in any way correlated with bodily ones) is limited by their physiology. Further, theists often claim that from time to time God intervenes in the natural order which he has made to prevent evil which would otherwise occur. So the theodicist can certainly claim that a good God stops too much suffering—it is just that he and his opponent draw the line in different places. The issue as regards the passive evils caused by men turns ultimately on the quantity of evil. To this crucial matter I shall return toward the end of the paper.

We shall have to turn next to the issue of passive evils not apparently caused by men. But, first, I must consider a further argument by the theodicist in support of the free-will defense and also an argument of the antitheodicist against it. The first is the argument that various evils are logically necessary conditions for the occurrence of actions of certain especially good kinds. Thus for a man to bear his suffering cheerfully there has to be suffering for him to bear. There have to be acts which irritate for another to show tolerance of them. Likewise it is often said, acts of forgiveness, courage, self-sacrifice, compassion, overcoming temptation, etc., can be performed only if there are evils of various kinds. Here, however, we must be careful. One might reasonably claim that all that is necessary for some of these good acts (or acts as good as these) to be performed is belief in the existence of certain evils, not their actual existence. You can show compassion toward someone who appears to be suffering, but is not really; you can forgive someone who only appeared to insult you, but did not really. But if the world is to be populated with imaginary evils of the kind needed to enable creatures to perform acts of the above specially good kinds, it would have to be a world in which creatures are generally and systematically deceived about the feelings of their fellows—in which the behavior of creatures generally and unavoidably belies their feelings and intentions. I suggest, in the tradition of Descartes (*Meditations* 4, 5 and 6), that it would be a morally wrong act of a creator to create such a deceptive world. In that case, given a creator, then, without an immoral act on his part, for acts of courage, compassion, etc., to be acts open to men to perform, there have to be various evils. Evils give men the opportunity to perform those acts which show men at their best. A world without evils would be a world in which men could show no forgiveness, no compassion, no self-sacrifice. And men without that opportunity are deprived of the opportunity to show themselves at their noblest. For this reason God might well allow some of his creatures to perform evil acts with passive evils as consequences, since these provide the opportunity for especially noble acts. Against the suggestion of the developed free-will defense that it would be justifiable for God to permit a creature to hurt another for the good of his or the other's soul, there is one natural objection which will surely be made. This is that it is generally supposed to be the duty of men to stop other men hurting each other badly. So why is it not God's duty to stop men hurting each other badly? Now the theodicist does not have to maintain that it is never God's duty to stop men hurting each other; but he does have to maintain that it is not God's duty in circumstances where it clearly is our duty to stop such hurt if we can—e.g., when men are torturing each other in mind or body in some of the ways in which they do this in our world and when, if God exists, he does not step in.

Now different views might be taken about the extent of our duty to interfere in the quarrels of others. But the most which could reasonably be claimed is surely this—that we have a duty to interfere in three kinds of circumstances—(1) if an oppressed person asks us to interfere and it is probable that he will suffer considerably if we do not, (2) if the participants are children or not of sane mind and it is probable that one or other will suffer considerably if we do not interfere, or (3) if it is probable that considerable harm will be done to others if we do not interfere. It is not very plausible to suppose that we have any duty to interfere in the quarrels of grown sane men who do not wish us to do, unless it is probable that the harm will spread. Now note that in the characterization of each of the circumstances in which we would have a duty to interfere there occurs the word "probable", and it is being used in the 'epistemic' sense—as "made probable by the total available evidence". But then the "probability" of an occurrence varies crucially with which community or individual is assessing it, and the amount of evidence which they have at the time in question. What is probable relative to your knowledge at t_1 may not be at all probable relative to my knowledge at t_2. Hence a per-

son's duty to interfere in quarrels will depend on their probable consequences relative to that person's knowledge. Hence it
follows that one who knows much more about the probable
consequences of a quarrel may have no duty to interfere where
another with less knowledge does have such a duty—and conversely. Hence a God who sees far more clearly than we do the
consequences of quarrels may have duties very different from
ours with respect to particular such quarrels. He may know
that the suffering that A will cause B is not nearly as great as
B's screams might suggest to us and will provide (unknown to
us) an opportunity to C to help B recover and will thus give C a
deep responsibility which he would not otherwise have. God
may very well have reason for allowing particular evils which it
is our bounden duty to attempt to stop at all costs simply because he knows so much more about them than we do. And
this is no ad hoc hypothesis—it follows directly from the characterization of the kind of circumstances in which persons have
a duty to interfere in quarrels.

We may have a duty to interfere in quarrels when God does
not for a very different kind of reason. God being our creator,
the source of our beginning and continuation of existence, has
rights over us which we do not have over our fellow-men. To
allow a man to suffer for the good of his or someone else's soul
one has to stand in some kind of parental relationship toward
him. I don't have the right to let some stranger Joe Bloggs suffer for the good of his soul or of the soul of Bill Snoggs, but I
do have *some* right of this kind in respect of my own children. I
may let the younger son suffer *somewhat* for the good of his and
his brother's soul. I have this right because in small part I am
responsible for his existence, its beginning and continuance. If
this is correct, then a fortiori, God who is, ex hypothesi, so
much more the author of our being than are our parents, has
so many more rights in this respect. God has rights to allow
others to suffer, while I do not have those rights and hence
have a duty to interfere instead. In these two ways the theodicist can rebut the objection that if we have a duty to stop certain particular evils which men do to others, God must have
this duty too.

In the free-will defense, as elaborated above, the theist seems to me to have an adequate answer to the suggestion that necessarily a good God would prevent the occurrence of the evil which men cause—if we ignore the question of the quantity of evil, to which I will return at the end of my paper. But what of the passive evil apparently not due to human action? What of the pain caused to men by disease or earthquake or cyclone, and what too of animal pain which existed before there were men? There are two additional assumptions, each of which has been put forward to allow the free-will defense to show the compatibility of the existence of God and the existence of such evil. The first is that, despite appearances, men are ultimately responsible for disease, earthquake, cyclone, and much animal pain. There seem to be traces of this view in Genesis 3:16–20. One might claim that God ties the goodness of man to the well-being of the world and that a failure of one leads to a failure of the other. Lack of prayer, concern, and simple goodness lead to the evils in nature. This assumption, though it may do some service for the free-will defense, would seem unable to account for the animal pain which existed before there were men. The other assumption is that there exist humanly free creatures other than men, which we may call fallen angels, who have chosen to do evil, and have brought about the passive evils not brought about by men. These were given the care of much of the material world and have abused that care. For reasons already given, however, it is not God's moral duty to interfere to prevent the passive evils caused by such creatures. This defense has recently been used by, among others, Plantinga. This assumption, it seems to me, will do the job, and is not *clearly* false. It is also an assumption which was part of the Christian tradition long before the free-will defense was put forward in any logically rigorous form. I believe that this assumption may indeed be indispensable if the theist is to reconcile with the existence of God the existence of passive evils of certain kinds, e.g., certain animal pain. But I do not think that the theodicist need deploy it to deal with the central cases of passive evils not caused by men—mental evils and the human pain that is a sign of bodily malfunctioning. Note, however, that if he does not attribute such passive evils to the free choice of some other agent, the theodicist must attribute them to the direct action of God himself, or rather, what he must say is that God created a universe in which passive evils must necessarily occur in certain circumstances, the occurrence of which is necessary or at any rate not within the power of a humanly free agent to prevent. The antitheodicist then naturally claims, that although a creator might be justified in allowing free creatures to produce various evils, nevertheless (P4) a creator is never justified in creating a world in which evil results except by the action of a humanly free agent. Against this the theodicist tries to sketch reasons which a good creator might have for creating a world in which there is evil not brought about by humanly free agents. One reason which he produces is one which we have already considered earlier in the development of the free-will defense. This is the reason that various evils are logically necessary conditions for the occurrence of actions of certain especially noble kinds. This was adduced earlier as a reason why a creator might allow creatures to perform evil acts with passive evils as consequences. It can also be adduced as a reason why he might himself bring about passive evils—to give further opportunities for courage, patience, and tolerance. I shall consider here one further reason that, the theodicist may suggest, a good creator might have for creating a world in which various passive evils were implanted, which is another reason for rejecting (P4). It is, I think, a reason which is closely connected with some of the other reasons which we have been considering why a good creator might permit the existence of evil.

A creator who is going to create humanly free agents and place them in a universe has a choice of the kind of universe to create. First, he can create a finished universe in which nothing needs improving. Humanly free agents know what is right, and pursue it; and they achieve their purposes without hindrance. Second, he can create a basically evil universe, in which everything needs improving, and nothing can be improved. Or, third, he can create a basically good but half-finished universe—one in which many things need improving, humanly free agents do not altogether know what is right, and their purposes are often frustrated; but one in which agents can come to know what is right and can overcome the obstacles to the achievement of their purposes. In such a universe the bodies of creatures may work imperfectly and last only a short time; and creatures may be morally ill-educated, and set their affections on things and persons which are taken from them. The universe might be such that it requires long generations of cooperative effort between creatures to make perfect. While not wishing to deny the goodness of a universe of the first kind, I suggest that to create a universe of the third kind would be no bad thing, for it gives to creatures the privilege of making their own universe. Genesis 1 in telling of a God who tells men to "subdue" the earth pictures the creator as creating a universe of this third kind; and fairly evidently—given that men are humanly free agents—our universe is of this kind.

Now a creator who creates a half-finished universe of this third kind has a further choice as to how he molds the humanly free agents which it contains. Clearly he will have to give them a nature of some kind, that is, certain narrow purposes which they have a natural inclination to pursue until they choose or are forced to pursue others—e.g., the immediate attainment of food, sleep, and sex. There could hardly be humanly free agents without some such initial purposes. But what is he to do about their knowledge of their duty to improve the world—e.g., to repair their bodies when they go wrong, so that they can realize long-term purposes, to help others who cannot get food to do so, etc.? He could just give them a formal hazy knowledge that they had such reasons for action without giving them any strong inclination to pursue them. Such a policy might well seem an excessively laissez-faire one. We tend to think that parents who give their children no help toward taking the right path are less than perfect parents. So a good creator might well help agents toward taking steps to improve the universe. We shall see that he can do this in one of two ways.

An action is something done for a reason. A good creator, we supposed, will give to agents some reasons for doing right actions—e.g., that they are right, that they will improve the universe. These reasons are ones of which men can be aware and then either act on or not act on. The creator could help agents toward doing right actions by making these reasons more effective causally; that is, he could make agents so that by nature they were inclined (though not perhaps compelled) to pursue what is good. But this would be to impose a moral character on agents, to give them wide general purposes which they naturally pursue, to make them naturally altruistic, tenacious of purpose, or strong-willed. But to impose a character on creatures might well seem to take away from creatures the privilege of developing their own characters and those of their fellows. We tend to think that parents who try too forcibly to impose a character, however good a character, on their children, are less than perfect parents.

The alternative way in which a creator could help creatures to perform right actions is by sometimes providing additional reasons for creatures to do what is right, reasons which by their very nature have a strong causal influence. Reasons such as improving the universe or doing one's duty do not necessarily have a strong causal influence, for as we have seen creatures may be little influenced by them. Giving a creature reasons which by their nature were strongly causally influential on a particular occasion on any creature whatever his character, would not impose a particular character on a creature. It would, however, incline him to do what is right on that occasion and maybe subsequently too. Now if a reason is by its nature to be strongly causally influential it must be something of which the agent is aware which causally inclines him (whatever his character) to perform some action, to bring about some kind of change. What kind of reason could this be except the existence of an unpleasant feeling, either a sensation such as a pain or an emotion such as a feeling of loss or deprivation? Such feelings are things of which agents are conscious, which cause them to do whatever action will get rid of those feelings, and which provide reason for performing such action. An itch causally inclines a man to do whatever will cause the itch to cease, e.g., scratch, and provides a reason for doing that action. Its causal influence is quite independent of the agent—saint or sinner, strong-willed or weak-willed, will all be strongly inclined to get rid of their pains (though some may learn to resist the inclination). Hence a creator who wished to give agents some inclination to improve the world without giving them a character, a wide set of general purposes which they naturally pursue, would tie some of the imperfections of the world to physical or mental evils.

To tie desirable states of affairs to pleasant feelings would not have the same effect. Only an existing feeling can be causally efficacious. An agent could be moved to action by a pleasant feeling only when he had it, and the only action to which he could be moved would be to keep the world as it is, not to improve it. For men to have reasons which move men of any character to actions of perfecting the world, a creator needs to tie its imperfections to unpleasant feelings, that is, physical and mental evils.

There is to some considerable extent such tie-up in our universe. Pain normally occurs when something goes wrong with the working of our body which is going to lead to further limitation on the purposes which we can achieve; and the pain ends when the body is repaired. The existence of the pain spurs the sufferer, and others through the sympathetic suffering which arises when they learn of the sufferer's pain, to do something about the bodily malfunctioning. Yet giving men such feelings which they are inclined to end involves the imposition of no character. A man who is inclined to end his toothache by a visit to the dentist may be saint or sinner, strong-willed or weak-willed, rational or irrational. Any other way of which I can conceive of giving men an inclination to correct what goes wrong, and generally to improve the universe, would seem to involve imposing a character. A creator could, for example, have operated exclusively by threats and promises, whispering in men's ears, "unless you go to the dentist, you are going to suffer terribly", or "if you go to the dentist, you are going to feel wonderful". And if the order of nature is God's creation, he does indeed often provide us with such threats and promises— not by whispering in our ears but by providing inductive evidence. There is plenty of inductive evidence that unattended cuts and sores will lead to pain; that eating and drinking will lead to pleasure. Still, men do not always respond to threats and promises or take the trouble to notice inductive evidence (e.g., statistics showing the correlation between smoking and cancer). A creator could have made men so that they naturally took more account of inductive evidence. But to do so would be to impose character. It would be to make men, apart from any choice of theirs, rational and strong-willed.

Many mental evils too are caused by things going wrong in a man's life or in the life of his fellows and often serve as a spur to a man to put things right, either to put right the cause of the particular mental evil or to put similar things right. A man's feeling of frustration at the failure of his plans spurs him either to fulfill those plans despite their initial failure or to curtail his ambitions. A man's sadness at the failure of the plans of his child will incline him to help the child more in future. A man's grief at the absence of a loved one inclines him to do whatever will get the loved one back. As with physical pain, the spur inclines a man to do what is right but does so without imposing a character—without, say, making a man responsive to duty, or strong-willed.

Physical and mental evils may serve as spurs to long-term co-operative research leading to improvement of the universe. A feeling of sympathy for the actual and prospective suffering of many from tuberculosis or cancer leads to acquisition of knowledge and provision of cure for future sufferers. Cooperative and long-term research and cure is a very good thing, the kind of thing toward which men need a spur. A man's suffering is never in vain if it leads through sympathy to the work of others which eventually provides a long-term cure. True, there could be sympathy without a sufferer for whom the sympathy is felt. Yet in a world made by a creator, there cannot be sympathy on the large scale without a sufferer, for whom the sympathy is felt, unless the creator planned for creatures generally to be deceived about the feelings of their fellows; and that, we have claimed, would be morally wrong.

So generally many evils have a biological and psychological utility in producing spurs to right action without imposition of character, a goal which it is hard to conceive of being realized in any other way. This point provides a reason for the rejection of (*P*4). There are other kinds of reason which have been adduced reasons for rejecting (*P*4)—e.g., that a creator could be justified in bringing about evil as a punishment—but I have no space to discuss these now. I will, however, in passing, mention briefly one reason why a creator might make a world in which certain mental evils were tied to things going wrong. Mental suffering and anguish are a man's proper tribute to losses and failures, and a world in which men were immunized from such reactions to things going wrong would be a worse world than ours. By showing proper feelings a man shows his respect for himself and others. Thus a man who feels no grief at the death of his child or the seduction of his wife is rightly branded by us as insensitive, for he has failed to pay the proper tribute of feeling to others, to show in his feeling how much he values them, and thereby failed to value them properly—for valuing them properly involves having proper reactions of feeling to their loss. Again, only a world in which men feel sympathy for losses experienced by their friends, is a world in which love has full meaning.

So, I have argued, there seem to be kinds of justification for the evils which exist in the world, available to the theodicist. Although a good creator might have very different kinds of justification for producing, or allowing others to produce, various different evils, there is a central thread running through the kind of theodicy which I have made my theodicist put forward. This is that it is a good thing that a creator should make a half-finished universe and create immature creatures, who are humanly free agents, to inhabit it; and that he should allow them to exercise some choice over what kind of creatures they are to become and what sort of universe is to be (while at the same time giving them a slight push in the direction of doing what is right); and that the creatures should have power to affect not only the development of the inanimate universe but the well-being and moral character of their fellows, and that there should be opportunities for creatures to develop noble characters and do especially noble actions. My theodicist has argued that if a creator is to make a universe of this kind, then evils of various kinds may inevitably—at any rate temporarily—belong to such a universe; and that it is not a morally bad thing to create such a universe despite the evils.

Now a morally sensitive antitheodicist might well in principle accept some of the above arguments. He may agree that in principle it is not wrong to create humanly free agents, despite the possible evils which might result, or to create pains as biological warnings. But where the crunch comes, it seems to me, is in the amount of evil which exists in our world. The antitheodicist says, all right, it would not be wrong to create men able to harm each other, but it would be wrong to create men able to put each other in Belsen. It would not be wrong to create backaches and headaches, even severe ones, as biological warnings, but not the long severe incurable pain of some diseases. In reply the theodicist must argue that a creator who allowed men to do little evil would be a creator who gave them little responsibility; and a creator who gave them only coughs and colds, and not cancer and cholera would be a creator who treated men as children instead of giving them real encouragement to subdue the world. The argument must go on with regard to particular cases. The antitheodicist must sketch in detail and show his adversary the horrors of particular wars and diseases. The theodicist in reply must sketch in detail and show his adversary the good which such disasters make possible. He must show to his opponent men working together for good, men helping each other to overcome disease and famine; the heroism of men who choose the good in spite of temptation, who help others not merely by giving them food but who teach them right and wrong, give them something to live for and something to die for. A world in which this is possible can only be a world in which there is much evil as well as great good. Interfere to stop the evil and you cut off the good.

Like all moral arguments this one can be settled only by each party pointing to the consequences of his opponent's moral position and trying to show that his opponent is committed to implausible consequences. They must try, too, to show that each other's moral principles do or do not fit well with other moral principles which each accepts. The exhibition of consequences is a long process, and it takes time to convince an opponent even if he is prepared to be rational, more time than is available in this paper. All that I claim to have *shown* here is that there is no *easy proof* of incompatibility between the existence of evils of the kinds we find around us and the existence of God. Yet my sympathies for the outcome of any more detailed argument are probably apparent, and indeed I may have said enough to convince some readers as to what that outcome would be.

My sympathies lie, of course, with the theodicist. The theodicist's God is a god who thinks the higher goods so worthwhile that he is prepared to ask a lot of man in the way of enduring evil. Creatures determining in cooperation their own character and future, and that of the universe in which they live, coming in the process to show charity, forgiveness, faith, and self-sacrifice is such a worthwhile thing that a creator would not be unjustified in making or permitting a certain amount of evil in order that they should be realized. No doubt a good creator would put a limit on the amount of evil in the world and perhaps an end to the struggle with it after a number of years. But if he allowed creatures to struggle with evil, he would allow them a real struggle with a real enemy, not a parlor game. The antitheodicist's mistake lies in extrapolating too quickly from *our* duties when faced with evil to the duties of a creator, while ignoring the enormous differences in the circumstances of each. Each of us at one time can make the existing universe better or worse only in a few particulars. A creator can choose the kind of universe and the kind of creatures there are to be. It seldom becomes us in our ignorance and weakness to do anything more than remove the evident evils—war, disease, and famine. We seldom have the power or the knowledge or the right to use such evils to forward deeper and longer-term goods. To make an analogy, the duty of the weak and ignorant is to eliminate cowpox and not to spread it, while the doctor has a duty to spread it (under carefully controlled conditions). But a creator who made or permitted his creatures to suffer much evil and asked them to suffer more is a very demanding creator, one with high ideals who expects a lot. For myself I can say that I would not be too happy to worship a creator who ex-pected too little of his creatures. Nevertheless such a God does ask a lot of creatures. A theodicist is in a better position to defend a theodicy such as I have outlined if he is prepared also to make the further additional claim—that God knowing the worthwhileness of the conquest of evil and the perfecting of the universe by men, shared with them this task by subjecting himself as man to the evil in the world. A creator is more jus-tified in creating or permitting evils to be overcome by his crea-tures if he is prepared to share with them the burden of the suffering and effort.

5

The Problem of Evil

D. Z. PHILLIPS

For practical purposes it would be considered unfortunate if two symposiasts agreed with each other on too many points. If disagreements are too extreme, however, there is a danger of them passing each other by. The first possibility in no way threatens the present symposium, but the second poses a real problem. Kierkegaard once depicted a source of confusion in philosophy as thoroughly investigating details of a road one should not have turned into in the first place. As far as I can see, Swinburne is far down such a road. Nevertheless, in my reply, I shall for the most part comment on features of the road on which he chooses to travel. My reason for doing so is that many of Swinburne's assumptions about the Great Architect must, on his own admission, pass the compatibility test with respect to what goes on in and what we know about the highways and byways of human life. If it can be shown that what Swinburne asks us to think about the roads he travels on and the people who live there distorts what we know or goes beyond the limits of what we are prepared to think, this in itself would be a reason against extrapolating possibilities of divine policy or reasoning from such dubious facts. I shall do no more than hint at some reasons why we should not turn into Swinburne's way in the first place. I fear that the extent of my disagreement makes it impossible to fulfill either task adequately, but at least I hope to indicate the various directions in which my misgivings lie.

Before we begin our travels, let us note Swinburne's terms of reference for the journey. Since various ills and misfortunes can be found in the streets where we live, religious believers are

faced with difficulties which are often referred to as the problem of evil: how are evils compatible with the existence of an
omnipotent, omniscient, all-good God? A theodicist is someone
who seeks to answer this question by justifying God's ways to
men, by showing us why things are as they are and, in particular, why that which appears to be evil to us has been sent or
created by God for the general good of mankind: a little evil
does no one any harm and even the greatest evil, on closer examination, turns out to be worth the price. With this context in
mind, let us follow Swinburne on his travels.

His first observation is that all men are guilty of some wrong
actions. Could men have been naturally good? This is a logical
and not a factual question. Does the supposition make sense? If
not, it makes no sense either to blame God for not creating perfect human beings. Swinburne holds that it is "not logically possible to create humanly free agents such that necessarily they
do not do morally evil actions" (p. 85). Let us first ask whether
we could have a world in which men always make the right
decisions and where no actual evil exists. If we are retaining, as
this talk may be doing, a world such as ours, where deliberations and temptations are what we know them to be, these assumptions soon run into conceptual difficulties. Consider the
following course of argument: Someone may say that acquiring
moral conceptions entails the existence of actual evil in the
world. For example, a child may be taught to condemn sel-
fishness by being restrained from performing a selfish action.
His arm may be pulled back as it reaches for a third cream bun.
Moral condemnation, it may be said, develops partly by commenting on what is actually taking place. To this it may be re-
torted that disdain of evil could be taught by means of hypothetical inference without actual evils taking place.[1] For
example, a child may be told that if human beings were killed
as animals are killed that would be a bad thing. Putting this
suggestion aside for the moment, how could evil thoughts be
eliminated? Someone may think that the possibility of saints
whose lives are characterized by spontaneous virtues constitutes
an answer to this question. Their generosity of spirit may be

1. This suggestion was put to me by Joseph L. Cowan.

such that they do not entertain such thoughts. This reply, however, does not work. The impressiveness of saints cannot be
explained by an attempt to isolate their characteristics in this
way. We are impressed by the generosity of spirit which saints
may possess, precisely because they possess it in a world where
it is all too easy to think otherwise of other human beings.
These observations about the saints admit of wider reference.
Generosity, kindness, loyalty, truth, etc., do get their identity in
a world where meanness, cruelty, disloyalty and lies are also
possible. We see the importance of virtues not in face of apparent or possible evils, but in face of actual evils. Swinburne himself rejects the possibility of a world where God has seen to it
that people only seem to be harmed, since God would be guilty
of deception if this were the case. The objection, however, is
logical, not moral. When we think we ought to be generous is it
in face of apparent need or real need? How would we know the
difference? The point is that we cannot, according to the argument. But this "cannot" is unintelligible, for no distinction between what can and cannot be known exists to give it any import. God, on this argument, suffers the same fate as
Descartes's malignant demon. If we now look again at the question, Could there be a world where men are naturally good? we
can see, for reasons already given, that such a world could not
contain people we would call good. Even so, would a world of
such people, whatever we call them, be a better world than the
world we know? I have no idea how to answer this question.

Swinburne doubts whether the notion of the best of all logically possible worlds makes sense, but even if it did, he cannot
see how God could have any obligation to create it. He does,
however, think it makes sense to compare a universe without
actual evil, a finished universe, with our own, a half-finished
universe. Swinburne says, "While not wishing to deny the
goodness of a universe of the first kind, I suggest that to create a
universe of the [other] kind would be no bad thing, for it gives
to creatures the privilege of making their own universe" (p.
95). Putting aside the dubious character of this privilege for the
moment, I take it that Swinburne would also say that God
could have no obligation to create such a universe. If Swin-

burne's conception of God were allowed, and that, as we shall see, is to allow a great deal, what can be made of Swinburne's defense of him? Swinburne asks, ". . . . to whom would he be doing an injustice if he did not?" (p. 84). The suggestion seems to be that God has no obligation to create a world of any particular kind, since prior to his act of creation, there are no people to harm! But this is no defense. If God were asked why he created such a world for people to live in instead of creating a better one, should his reply be, "They wouldn't know the difference", an appropriate reply, even if it could not be uttered, would be, "No, but you did!"

Having raised some difficulties concerning the possibility of a world of naturally good men which contains no actual evil and Swinburne's claim that God could not have an obligation to create the best of all possible worlds if that notion made sense, we see that new difficulties arise in the light of Swinburne's further observations. His strategy is placed in the context of the free-will defense, a defense which "must claim that it is a good thing that there exist free agents with the power and opportunity of choosing between morally good and morally evil actions, agents with sufficient moral discrimination to have some idea of the difference and some (though not overwhelming) temptation to do other than the morally good" (p. 85). Objections have been made to this defense by some philosophers who ask why God has not ensured or seen to it that men as a result of their free deliberations always make the right decisions. Swinburne says that God has not done this because it would be an imposition of character on man and therefore morally wrong. My difficulty is that I have the prior problem of not knowing what it means to speak of God either ensuring or not ensuring, seeing to it or not seeing to it, where the development of human character is concerned. My difficulties can be discussed in two contexts: first, the difficulty of the metaphysical level at which the "ensuring" or "seeing to it" is supposed to take place, and second, the difficulty of knowing what it would be to see to or ensure the formation of human character.

First, then, the question of the metaphysical character of God ensuring that human beings have such-and-such characters. There is no difficulty in locating natural events or intentional acts which have influenced a person's character in specific ways. But here I can say that there may or may not have been such effects, or that some people were affected and others not or that different people were affected in different ways. Even if we say that such-and-such an event or action must have an effect of a specifiable kind, there is still a question of how such an effect is taken up into the rest of a person's life. If I want to speak of "ensuring" or "seeing to it" that a person exhibits a certain "character" then I'd think of something akin to post-hypnotic suggestion. Here, although the person so influenced "obeys the command" and "gives reasons" for his conduct, we do not accept such behavior without reservation as an instance of what we would call obeying a command or giving reasons. There are features of his behavior which lead us to detect rationalization. Of course, on a given occasion, one may be taken in. A man may exhibit anger as the result of a suggestion made to him while under hypnosis in a situation where anger would have been a natural response in any case. The point to stress is not that the seeing to it or the ensuring is always detected, but that we know what it means to speak of detecting it. Add to this the possibility of our having independent knowledge of the hypnosis in the first place. Such direct knowledge is not given to us in God's case, and so we are trying to contemplate what God may or may not have done on the basis of what we already know. My difficulty is to find a discernible difference in human affairs which would confirm or refute these speculations. Those who think it makes sense to speak of God ensuring that men, after free deliberation, always make the right decisions, do not want to think of God as the divine hypnotist since (a) that is not the kind of behavior God is said to ensure and (b) God's ensuring is not something we can clearly discern as sometimes present and sometimes absent in human affairs, but as that which ensures that human affairs are what they are in the first place. My difficulty, I suppose, concerns the intelligibility of thinking of creation as an act of ensuring or seeing to things, similar in character to acts of ensuring or seeing to things that we know, different only in the resources available and the scale of operation.

Second, I find difficulty in knowing what it means to speak of someone ensuring or seeing to it that human characters are of such-and-such a kind. Swinburne does not find this difficult to imagine. He simply thinks it would be a bad thing for God to do, just as it would be a bad thing for parents to do:

> The creator could help agents toward doing right actions by making these reasons more effective causally; that is, he could make agents so that by nature they were inclined (though not perhaps compelled) to pursue what is good. But this would be to impose a moral character on agents, to give them wide general purposes which they naturally pursue, to make them naturally altruistic, tenacious of purpose, or strong-willed. But to impose a character on creatures might well seem to take away from creatures the privilege of developing their own characters and those of their fellows. We tend to think that parents who try too forcibly to impose a character, however good a character, on their children, are less than perfect parents (p. 96).

Someone might well argue from the same facts to the opposite conclusion. A parent who wants to ensure or see to it that his child has one sort of character rather than another, it may be said, is not necessarily interfering with the freedom of the child. If we do not regard such measures as an interference with freedom, despite our ignorance and all the mistakes we make, why should a logical or moral limit be drawn on God, who is not ignorant nor liable to error, seeing to it that human beings freely develop in the right way? [2] I do not want to enter the dispute over whether either program for parental attitudes is right or wrong, since my difficulties over the intelligibility of the program remain.[3] I am not denying that measures taken by parents may influence the development of their children in the way hoped for by the parents. I deliberately speak in the subjunctive mood and speak of hope, since I think it important to distinguish between the retrospective judgment, "I influenced the development of my child's character" or "I did what I

2. This possibility was put to me in discussion by Renford Bambrough.
3. I am indebted to Peter Winch in the discussion referred to in the previous footnote for suggesting that the unintelligibility lies in this direction.

could" with the claim, "I ensured or saw to it that my child's character developed in a certain way". Measures taken in hope recognize that such measures are taken in contexts where a great deal is outside the control of the agent, and a wise parent may recognize that this does not simply happen to be true. He would not know what it would mean if someone wanted to talk of parental influence on development of character in any other way. Greater control would recall visions of posthypnotic behavior, something we wouldn't include in developments of character at all. Thus the wise parent may say, "I thank my lucky stars that I was able to help the development of my child's character" or "I thank God that I was able to help my child". These references to God or lucky stars, here, are not references to those agents who *did* ensure the outcome. On the contrary, these utterances are themselves reactions to the fact that what is contingent, in the hands of God, we might say, has gone in a certain way. It is ironic that the debate about whether God should or should not have seen to the development of human characters, uproots the language of things being in God's hands from one of its natural contexts, a context which gets much of its force from the fact that talk of ensuring or seeing to it that outcomes are of one sort or another has no place in it.

Having spent a little time considering Swinburne's treatment of the question whether men could have been naturally good and whether God could have seen to it that men developed freely in this direction, I want now to consider his defense of God based on more specific evils which he has observed. This shift of attention corresponds to the first two moral principles of the antitheodicist which Swinburne wants to attack. So far he would claim to have disposed of the principle "that a creator able to do so ought to create only creatures such that necessarily they do not do evil actions" (p. 84). He intends next to consider the modified second principle, namely, "that a creator able to do so ought always to ensure that any creature whom he creates does not cause passive evils, or at any rate passive evils which hurt creatures other than himself" (p. 87). Swinburne's general theodicist strategy within which he attempts to show the implausibility of this principle is "that it is not morally wrong for God to create or permit the various evils, normally on the grounds that doing so is providing the logically necesary conditions of greater goods" (p. 82). What is the greater good which justifies the harm that we do to others? Swinburne replies,

A world in which no one except the agent was affected by his evil actions might be a world in which men had freedom but it would not be a world in which men had responsibility. . . . So then the theodicist objects . . . on the grounds that the price of possible passive evils for other creatures is a price worth paying for agents to have great responsibilities for each other. It is a price which (logically) must be paid if they are to have those responsibilities (pp. 87–88).

Swinburne's anlaysis is not an analysis of moral responsibility, but of pseudoresponsibility; it involves a vulgarization of the concept. From the truth that we could not feel responsible unless we were responsible to someone or for something, it does not follow that someone or something should be regarded as opportunities for us to feel responsible. If we remind someone of his responsibilities, we are directing his attention to concerns other than himself. Swinburne's analysis makes these concerns the servants of that self. Compare: "He recognizes the importance of his job" with "His job makes him feel important". Similarly, instead of sometimes feeling responsible for or a responsibility toward the afflictions of others, we would, in terms of Swinburne's analysis, look on those afflictions as opportunities for feeling responsible. It is as if the Parable of the Good Samaritan were thought to show that unlike the priest and the levite, the Samaritan did not pass by an opportunity of feeling responsible.

Furthermore, even if the feeling of responsibility had not been vulgarized in Swinburne's analysis, it would not follow that a responsible reaction justifies the evil or suffering which occasions it. This has been well expressed by W. Somerset Maugham:

It may be that courage and sympathy are excellent and that they could not come into existence without danger and suffering. It is hard to see how the Victoria Cross that rewards the soldier who has risked his life to save a blinded man is going to solace *him* for the loss of his sight. To give alms shows charity, and charity is a virtue, but does *that* good compensate for the evil of the cripple whose poverty has called it forth? [4]

Let us go further down Swinburne's road. He has noticed already that men intentionally bring evil to others, but now he also notices that there is quite a lot of evil around. Therefore he feels that a third moral principle advanced by the antitheodicist needs answering, namely, "that a creator able to do so ought to ensure that any creature whom he creates does not cause passive evils as many and as evil as those in our world" (p. 89). God may have laid out a moral obstacle race for mankind, but are the obstacles too difficult? A defender of the third moral principle "says that in our world freedom and responsibility have gone too far—produced too much physical and mental hurt. God might well tolerate a boy hitting his younger brother, but not Belsen" (p. 89). Swinburne admits that this would be a telling criticism if true, but as he looks around him he does not believe it is true. On the contrary, Swinburne believes that God has created a world where the men are sorted out from the boys. It means "that the creator must create them immature, and allow them gradually to make decisions which affect the sort of beings they will be" (p. 89). This is why Swinburne calls our world "a half-finished universe". The words are well chosen, since the picture is of a finishing school with God as the benevolent headmaster setting the tests. But does Swinburne's God pass the test of benevolence? It is hard to see that he does when we hear Swinburne's argument to show that in allowing evil God has not gone too far:

There are limits to the amount and degree of evil which is possible in our world. Thus there are limits to the amount of pain which a person can suffer—persons only live in our world so many years and the amount which they can suffer at any given time (if mental goings-on are in any way correlated with bodily ones) is limited by their physiology. . . . So the theodicist can certainly claim that a good God stops too much suffering—it is just that he and his opponent draw the line in different places (pp. 89–90).

4. W. Somerset Maugham, *The Summing Up* (Collected edition: London, 1948), p. 259.

Can the theodicist make such a claim on the basis of Swinburne's argument? I think not. There is an unwarrantable transition in the argument from talk of the world to talk about
human beings, and, more important, from conceivable limits to
actual limits. Of course, for any evils in the world we mention,
more can be conceived of, but this is neither here nor there as
far as the question of whether human beings are visited with
greater afflictions than they can bear is concerned. Swinburne
argues that since any human being can stand only so much suffering and we can conceive of more, it follows that God has not
produced unlimited suffering and therefore has not gone too
far. But, clearly, he has produced too much suffering for that
human being and has gone too far for him. Such questions cannot be answered in an abstract or global way. What constitutes
a limit or going too far for one person may not do so for
another. In order to judge whether a human being has suffered more than he can bear, we need to refer to actual limits,
not conceivable limits. By judging actual limits as if they were
conceivable limits, Swinburne could deny that even a person's
death could count as going too far in his case. "After all," he
might say, "he could have died a worse death"! I find this
whole defense rather perverse. God's finishing school is one
where everyone is finished in one sense or another. Either they
are well finished, educated to maturity by their experience in
the moral obstacle race, or they are finished off completely by
it. If the finishing off were done by someone who was solely the
bringer of death, then, in certain circumstances, he could be
described as the bringer of welcome release. But this is not true
of Swinburne's God. Since the bringer of death is also the
bringer of afflictions, he who devised the whole fiendish obstacle race, one cannot even attribute to him the compassion
with which a dog may be put out of his misery. On the contrary, as each candidate fails to make the grade, it is surely
more appropriate to say with Thomas Hardy that thus God has
ended his play. Let us hurry from this scene.

As he goes further down his road, Swinburne thinks that the
possibility of evil can be justified in terms of the opportunities
for noble actions it provides:

given a creator, then, without an immoral act on his part, for acts of courage, compassion, etc., to be acts open to men to perform, there have to be various evils. Evils give men the opportunity to perform those acts which show men at their best. A world without evils would be a world in which men could show no forgiveness, no compassion, no self-sacrifice. And men without that opportunity are deprived of the opportunity to show themselves at their noblest. For this reason God might well allow some of his creatures to perform evil acts with passive evils as consequences, since these provide the opportunity for especially noble acts (pp. 90–91).

This argument ignores a great deal, its main defect being its one-sided optimism. Why should evil beget good? One cannot feel remorse without having done wrong, but evil may give one an appetite for more. One cannot show forgiveness without something to forgive, but that something may destroy or prompt savage reactions. In a man's own life natural evils such as illness or social evils such as poverty may debase and destroy him. Swinburne says,

Pain normally occurs when something goes wrong with the working of our body which is going to lead to further limitation on the purposes which we can achieve; and the pain ends when the body is repaired. The existence of the pain spurs the sufferer, and others through the sympathetic suffering which arises when they learn of the sufferer's pain, to do something about the bodily malfunctioning. Yet giving men such feelings which they are inclined to end involves the imposition of no character (p. 97).

Swinburne is faced with formidable contrary testimony often expressed in art or from recollection of experience. Here are some of Settembrini's comments to Hans Castorp in Thomas Mann's *The Magic Mountain:*

You said that the sight of dullness and disease going hand in hand must be the most melancholy in life. I grant you, I grant you that. I too prefer an intelligent ailing person to a consumptive idiot. But I take issue where you regard the combination of disease with dullness as a sort of aesthetic inconsistency, an error in taste on the part of nature, a "dilemma for the human feelings", as you were pleased to express yourself. When you professed to regard disease as something so refined, so—what did you call it?—possessing a "certain dignity"— that it doesn't "go with" stupidity. That was the expression you used. Well, I say no! Disease has nothing refined about it, nothing dignified.

Such a conception is in itself pathological, or at least tends in that direction. . . . Do not, for heaven's sake, speak to me of the ennobling effects of physical suffering! A soul without a body is as inhuman and horrible as a body without a soul—though the latter is the rule and the former the exception. It is the body, as a rule, which flourishes exceedingly, which draws everything to itself, which usurps the predominant place and lives repulsively emancipated from the soul. A human being who is first of all an invalid is *all* body; therein lies his inhumanity and his debasement. In most cases he is little better than a carcass.[5]

Here too are W. Somerset Maugham's recollections of what he saw in hospital wards as he trained for the medical profession:

At that time (a time to most people of sufficient ease, when peace seemed certain and prosperity secure) there was a school of writers who enlarged upon the moral value of suffering. They claimed that it was salutary. They claimed that it increased sympathy and enhanced the sensibilities. They claimed that it opened to the spirit new avenues of beauty and enables it to get into touch with the mystical kingdom of God. They claimed that it strengthened the character, purified it from its human grossness, and brought to him who did not avoid but sought it a more perfect happiness . . . I set down in my note-books, not once or twice, but in a dozen places, the facts that I had seen. I knew that suffering did not ennoble; it degraded. It made men selfish, mean, petty, and suspicious. It absorbed them in small things. It did not make them more than men; it made them less than men; and I wrote ferociously that we learn resignation not by our own suffering, but by the suffering of others.[6]

Not only need evil not occasion goodness, but goodness itself may occasion evils. Swinburne does not consider these possibilities. The depth of a man's love may lead him to kill his wife's lover or to be destroyed when the object of his love is lost to him. A man whose love was mediocre would not have done either of these things. Love has as much to do with the terrible as with the wonderful. The presence of goodness in some may be the cause of hatred in others. Budd's goodness is more than Claggart can bear and it is the very possibility that deep love may be a reality which Iago cannot admit into his dark soul.

5. Thomas Mann, *The Magic Mountain,* trans. H. T. Lowe-Porter (London, 1965), pp. 98–100.
6. *The Summing Up,* p. 62.

On his travels Swinburne has seen how human beings intervene from time to time to help each other in their troubles.
Sometimes, when fortunate, they can prevent those troubles occurring, and they often try to prevent things getting worse. He
realizes then that he has to answer the question why his God
does not intervene in circumstances where mere mortals would
not hesitate. His answers are not encouraging. Roughly, they
amount to saying that just as parents know more than their
children and are often right not to act when their offspring beg
them to do so, so God, the Father of us all, knowing more than
we know, refrains from acting despite the cries of the afflicted.
Here is a sample:

> Hence a God who sees far more clearly than we do the consequences
> of quarrels may have duties very different from ours with respect to
> particular such quarrels. He may know that the suffering that A will
> cause B is not nearly as great as B's screams may suggest to us and will
> provide (unknown to us) an opportunity to C to help B recover and
> will thus give C a deep responsibility which he would not otherwise
> have (p. 92).

I have already commented on the character of such a sense of
responsibility, and that is not my purpose now. It is true that
sometimes considering a matter further is a sign of reasonableness and maturity. But this cannot be stated absolutely,
since at other times readiness to be open-minded about matters
is a sign of a corrupt mind. There are screams and screams,
and to ask of what use are the screams of the innocent, as Swinburne's defense would have us do, is to embark on a specula-
tion we should not even contemplate. We have our reasons,
final human reasons, for putting a moral full stop at many
places. If God has other reasons, they are his reasons, not ours,
and they do not overrule them. That is why, should he ask us
to consider them, we, along with Ivan Karamazov, respectfully,
or not so respectfully, return him the ticket. So when Swinburne says, "The argument must go on with regard to particular cases. . . . The exhibition of consequences is a long process,
and it takes time to convince an opponent even if he is prepared to be rational, more time than is available in this paper"
(pp. 100f.), one must not be misled by apparent reasonableness.

Being prepared to consider the consequences of doing something is not the hallmark of moral reasonableness. Often, when
the invitation to consider consequences is made, the appropriate reply is "Get thee behind me, Satan!" And if there is a
"higher" form of reasoning among God and his angels, where
such matters are open for compromise and calculation, then so
much the worse for God and his angels. If they reason in this
way in the heavenly places, we can say with Wallace Stevens,
"Alas that they should wear our colors there".

Swinburne notices that there are natural and mental evils
which are not the results of intentional actions. How are these
to be justified? The answer is that pains give men additional
reasons for changing states of affairs without imposing a character on them.

An itch causally inclines a man to do whatever will cause the itch to
cease, e.g., scratch, and provides a reason for doing that action. Its
causal influence is quite independent of the agent—saint or sinner,
strong-willed or weak-willed, will all be strongly inclined to get rid of
their pains (though some may learn to resist the inclination). Hence a
creator who wished to give agents some inclination to improve the
world without giving them a character, a wide set of general purposes
which they naturally pursue, would tie some of the imperfections of
the world to physical or mental evils (pp. 96–97).

This is a strange argument. Insofar as these causal effects become reasons for a man, one will have to take account of the
man's character to appreciate what role the reason plays in his
life, how it connects up with other considerations he thinks important. Even if the causal influence of certain pains is undeni-
able, one cannot, as we have seen already, argue for an easy
transition between this recognition and its becoming a reason
for working toward improvement. The character of the transition, or whether there is one at all, cannot be wholly determined without reference to the character of the person concerned. Kierkegaard provides a good example of what I mean
in the case of the calculating rake: "Indeed, fear of the body's
infirmities has taught the voluptuary to observe moderation in
debauchery . . . but it has never made him chaste." [7] Further-

7. Søren Kierkegaard, *Purity of Heart*, trans. Douglas Steere (London, 1961),
p. 72.

more, if a man's life were governed by the calculation of the acquiring or avoiding of such pains in relation to the policy of moral or immoral conduct, surely the character at work would be a servile one.[8]

Similar conclusions can be drawn regarding Swinburne's remarks on mental evils. He says,

Many mental evils too are caused by things going wrong in a man's life or in the life of his fellows and often serve as a spur to a man to put things right, either to put right the cause of the particular mental evil or to put similar things right. A man's feeling of frustration at the failure of his plans spurs him either to fulfill those plans despite their initial failure or to curtail his ambitions. A man's sadness at the failure of the plans of his child will incline him to help the child more in the future. A man's grief at the absence of a loved one inclines him to do whatever will get the loved one back. As with physical pain, the spur inclines a man to do what is right but does so without imposing a character—without say, making a man responsive to duty, or strong-willed (p. 98).

We have seen already that Swinburne's analysis does not work in the case of physical pains, save in simple, straightforward cases. If a man has toothache, normally, he wants it attended to. Yet, one will not get very far by suggesting that mental evils stand to behavior as toothache stands to the search for a remedy. Karenin was in mental anguish at the loss of Anna to Vronsky. He was certainly frustrated at the failure of his plans. He was spurred on to fulfill those plans. Nevertheless, it would be absurd to think that an account could be given of his anguish or frustration without introducing considerations of character, considerations internally related to the nature of his subsequent behavior.

Having traveled with Swinburne to the end of the road he has chosen to go down, noting various ills and misfortunes to which human beings are subject, we are now in a position to summarize the answer to the problem of evil which he brings before us: There are doubts as to whether it makes sense to imagine men who are naturally good without actual evils in the

---

8. Swinburne recognizes this when he supports my criticisms of Peter Geach's appeal to divine power as a justification for obeying God's commands. See Richard G. Swinburne, "Duty and the Will of God," *Canadian Journal of Philosophy*, 4 (1974).

world. It is equally doubtful to say that God ought to have seen to it that men freely reach the right decisions. Even if the notion of the best of all logically possible worlds made sense, God would have no obligation to create such a world, for whom would he harm if he did not? There are good reasons for saying that the various evils in the world are compatible with the existence of an omnipotent, omniscient, all-good God. Such evils as we bring on others give us the opportunity of feeling responsible, and that is a good thing. After all, such evils are not unlimited, since there is a limit to what anyone can stand. Evils give us an opportunity to be seen at our best in reacting to them. God does not intervene to prevent evil when any decent human being would, because he has a wider knowledge of the situations in which evils occur. In order to prompt us in the right direction without imposing characters on us, God has seen to it that physical and mental evils are linked to things going wrong. Looking back at the details of his case, Swinburne says that "a morally sensitive antitheodicist might well in principle accept some of the above arguments" (p. 100). This conclusion is a somewhat embarrassing one since it is evident from my comments that one of the strongest criticisms available to the antitheodicist would be the moral insensitivity of the theodicist's case. There is an example in Billie Holiday's autobiography which combines many of the circumstances to which Swinburne calls our attention but which also sums up the fragility of his optimistic analyses. She tells of a well-known jazz personality who was a drug addict:

I can tell you about a big-name performer who had a habit and a bad one. There were times when he had it licked. And other times it licked him. It went around that way for years. He was well known, like me, which makes it worse. He had bookings to make, contracts to fulfil. In the middle of one engagement he was about to crack up and go crazy because he had run out of stuff. There was no way in God's world that he could kick cold turkey and make three shows a day. There wasn't a doctor in town who would be seen looking at him. His wife got so scared he'd kill himself that she tried to help him the only way she knew—by risking her own neck and trying to get him what he needed. She went out in the street like a pigeon, begging everyone she knew for help. Finally she found someone who sold her some stuff for an arm and a leg. It was just her luck to be carrying it back to her old man when she was arrested.

She was as innocent and clean as the day she was born. But she knew that if she tried to tell that to the cops it would only make her a "pusher" under the law, liable for a good long time in jail. She thought if she told them she was a user, and took some of the stuff in her pocket to prove it, they might believe her, feel sorry for her, go easy on her. And she could protect her man. So that's what she did. She used junk for the first time to prove to the law she wasn't a pusher. And that's the way she got hooked. She's rotting in jail right now. Yes siree bob, life is just a bowl of cherries.[9]

Later, Billie Holiday sums up her own attitude, "If you expect nothing but trouble, maybe a few happy days will turn up. If you expect happy days, look out." [10]

In replying to Swinburne's arguments I have chosen in the main to comment on his reading of the fortunes and misfortunes of human life, a reading which is to serve in the construction of a theodicy. Theodicies, such as Swinburne's, are marked by their order, optimism and progress. If we want to appreciate why Swinburne should not have turned down the road on which he chooses to travel in the first place, this, above all, is what has to be put aside. Throughout Swinburne's paper, the main emphasis, with only an occasional hint of difficulties, is on the world as a God-given setting in which human beings can exercise rational choices which determine the kind of people they are to become. This is neither the world I know, nor the world in which Swinburne lives. Ours is a world where disasters of natural and moral kinds can strike without rhyme or reason. Where, if much can be done to influence character, much can also bring about such influence over which we have no control. Character has as much, and probably more, to do with reacting to the unavoidable, as with choosing between available alternatives. Commenting on a similar order, progress and optimism to Swinburne's in recent moral philosophy, I had reason to quote Hardy's comments on the limits which life placed on Tess's endeavors:

9. Billie Holiday with William Dufty, *Lady Sings The Blues* (London, 1975), pp. 183–184.
10. Ibid., p. 187.

Nature does not often say "See!" to her poor creature at a time when
seeing can lead to happy doing; or reply "Here!" to a body's cry of
"Where?" till the hide-and-seek has become an irksome, outworn
game. We may wonder whether at the acme and summit of the human
progress these anachronisms will be corrected by a finer intuition, a
closer interaction of the social machinery than that which now jolts us
round and along; but such completeness is not to be prophesied, or
even conceived as possible.[11]

And yet, even such poor creatures are heard to talk of God. In
the context of this reply I can only hint at the import of such
talk, talk which I do not claim is all of a piece or capable of
being fitted into a neat theological system. I have already suggested in discussing what might be meant by someone who said
the outcome was in the hands of God, that the force of the
belief depends on the absence of the kind of higher level plan-
ning so essential to Swinburne's theodicy. The same is true of
talk of God's grace in face of life's evils. In order even to reach
the threshold of understanding what might be meant here, the
sheer pointlessness of those evils has to be admitted. One has to
see, for example, that there is no reason why these natural disasters should have come our way. One has to be ready to answer in face of one's cry, "Why is this happening to me?", "Why
shouldn't it?" This recognition of the pointlessness of suffering
in this sense can lead in various directions. It has led some to
speak of the absurd, but it has led others to speak of all things
as God's gifts, and of things not being one's own by right or
reason, but by the grace of God. It is not my purpose to advocate these uses of language, but simply to note their existence. Again, in other contexts, a person may wonder in relation to his own character what he can do something about and
what has been given by God; that is, what cannot be changed,
but which he must come to terms with. On wider issues there
may be much agonizing over whether something, marriage, for
example, is of God, something fixed and unalterable with
which we must come to terms, or whether we are confusing a
human institution with God's will and erecting a barrier with

11. *Tess of the D'Urbervilles* (London, 1912), p. 49. Quoted in "Some Limits To
Moral Endeavour," Inaugural Lecture, published by University College of
Swansea, 1971.

no more than a nominal reality which prevents us receiving God's gifts of happiness. Such contexts as these do not imply the dismissal of those considerations which have led people to talk of the problem of evil. On the contrary, without the human cry from the midst of afflictions no sense can be made of these religious responses, and there may be constant tensions of various kinds between the responses and the evils which surround them. The responses are not, however, recognitions of a higher order, but one way of understanding the lack of such an order. Even when the response is understood in this way, it may well be regarded by those who cannot share it as an evil response.

Hardy complains ironically in face of the limits and limitations Tess had to face or fail to face, that "why so often the coarse appropriates the finer . . . the wrong man the woman, the wrong woman the man, many thousand years of analytical philosophy have failed to explain to our sense of order" (p. 91). In the context already mentioned I commented that Hardy, of course, was not looking for explanations. Swinburne looks for explanations. Any sense of order with which one would have been satisfied would be defective just for that reason. That must be my verdict on Swinburne's theodicy. Swinburne admits that his God does ask a lot of his creatures, but says,

A theodicist is in a better position to defend a theodicy such as I have outlined if he is prepared also to make the further additional claim— that God knowing the worthwhileness of the conquest of evil and the perfecting of the universe by men, shared with them this task by subjecting himself as man to the evil in the world. A creator is more justified in creating or permitting evils to be overcome by his creatures if he is prepared to share with them the burden of the suffering and effort (p. 102).

Not so, for if the visit to our world were by a God such as Swinburne describes, those who said that there was no room at the inn would be right. We should not be at home to such callers. And if perchance we were asked to choose between this visitor and another, we should unhesitatingly demand, "Give us Prometheus!"

6

Remarks

JOHN HICK

In his paper Swinburne traces out what I expect he would
agree is only the bare bones of a possible theodicy. Phillips
rejects this theodicy, and indeed I think rejects the very idea of
a theodicy in the sense of a theory which seeks to show how the
realities of suffering and wickedness may be compatible with
the existence of an all-powerful and limitlessly loving God.
Thus far the difference between them might seem to be that
while they agree as to the reality both of evil and of God, Swinburne thinks that it is and Phillips that it is not possible to *show*
the compatibility between them. But I fancy that their difference is really much deeper than this. For reading Phillips's
paper, in the light of his other writings, I take it that he denies
the existence of an all-powerful and limitlessly loving God. I
take it, that is, that he denies that in addition to all the many
human consciousnesses there is another consciousness which is
the consciousness of God, and that this God is the creator of
the universe and is both all-powerful and limitlessly loving. I
take it that he rejects this belief as a crude misunderstanding of
religious language and holds that, rightly understood, the 'existence of God' consists in man's use of theistic language within
the context of a pattern of religious life. If so, his fundamental
objection to theodicies is the radical and wholesale objection
that since there is no *theos* there can be no theodicy. I think it
worthwhile to bring this out, because it is important to insist
that the serious and honest theist must face the challenge which
the fact of evil, and above all the fact of undeserved human
suffering, pose to his faith in God. He cannot dispose of this
challenge along the lines hinted at toward the end of Phillips's

paper. For while some fortunate, or noble, souls do indeed react to life's tragedies acceptingly—saying, not 'Why is this happening to me?' but 'Why shouldn't it?'—others (as Phillips himself insists) do not, and are instead embittered or driven to black despair. If there is no God—except as a thought in men's minds, a concept operating within our theistic language—then the destructive power of suffering is just a dreadful fact, and that's that. But if we believe that behind the existence of this world and of our life within it there lies a sovereign purpose of love, then we have on our hands the well-known problem of evil. The religious, as well as philosophical, importance of a theodicy is that it may show faith in God to be, even in face of this challenge, still a possibility for a rational person. So let us look at Swinburne's outline of a theodicy and at Phillips's comments on it.

Seen against the background of the long history of thought on this subject, Swinburne's theodicy is of what has been called the Irenaean as distinguished from the Augustinian type. Its approach falls broadly within a tradition which began with some of the Greek-speaking Fathers of the Church, and particularly Irenaeus, who was a Christian thinker active toward the end of the second century. I think that a theodicy of this kind is probably viable. I am therefore interested to notice how Phillips, even while attacking it, gives it backhanded support at certain key points. For where Swinburne argues that God could not have done such-and-such because this would have been incompatible with the value that he is said to put upon the existence of free creatures, Phillips says that God could not have done that same thing because it does not make sense to speak of its being done—it is logically undoable. Swinburne's theodicy gains either way. For if Phillips is right, he has supplied an even stronger argument for Swinburne's conclusion. In this way Phillips contributes arguments for the two important contentions (a) that God could not have created a world in which men are naturally good and which contains no evil and (b) that God could not have ensured that men as a result of their free deliberations always make the right choice. As to the first, Phillips claims that the notion of moral goodness only makes sense in a world in which there are temptations and difficulties (pp. 104–105); and as to the second, he claims the notion of God's 'ensuring' or 'seeing to it' that men develop morally in a certain way makes no sense (p. 106). These constitute alternative arguments for important elements in Swinburne's theodicy.

Let us remember at this point what a theodicy is. It consists in a 'picture' of the universe or a hypothesis about the nature of the universe, a hypothesis or 'picture' in which evil can be seen as ultimately serving a good and justifying purpose. The interest of such a 'picture' largely depends, I would suggest, upon its connection with an actual living tradition of religious faith, rather than being a mere ad hoc invention of philosophers. For the context within which the theodicy problem arises, for most of us at any rate, is an inquiry concerning the rational possibility of an actual form of religious faith, such as the Christian faith. What we are asking is whether there are resources within that faith for meeting the problem of evil. Let me, then, now point very briefly to four aspects of the Christian tradition, mainly in its Irenaean development, which I think help to fill out the outline theodicy which Swinburne has offered.

First, when we ask whether this world is good, or good enough, or the best possible, we have also to ask, good for what? good in relation to what purpose? A great deal of antitheodicy has assumed the 'picture' of God intending to create a paradise, a flawless environment for his creatures, and has pointed to the world's evils as manifest failures within such a program. The Christian tradition, on the other hand, in its Irenaean form, presents this world as part of a vast ongoing act of soul making or, better, person making. God has, through the long evolutionary process, produced the human animal and is now producing out of human animals 'children of God'. Man as intelligent, ethical and religious animal exists in what Irenaeus called the image of God, and is now being brought through his own free responses into what Irenaeus called the finite likeness of God, which is the ultimate fulfillment of the human potentiality. Within this 'picture' man is seen as an immature creature, undergoing a further development which is spiritual rather than physical. At this midpoint of his creation man is, in traditional religious language, a 'sinner', a 'fallen' creature. For, as Kierkegaard so vividly insisted, the 'problem' facing the infinite God in his creation of finite persons is to give them genuine freedom over against himself. If man were brought into being in the direct presence of God, unable not to be conscious of his maker, how could he ever be free in relation to God? But man has been brought into being at an epistemic distance from God through his emergence as part of an autonomous world in which God is not overwhelmingly evident—a world which is, as Dietrich Bonhoeffer said, *etsi deus non daretur*. In such a world man is not compelled to know God but is at the same time free to come to know him by faith. Formed in this way, man is an animal, responsible for his individual survival, and thus basically self-concerned; and this instinctive self-concern is the source of what in the Christian tradition is called sin. Accordingly man, as animal in process of becoming 'child of God', is inevitably morally immature and imperfect, and the occurrence of moral evil is at this stage integral to the divine creative work. This does not, of course, mean that particular wrong acts are in accordance with God's purposes, but that the existence of man as self-centered animal in process of becoming a 'child of God' is in accordance with God's purpose.

Second, given this conception of a divine intention behind the existence of man in this world, it is not only evident why there is moral evil but also why there is natural evil. For man could not develop morally and spiritually in a paradise. The best of all possible worlds for his present comfort and pleasure might well be the worst of all possible worlds for his growth into a higher quality of existence. Moral and spiritual growth are not spontaneous but come in response to challenges, in the making of choices, in the facing of difficulties and problems, and through the experience of coping with setbacks and failures as well as enjoying success and achievement. Hence something like our present imperfect world, with its contingencies

and uncertainties, is an environment more apt for person making than would be a stress-free paradise. Once again, the
suggestion is not that God ordains the specific challenges and
the specific good and bad fortunes which each individual
meets, but that he has ordained a world involving genuine contingencies as an environment in which the human animal may
begin to become a 'child of God'.

Third, if this is so the theodicy problem becomes, as Swinburne suggests, a question of the actual concrete character and
incidence of evil in the world. There are two main aspects of
this. One is the age-old offense of the wicked prospering while
the righteous suffer. All manner of accidents and misfortune
strike randomly and therefore unjustly, without relation to
human desert. But suppose that instead they occurred justly
and therefore nonrandomly, so that the evil were always pun-
ished and the virtuous rewarded. Such a system would not
serve a person-making purpose. As Kant pointed out in the
Critique of Practical Reason (Pt. I, Bk. II, sec. 9), it would undermine the moral life, since men would then act rightly for hope
of reward or fear of punishment. In other words, moral responsibility and hence moral growth require a world in which
there are genuine contingencies which distribute good and bad
fortune not on the basis of desert. The other aspect of the
problem concerns the degree of misfortune that can occur, the
sheer intensity of human suffering. Is this not often too great
to serve any constructive purpose? Yes indeed, sometimes, and
indeed all too often, the effect of some crushing tragedy, as we
see it in this life, *is* morally and spiritually destructive. The
Irenaean theodicy claims that beyond this destruction there will
be further creation, leading at last to the formation of a perfect
being. I will return in a moment to the way in which the picture
changes when we remove the restrictive assumption, which
Phillips clearly makes, that there is no continued personal existence, with the possibility of further change and growth,
beyond this life. But thinking for the moment only of this
earthly life, let us consider what it would be for life's challenges
and tragedies *not* sometimes to be too great. Let us make a
thought experiment and suppose the worst form of human suf-

fering, whatever it may be, not to exist. Something else would then be the worst form of suffering; and if that did not exist, then something else again. But if in imagination we reduce the possibilities of human pain and suffering to an acceptable level, with nothing worse occurring than, say, an itch as physical pain and a mild feeling of regret as mental pain, it will turn out that we have imagined a world which does not allow for real moral responsibility or therefore for the possibility of moral growth. For note that in such a world no one will be able to hurt anyone else, either physically or mentally. And since it will be impossible to harm anyone, there will be no such thing as a wrong action, or therefore a right action. Again, the caring and sacrificial aspects of human love will not exist, nor sympathy and mutual aid. It will in fact be a world in which ethical concepts have no use; and such a world could not serve any purpose of moral and spiritual person making. And yet when we turn back to the real world, in which moral progress—and also regress—does occur, we are back in an environment in which suffering can rise to unacceptable levels. For there is, I suggest, a deep connection between morality and suffering such that a world without the possibility of real—and therefore unacceptable—suffering could not be inhabited by morally growing beings. We may be tempted to feel that if morality and evil go together in this way, God should not have created moral beings. But to reject this temptation is to begin to see the possibility of the Irenaean type of theodicy.

This brings me to my fourth and last point. This is that the picture of the world as the scene of a person-making process can make sense only if we see this life as part of a much larger existence in which that creative process continues to completion beyond this world. In other words, human immortality is essential to this type of theodicy. For it is quite evident that the creating of human animals into children of God is not usually completed by the moment of bodily death and that if it is ever to be completed it must continue beyond this life. I think that many philosophers are inclined to regard a reference at this point to life after death as a kind of cheating, a breaking of the rules of the game. But if we are trying to test the rational possibility of the Christian faith, this is not a game but an examination of the actual beliefs of a living community; and these undoubtedly include the belief in an afterlife. The life everlasting has always been recognized as a central implicate of the Christian doctrine of the love of God for his human creatures, and is thus one of the essential resources of Christianity in face of the problem of evil. For the justification of evil, according to this Irenaean type of theodicy, is that it is a necessary part of a process whose end product is to be an infinite good—namely, the perfection and endless joy of all finite personal life. This implies, in traditional Christian terms, universal salvation, and an eternal heavenly life eventually supervening upon an intermediate or purgatorial postmortem existence.

Obviously the notion of immortality opens up many and vast questions. How can man live after the death of his body? Is such an afterlife disembodied or reembodied? How may men continue to grow beyond this life as moral agents? What guarantee can there be that the person-making process will ever fully succeed, however much time is available? I do not think that these questions are unanswerable, and it may be that some of them will be answered in this symposium's session on Immortality; but I must not divert us onto these questions now.

Postscript

RICHARD SWINBURNE

I shall make one general comment on Phillips's paper and a number of brief comments on points of detail. The major strategy of his paper seems to me to be to draw our attention to much of the evil in life and to its apparent pointlessness. I hope that I am not insensitive to the evil in life, but I do not share Phillips's conviction that the evil is pointless, and I do not find enough *argument* in Phillips's paper to show that it is. Thus to illustrate his points, Phillips quotes at me the example from Billie Holiday's autobiography. But I cannot see that the production of this example of evil settles anything. To start with, we just don't know some of the crucial factors involved—could the "performer" have resisted his "habit"? And could his wife have resisted the temptation to use "junk" on occasions subsequent to the first? If the answers to these questions are yes, clearly the performer and his wife have some share in the responsibility for her troubles. But, whatever the answers to these questions, quite obviously a considerable number of other human beings have a large share of responsibility for the wife's troubles—the drug pushers, the doctors who "wouldn't be seen looking at" the performer, the legislators who passed such lousy drug legislation, the people of the state who were too busy with their own concerns to press their legislators into doing anything about the legislation, etc. Now the issue is—is there a moral obligation on a creator to ensure that agents have no opportunity to exercise the kind and amount of responsibility which will allow this sort of thing to happen? If there is a creator, has he given men too much responsibility? I don't find in Phillips's discussion of this case any arguments to show that he has. Horrifying as the circumstances undoubtedly are, the alternative is a world where men have a great deal less responsibility for their fellows than they do in our world. That men should have much responsibility for their fellows and for the world seems in itself quite evidently an extremely good thing. In view of this, the moral obligations in this matter of a creator are in no way obvious, and I wait for further arguments on the matter, which Phillips does not give. Phillips will, I suspect, say that it is so obvious that a creator ought not to permit such things to happen that it is, in his phrase a "sign of a corrupt mind" on my part to suppose anything else.

My answer to the paragraph on p. 115 in which this phrase occurs is as follows. It is indeed often the case in life that we have to make decisions in the light of the evidence as we have it and of the moral judgments which we are initially inclined to make. There is often no time to consider the moral issues further, for if we did we should fail to take the action which we ought morally to take instantly. Here indeed delay is the sign of a corrupt mind. But that is not our situation today. We are not delaying essential action by insisting on moral theorizing. We are doing philosophy. And, when we are doing philosophy and are justified in doing so (as I hope that we are now), it is *never* a "sign of a corrupt mind" to be open-minded about things. In all areas of life what seems most obviously true sometimes turns out to be false, and it is not the sign of a corrupt mind but the sign of a seeker after truth to examine carefully views which initially seem obviously true. It seemed to many men obvious that the Earth was flat; we may, however, be grateful that despite this, they were prepared to listen to arguments to the contrary. Sometimes, too, moral judgments which seem obviously true turn out on investigation not to be so at all—and this both for moral and factual reasons. It seemed to many obviously right that heretics should be tortured. Nevertheless, some who held this view were prepared to listen to arguments and to look at consequences, and this process may have led them to change their views. Think too of what the initial moral indignation of some of us would be if we saw a man sawing off another's leg, and yet our initial moral indignations might have been quite misplaced—maybe the man was doing his utmost to save an-

other's life, removing a wounded leg in the absence of anaes-
thetics. Detailed knowledge of the circumstances (and that
doesn't mean only knowledge of effects) may rightly make us
withdraw initial moral judgments, and that applies to almost all
initial moral judgments of which you like to think. The evils of
this world which seem pointless may have a point despite appearances. Whether they do or not depends in part on the circumstances which do not lie open to view—has some sufferer
brought the evil on himself, is it giving him an opportunity to
do greater good, is there life after this life (a possible circumstance to which John Hick has drawn our attention), etc.? It
also depends on just how desirable are the logically possible alternatives to those evils, which lie within the power of a creator
to create—if the only logically possible alternative available to a
creator to allowing the events recorded in Billie Holiday's nar-
rative is for the creator to act as Big Brother and weigh out for
all rations of a certain amount of pleasure and no pain, then
perhaps a creator's actions in creating a world in which these
events lay within the power of creatures to bring about was not
so evil after all. Phillips just begs the question by claiming that
"ours is a world where disasters of natural and moral kinds can
strike without rhyme or reason". We need argument here to
counter the kinds of suggestion which I put forward, to show
that they don't provide adequate "reason" to justify the disasters. Otherwise maybe there is, despite first appearances,
rhyme or reason in these disasters.

I pass to making some very brief comments on some of Phillips's less central points. On pp. 113f. Phillips points out that evil
may beget evil as well as good. Of course it may. But all that I
said was that certain kinds of evil give men the opportunity
which they could not otherwise have to perform good actions
of certain kinds. Better a world with opportunity for both kinds
of humanly free action than one with opportunity for neither,
surely? On p. 115 he points out that good may beget evil. So
indeed it may. But is Phillips seriously suggesting that a good
creator ought to immunize men from a whole variety of possible free responses to love? On p. 110 (and again on p. 113) Phillips seems to think that I am suggesting that afflictions provide
opportunities for "*feeling* responsible". I certainly wrote no

such thing. What I claimed was the opportunity to do to others either good or evil allowed men to exercise responsibility; not to feel responsible, but to *be* responsible. On p. 112 Phillips writes that I argue that "since any human being can stand only so much suffering and we can conceive of more, it follows that God has not produced unlimited suffering and therefore has not gone too far." Although the first conclusion follows, the second does not (although, of course, what the conclusion says may nevertheless be true) and I certainly did not mean to suggest that it did. When I look at the text of my p. 89, however, I can see that I expressed myself badly. All that I *meant* to say in the second sentence of the last paragraph is that if God made our world, he has clearly limited the amount of suffering. For this unclarity I apologize. The issue, as I made clear in the penultimate sentence, is whether the actual amount of evil is nevertheless too great. This is, I have suggested throughout my paper, not a question which admits of a quick answer—certainly not the quick answer which Phillips gives in the middle of his p. 112, that *"clearly"* since God "has produced too much suffering for that human being"—which one? presumably one who has collapsed morally under the suffering—God "has gone too far for him". But that follows only if we know that he couldn't help collapsing, that he hasn't given in to forces which he could have resisted—and that's just what we don't know until philosophers and scientists together have solved the free-will problem.

I could comment on many other details of Phillips's paper, but time does not allow. I would like instead in conclusion to make again the kind of point which I make in my paper, in a more rhetorical and less rigorous way. Let me do this by asking you to consider what kind of a world you would think it right to create if you had unlimited power and knowledge. At first the kind of answer we give to this question is overinfluenced by thought of how we would improve this world if we were a bit more powerful and knowledgeable. We would, we say, make certain that everybody had long years of food, drink, sleep, sex, clothes, music, drama, philosophy, etc.; plenty of opportunity to enjoy themselves. But a little reflection will suggest that this is a pretty mediocre way of treating creatures. Creatures would rightly want something more—the privilege of running things for themselves; of finding out for themselves how the world works, of teaching and learning from each other; of choosing (without predetermination by a creator) between alternative blueprints for parts of the Universe, of putting their plans into practice through much hard work, of affecting the destiny of their fellows. These privileges logically bring with them other privileges—less immediately recognized as such, but great privileges all the same—such as the privilege of being able to give in, of sinking to the level of the beasts; the privilege of being able to spit at God in the face and get away with it for a time; the privilege of making one's own mistakes; the privilege of being able to mold other men for ill as well as for good; the privilege of having something to live for, and something to die for. The latter is the privilege of being able to give away everything without expectation of reward. "Greater love has no man than this that a man lay down his life for his friends"—does Phillips really want a world in which men had no opportunity to show love of that greatness? The latter set of privileges go with the former set, and they carry with them of logical necessity either the existence of evil or the possibility of its occurrence without a creator preventing it. Those who follow Phillips in rejecting theodicy ought to give a serious and detailed answer to the question of what kind of world they would think it right to create if they themselves had unlimited power and knowledge. And they ought then to ask themselves whether that world has the scope for love and learning, sacrifice, patience, and faith which there is in our world; and, if it does not, whether their world is really better. Clearly a world in which there was nothing but scope for exercise of these virtues and no food and rest, family and nature, literature and dancing would be a dubiously desirable, if not somewhat incoherent, world (what would be the point of laying down your life for your friends unless they were likely in consequence to be able to enjoy some of these primary pleasures?). But then equally clearly our world is not like that.

Postscript

D. Z. PHILLIPS

These remarks are based on the opening comments made by
Hick as chairman of the symposium, Swinburne's comments on
my original reply, and various points made in the course of the
discussion.

Hick thinks that the real difference between Swinburne and
myself is that Swinburne believes in the existence of God and I
do not. I do not think we are concerned with the personal
beliefs of either of us. Hick thinks I would object to someone
saying that he believed in "the existence of an all-powerful and
limitlessly loving God". Anyone who has this belief believes, according to Hick, "that in addition to all the many human consciousnesses there is another consciousness which is the consciousness of God". That I should certainly contest. I contest it
as a philosopher's gloss on the nature of religious belief. For
Hick, my views entail atheism. He says that my "fundamental
objection to theodicies is the wholesale one that since there is
no *theos* there can be no theodicy". But, on the contrary, my
claim is that the urge to construct theodicies is itself the result
of a confused view of what must be the relation between the
will of God and the lives of men and women. Hick claims that
for me, "the 'existence of God' consists in man's use—his spontaneous and committed use—of theistic language". These
words are puzzling. Clearly, a man's commitment to God shows
itself in the language he uses, not only about God, but about
the world and in his general behavior. That he is able to have
such a commitment depends on there being a shared language
and shared practices in which he can partake. But if Hick is
saying that for me commitment to God *means* commitment to

language, the results would obviously be absurd. I do not think 'I believe in the language almighty' would strike a responsive chord in many and I certainly would not recognize it as an account of religious belief.

The puzzle deepens when Hick presents philosophers with the exclusive choice of thinking of God either as an additional consciousness or as a thought in men's minds. I may think about sticks and stones. I must master certain techniques of reference and identity in order to do so. But when I think about sticks and stones, I do not think that sticks and stones are mere thoughts in my mind. Even when the empiricists said that bodies were collections of ideas they wanted to distinguish between perceiving a dagger and the dagger which is a mere thought in my mind. In mathematical reasoning we do not find notions of reference comparable to those operative in our talk of physical objects, and yet when we think of mathematical concepts we do not think they are thoughts in our mind. Except the poor mad accountant, of course, who kept on adding the same column of figures again and again, in the grip of the obsession that no matter how many times he reached the same answer it might be only a thought in his mind. And those philosophers who stress that pain is a mental concept do not say that pain is a thought in the mind. We may say of someone, "His pain is all in his mind", which suggests that he is not in pain at all. Again, the lover who keeps his love for a woman secret in his own heart, never to be expressed to anyone, does not think that his love is a thought in his mind. If he did, he'd pull himself together, perhaps, and say, "Snap out of it, it's just infatuation". A religious believer, of course, may come to think that "God" is a thought in his mind. He may say, "Why shouldn't I enjoy myself? There's no one there to stop me or to punish me". Here, we would say not that the person is wrong because there is someone there, but that he was far away from what is meant by the fear of God. A philosopher too might say, "If God is not an additional consciousness to all human consciousness, isn't he just a thought in my mind?" I can imagine how a philosopher can get into that state of mind. Clearly, however, when I have spoken of belief in God I have not been saying that God is a thought in my mind or anyone else's in any of these senses, so it is unclear to me what Hick is wanting to attribute to me.

I shall now say a brief word about the strategy of my reply to Swinburne. I take note of the various moral notions he invokes in constructing his theodicy and argue that in his hands they become distorted and sometimes unrecognizable. I do this for a reason which Peter Winch mentions in his paper, namely, "the importance of being able to confront religious beliefs with reality". The realities in question, in Swinburne's paper, are, for the most part, moral realities. My claim is that there is no genuine confrontation since these realities are distorted.

Swinburne claims that in attributing to him the view that God allows evil to provide us with opportunities of *feeling* responsible I was mistaken. What God provides us with, Swinburne says, is an opportunity of *being* responsible. No matter. The Good Samaritan would be no less objectionable if he regarded the man who had fallen among thieves as an opportunity to be responsible than if he regarded him as an opportunity to feel responsible. The objection has to do with regarding the victim as an *opportunity* for me in this way.

It was suggested in discussion that such an attitude in a theodicy belongs to God and not to men and that therefore my criticisms are misdirected. Even if this were true, it would have the consequence, in the light of my previous criticism, of ascribing to God a moral description which would make him morally inferior to his creatures. He would see men as opportunities, in the sense described, but his creatures would not. Yet, as a matter of fact, in entertaining theodicies, one does think of God and of the evil which occurs in life in this way. This brings us back to the consideration of particular cases.

Swinburne wanted to say in face of particular examples that we needed more information and that we could not rule out a priori that some point to evil could emerge even in the most horrific cases. Yet, if one cannot rule out a priori the possibility of something turning up, neither can one rule out a priori the possibility that nothing will turn up. Swinburne sometimes seemed to suggest that we can *never* be sure that people have reached the limit of pointless suffering. But this claim is a metaphysical one and is not informative in any way. Nothing counts for or against it; it is an example of language idling. I certainly find Swinburne's claim that we just do not know whether people had to give in to the forces operating on them until philosophers and scientists have solved the free-will problem an incredible claim. Our knowledge of people who have been crushed by circumstances in their lives, people who had more than they could bear, does not wait on philosophy and science.

It was suggested that my strategy in argument is as follows: I'd present an example of pointless evil. Swinburne would give it a point. I would then find another example. This misses my main point. My point is that in certain cases searching for a point to the evil is not to make matters better, but to make them worse. Of course, I am not saying that a consideration of consequences is never morally desirable. What I am saying is that *sometimes* a readiness to do so is a sign of corruption. The same is true of being open-minded.

The main difference between Swinburne and me is that he thinks it meaningful and desirable to discover a system or an order in human affairs. Belief in God demands such an order. I do not think it makes sense to look for such an order and that belief in God is connected with a recognition of this fact.

My criticisms of Swinburne's treatment of moral realities do not depend on holding any particular moral point of view. Furthermore, if these moral realities had not been distorted, they would not have provided rational grounds either for or against religious belief. They would not be the handmaids of a theodicy. But would not such a view seal off religion from any conceivable challenge, and lead to the view, which, Winch says, he has not always been careful enough to avoid, namely, that "religion is something people engage in part of the time, taking care not to let it be confronted with what they are thinking and doing the rest of the week"? Not at all. What it would get us to see is that whereas indeed all serious faith is tried, the defense against trials is not the construction of a theodicy. Hick says that the interest of a theodicy depends on "its connection with an actual living tradition of religious faith, rather than being a

mere ad hoc invention of philosophers". He says that "the theodicy problem arises, for most of us at any rate", as "an inquiry
concerning the rational possibility of an actual form of religious
faith, such as the Christian faith". It is not clear whether the
majority Hick refers to here is the majority of philosophers of
religion or the majority of believers. He takes himself to be simply restating his point when he says, "What we are asking is
whether there are resources within that faith for meeting the
problem of evil". I do not deny that when a believer in face of
evil says, "Lord, I believe, help thou mine unbelief" he is
searching for such resources. What I deny is that those resources are the resources of a theodicy.

I gave a brief outline of a believer's response to evil at the
end of my paper. Hick talks of my disposing of the challenge as
though I did not allow for its reality. But in meeting a challenge the believer recognizes its reality, otherwise there would
be no need to meet it. His faith is tried and it may be defeated.
That is why, although agreeing with Colin Lyas's remarks
about the inadequacy of probabilistic conceptions of God to account for faith, I think one needs to show what is involved in
the loss of a faith which was not, when strong, based on probabilities.

But no one is denying the fact that faith is tried by evils of
various kinds. I think Winch was premature in his admission of
lack of care. In face of familiar objections to philosophers of
religion influenced by Wittgenstein I recently underwent the
self-inflicted penance of rereading what I had said on these
topics. I found no evidence of my having said that faith could
not be challenged or overthrown by nonreligious factors. On
the contrary, the account I gave of prayers, for example, would
make no sense without connections with features of human life
intelligible independently of religion. At the end of an early
chapter in *The Concept of Prayer* I said: "Religious concepts,
however, are not *technical* concepts; they are not cut off from
the common experiences of human life, joy and sorrow, hope
and despair. Because this is so, an attempt can be made to clar-
ify their meaning" (p. 40). What was rejected was a certain kind
of defense and attack of religion emanating from scientism and

rationalism. I think the same holds for Winch's writings. I suspect that we have heard so-called fideistic (a term which, unfortunately, has come to stay) views attributed to us so often that
we have almost come to believe in their accuracy ourselves
without checking it!

Theodicies are part of the rationalism which I believe clouds
our understanding of religious belief. I doubt whether any
believer would deny that Jesus faced evil of a certain kind in
the Garden of Gethsemane. And in asking that if possible the
bitter cup should pass from him, he came to see his own survival as a mere possibility subject to the will of God. He came to
see that the will of God meant, for him, the Cross. If anyone
said that the Son of God met the evil in a reasonable way I
would not know what to make of him. And if a philosopher attempts, as John Wisdom did once, to show that the forgiveness
from the Cross is reasonable, he gets into terrible trouble. I'd at
least venture to say that talk of reasonableness and rationality is
not the most natural response of most Christians to the central
act of their faith.

PART THREE

THE RATIONALITY OF

RELIGIOUS BELIEF

7

The Groundlessness
of Belief

NORMAN MALCOLM

I

In his final notebooks Wittgenstein wrote that it is difficult "to realize the groundlessness of our believing." [1] He was thinking of how much mere acceptance, on the basis of no evidence, forms our lives. This is obvious in the case of small children. They are told the names of things. They accept what they are told. They do not ask for grounds. A child does not demand a proof that the person who feeds him is called "Mama." Or are we to suppose that the child reasons to himself as follows: "The others present seem to know this person who is feeding me, and since they call her 'Mama' that probably is her name"? It is obvious on reflection that a child cannot consider evidence or even doubt anything until he has already learned much. As Wittgenstein puts it: "The child learns by believing the adult. Doubt comes *after* belief" (*OC*, 160).

What is more difficult to perceive is that the lives of educated, sophisticated adults are also formed by groundless beliefs. I do not mean eccentric beliefs that are out on the fringes of their lives, but fundamental beliefs. Take the belief that fa-

1. Ludwig Wittgenstein, *On Certainty*, ed. G. E. M. Anscombe and G. H. von Wright; English translation by D. Paul and G. E. M. Anscombe (Oxford, 1969), paragraph 166. Henceforth I include references to this work in the text, employing the abbreviation "*OC*" followed by paragraph number. References to Wittgenstein's *The Blue and Brown Books* (Oxford, 1958) are indicated in the text by "*BB*" followed by page number. References to his *Philosophical Investigations*, ed. G. E. M. Anscombe and R. Rhees; English translation by Anscombe (Oxford, 1967) are indicated by "*PI*" followed by paragraph number. In *OC* and PI, I have mainly used the translations of Paul and Anscombe but with some departures.

miliar material things (watches, shoes, chairs) do not cease to exist without some physical explanation. They don't "vanish in thin air." It is interesting that we do use that very expression: "I *know* I put the keys right here on this table. They must have vanished in thin air!" But this exclamation is hyperbole; we are not speaking in literal seriousness. I do not know of any adult who would consider, in all gravity, that the keys might have inexplicably ceased to exist.

Yet it is possible to imagine a society in which it was accepted that sometimes material things do go out of existence without having been crushed, melted, eroded, broken into pieces, burned up, eaten, or destroyed in some other way. The difference between those people and ourselves would not consist in their *saying* something that we don't say ("It vanished in thin air"), since we say it too. I conceive of those people as acting and thinking differently from ourselves in such ways as the following: If one of them could not find his wallet he would give up the search sooner than you or I would; also he would be less inclined to suppose that it was stolen. In general, what we would regard as convincing circumstantial evidence of theft those people would find less convincing. They would take fewer precautions than we would to protect their possessions against loss or theft. They would have less inclination to save money, since it too can just disappear. They would not tend to form strong attachments to material things, animals, or other people. Generally, they would stand in a looser relation to the world than we do. The disappearance of a desired object, which would provoke us to a frantic search, they would be more inclined to accept with a shrug. Of course, their scientific theories would be different; but also their attitude toward experiment, and inference from experimental results, would be more tentative. If the repetition of a familiar chemical experiment did not yield the expected result this *could* be because one of the chemical substances had vanished.

The outlook I have sketched might be thought to be radically incoherent. I do not see that this is so. Although those people consider it to be possible that a wallet might have inexplicably ceased to exist, it is also true that they regard that as unlikely.

For things that are lost usually do turn up later; or if not, their fate can often be accounted for. Those people use pretty much the same criteria of identity that we do; their reasoning would resemble ours quite a lot. Their thinking would not be incoherent. But it would be different, since they would leave room for some possibilities that we exclude.

If we compare their view that material things do sometimes go out of existence inexplicably, with our own rejection of that view, it does not appear to me that one position is supported by *better evidence* than is the other. Each position is compatible with ordinary experience. On the one hand it is true that familiar objects (watches, wallets, lawn chairs) occasionally disappear without any adequate explanation. On the other hand it happens, perhaps more frequently, that a satisfying explanation of the disappearance is discovered.

Our attitude in this matter is striking. We would not be willing to consider it as even improbable that a missing lawn chair had "just ceased to exist." We would not entertain such a suggestion. If anyone proposed it we would be sure he was joking. It is no exaggeration to say that this attitude is part of the foundations of our thinking. I do not want to say that this attitude is *un*reasonable; but rather that it is something that we do not *try* to support with grounds. It could be said to belong to "the framework" of our thinking about material things.

Wittgenstein asks: "Does anyone ever test whether this table remains in existence when no one is paying attention to it?" (*OC*, 163). The answer is: Of course not. Is this because we would not call it "a table" if that were to happen? But we do call it "a table" and none of us makes the test. Doesn't this show that we do not regard that occurrence as a possibility? People who did so regard it would seem ludicrous to us. One could imagine that they made ingenious experiments to decide the question; but this research would make us smile. Is this because experiments were conducted by our ancestors that settled the matter once and for all? I don't believe it. The principle that material things do not cease to exist without physical cause is an unreflective part of the framework within which physical investigations are made and physical explanations arrived at.

Wittgenstein suggests that the same is true of what might be called "the principle of the continuity of nature":

Think of chemical investigations. Lavoisier makes experiments with substances in his laboratory and now concludes that this and that takes place when there is burning. He does not say that it might happen otherwise another time. He has got hold of a world-picture—not of course one that he invented: he learned it as a child. I say world-picture and not hypothesis, because it is the matter-of-course (*selbstverständliche*) foundation for his research and as such also goes unmentioned (*OC*, 167).

But now, what part is played by the presupposition that a substance A always reacts to a substance B in the same way, given the same circumstances? Or is that part of the definition of a substance? (*OC*, 168).

Framework principles such as the continuity of nature or the assumption that material things do not cease to exist without physical cause belong to what Wittgenstein calls a "system." He makes the following observation, which seems to me to be true: "All testing, all confirmation and disconfirmation of a hypothesis takes place already within a system. And this system is not a more or less arbitrary and doubtful point of departure for all our arguments: no, it belongs to the nature of what we call an argument. The system is not so much the point of departure, as the element in which arguments have their life" (*OC*, 105).

A "system" provides the boundaries within which we ask questions, carry out investigations, and make judgments. Hypotheses are put forth, and challenged, *within* a system. Verification, justification, the search for evidence, occur *within* a system. The framework propositions of the system are not put to the test, not backed up by evidence. This is what Wittgenstein means when he says: "Of course there is justification; but justification comes to an end" (*OC*, 192); and when he asks: "Doesn't testing come to an end?" (*OC*, 164); and when he remarks that "whenever we test anything we are already presupposing something that is not tested" (*OC*, 163).

That this is so is not to be attributed to human weakness. It is a conceptual requirement that our inquiries and proofs stay within boundaries. Think, for example, of the activity of calculating a number. Some steps in a calculation we will check for

correctness, but others we won't: for example, that $4+4=8$.
More accurately, some beginners might check it, but grown-ups
won't. Similarly, some grown-ups would want to determine by
calculation whether $25 \times 25 = 625$, whereas others would
regard that as laughable. Thus the boundaries of the system
within which *you* calculate may not be exactly the same as *mine*.
But we do calculate; and, as Wittgenstein remarks, "In certain
circumstances . . . we regard a calculation as sufficiently
checked. What gives us a right to do so? . . . Somewhere we
must be finished with justification, and then there remains the
proposition that *this* is how we calculate" (*OC*, 212). If someone
did not accept any boundaries for calculating this would mean
that he had not learned *that* language-game: "If someone supposed that *all* our calculations were uncertain and that we
could rely on none of them (justifying himself by saying that
mistakes are always possible) perhaps we would say he was
crazy. But can we say he is in error? Does he not just react differently? We rely on calculations, he doesn't; we are sure, he
isn't" (*OC*, 217). We are taught, or we absorb, the systems
within which we raise doubts, make inquiries, draw conclusions.
We grow into a framework. We don't question it. We accept it
trustingly. But this acceptance is not a consequence of reflection. We do not decide to accept framework propositions. We
do not decide that we live on the earth, any more than we
decide to learn our native tongue. We do come to adhere to a
framework proposition, in the sense that it forms the way we
think. The framework propositions that we accept, grow into,
are not idiosyncrasies but common ways of speaking and thinking that are pressed on us by our human community. For our
acceptances to have been withheld would have meant that we
had not learned how to count, to measure, to use names, to
play games, or even *to talk*. Wittgenstein remarks that "a
language-game is only possible if one trusts something." Not
can, but *does* trust something (*OC*, 509). I think he means by
this trust or acceptance what he calls belief "in the sense of
religious belief" (*OC*, 459). What does he mean by belief "in the
sense of religious belief"? He explicitly distinguishes it from
conjecture (*Vermutung*: ibid.). I think this means that there is

nothing tentative about it; it is not adopted as a hypothesis that might later be withdrawn in the light of new evidence. This also makes explicit an important feature of Wittgenstein's understanding of belief, in the sense of "religious belief," namely, that it does not rise or fall on the basis of evidence or grounds: it is "groundless."

II

In our Western academic philosophy, religious belief is commonly regarded as unreasonable and is viewed with condescension or even contempt. It is said that religion is a refuge for those who, because of weakness of intellect or character, are unable to confront the stern realities of the world. The objective, mature, *strong* attitude is to hold beliefs solely on the basis of *evidence*.

It appears to me that philosophical thinking is greatly influenced by this veneration of evidence. We have an aversion to statements, reports, declarations, beliefs, that are not based on grounds. There are many illustrations of this philosophical bent.

For example, in regard to a person's report that he has an image of the Eiffel Tower we have an inclination to think that the image must *resemble* the Eiffel Tower. How else could the person declare so confidently what his image is *of? How could he know?*

Another example: A memory-report or memory-belief must be based, we think, on some mental *datum* that is equipped with various features to match the corresponding features of the memory-belief. This datum will include an image that provides the *content* of the belief, and a peculiar feeling that makes one refer the image to a *past* happening, and another feeling that makes one believe that the image is an *accurate* portrayal of the past happening, and still another feeling that informs one that it was *oneself* who witnessed the past happening. The presence of these various features makes memory-beliefs thoroughly reasonable.

Another illustration: If interrupted in speaking one can usually give a confident account, later on, of what one had been *about* to say. How is this possible? Must not one remember *a feeling of tendency to say just those words?* This is one's basis for knowing what one had been about to say. It justifies one's account.

Still another example: After dining at a friend's house you announce your intention to go home. How do you know your intention? One theory proposes that you are presently aware of a particular mental state or bodily feeling which, as you recall from your past experience, has been highly correlated with the behavior of going home; so you infer that *that* is what you are going to do now. A second theory holds that you must be aware of some definite mental state or event which reveals itself, not by experience but *intrinsically,* as the intention to go home. Your awareness of that mental item *informs* you of what action you will take.

Yet another illustration: This is the instructive case of the man who, since birth, has been immune to sensations of bodily pain. On his thirtieth birthday he is kicked in the shins and for the first time he responds by crying out, hopping around on one foot, holding his leg, and exclaiming, "The pain is terrible!" We have an overwhelming inclination to wonder, "How could he tell, *this first time,* that what he felt was *pain?*" Of course, the implication is that *after* the first time there would be *no* problem. Why not? Because his first experience of pain would provide him with a sample that would be preserved in memory; thereafter he would be equipped to determine whether any sensation he feels is or isn't pain; he would just compare it with the memory-sample to see whether the two match! Thus he will have a justification for believing that what he feels is pain. But the *first time* he will not have this justification. This is why the case is so puzzling. Could it be that this first time he *infers* that he is in pain from his own behavior?

A final illustration: Consider the fact that after a comparatively few examples and bits of instruction a person can go on to carry out a task, apply a word correctly in the future, continue a numerical series from an initial segment, distinguish grammatical from ungrammatical constructions, solve arithmetical problems, and so on. These correct performances will be dealing with new and different examples, situations, combinations. The performance output will be far more varied than the instruction input. How is this possible? What carries the person from the meager instruction to his rich performance? The explanation has to be that an effect of his training was that he abstracted the Idea, perceived the Common Nature, "internalized" the Rule, grasped the Structure. What else could bridge the gap between the poverty of instruction and the wealth of performance? Thus we postulate an intervening mental act or state which removes the inequality and restores the balance.

My illustrations belong to what could be called the *pathology* of philosophy. Wittgenstein speaks of a "general disease of thinking" which attempts to explain occurrences of discernment, recognition, or understanding, by postulating mental states or processes from which those occurrences flow "as from a reservoir" (*BB,* p. 143). These mental intermediaries are assumed to contribute to the causation of the various cognitive performances. More significantly for my present purpose, they are supposed to *justify* them; they provide our *grounds* for saying or doing this rather than that; they *explain how we know.* The Image, or Cognitive State, or Feeling, or Idea, or Sample, or Rule, or Structure, *tells* us. It is like a road map or a signpost. It guides our course.

What is "pathological" about these explanatory constructions and pseudoscientific inferences? Two things at least. First, the movement of thought that demands these intermediaries is circular and empty, unless it provides criteria for determining their presence and nature *other than* the occurrence of the phenomena they are postulated to explain—and, of course, no such criteria are forthcoming. Second, there is the great criticism by Wittgenstein of this movement of philosophical thought: namely, his point that no matter what kind of state, process, paradigm, sample, structure, or rule, is conceived as giving us the necessary guidance, *it* could be taken, or understood, as indicating a *different* direction from the one in which we actually did go. The assumed intermediary Idea, Structure, or Rule, does not and cannot reveal that because of it we went

in the only direction it was reasonable to go. Thus the internalized intermediary we are tempted to invoke to bridge the
gap between training and performance, as being that which
shows us what we must do or say if we are to be rational, cannot do the job it was invented to do. It cannot fill the epistemological gap. It cannot provide the bridge of justification. It
cannot put to rest the How-do-we-know? question. Why not?
Because it cannot tell us how *it itself* is to be taken, understood,
applied. Wittgenstein puts the point briefly and powerfully:
"Don't always think that you read off your words from facts;
that you portray these in words according to rules. For even so
you would have to apply the rule in the particular case without
guidance" (*PI*, 292). Without guidance! Like Wittgenstein's
signpost arrow that cannot tell us whether to go in the direction
of the arrow tip or in the opposite direction, so too the Images,
Ideas, Cognitive Structures, or Rules, that we philosophers
imagine as devices for guidance, cannot interpret themselves to
us. The signpost does not tell the traveler how to read it. A second signpost might tell him how to read the first one; we can
imagine such a case. But this can't go on. If the traveler is to
continue his journey he will have to do something on his own,
without guidance.

The parable of the traveler speaks for *all* of the language-
games we learn and practice; even those in which there is the
most disciplined instruction and the most rigorous standards of
conformity. Suppose that a pupil has been given thorough
training in some procedure, whether it is drawing patterns,
building fences, or proving theorems. But then he has to carry
on by himself in new situations. How does he know what to do?
Wittgenstein presents the following dialogue: " 'However you
instruct him in the continuation of a pattern—how can he *know*
how he is to continue by himself?'—Well, how do *I* know?—If
that means 'Have I grounds?', the answer is: the grounds will
soon give out. And then I shall act, without grounds" (*PI*, 211).
Grounds come to an end. Answers to How-do-we-know? questions come to an end. Evidence comes to an end. We must
speak, act, live, without evidence. This is so, not just on the
fringes of life and language, but at the center of our most regu-

larized activities. We do learn rules and learn to follow them. But our training was in the past! We had to leave it behind and proceed on our own.

It is an immensely important fact of nature that as people carry on an activity in which they have received a common training, they do largely *agree* with one another, accepting the same examples and analogies, taking the same steps. We agree in what to say, in how to apply language. We agree in our responses to particular cases.

As Wittgenstein says: "That is not agreement in opinions but in form of life" (*PI, 241*). We cannot explain this agreement by saying that we are just doing what the rules tell us—for our agreement in applying rules, formulae, and signposts is what gives them their *meaning*.

One of the primary pathologies of philosophy is the feeling that we must *justify* our language-games. We want to establish them as well-grounded. But we should consider here Wittgenstein's remark that a language-game "is not based on grounds. It is there—like our life" (*OC, 559*).

Within a language-game there is justification and lack of justification, evidence and proof, mistakes and groundless opinions, good and bad reasoning, correct measurements and incorrect ones. One cannot properly apply these terms to a language-game itself. It may, however, be said to be "groundless," not in the sense of a groundless opinion, but in the sense that we accept it, we live it. We can say, "This is what we do. This is how we are."

In this sense religion is groundless; and so is chemistry. Within each of these two systems of thought and action there is controversy and argument. Within each there are advances and recessions of insight into the secrets of nature or the spiritual condition of humankind and the demands of the Creator, Savior, Judge, Source. Within the framework of each system there is criticism, explanation, justification. But we should not expect that there might be some sort of rational justification of the framework itself.

A chemist will sometimes employ induction. Does he have evidence for a Law of Induction? Wittgenstein observes that it would strike him as nonsense to say, "I know that the Law of Induction is true." ("Imagine such a statement made in a law court.") It would be more correct to say, "I believe in the Law of Induction" (*OC*, 500). This way of putting it is better because it shows that the attitude toward induction is belief in the sense of "religious" belief—that is to say, an acceptance which is not conjecture or surmise and for which there is no reason—it is a groundless acceptance.

It is intellectually troubling for us to conceive that a whole system of thought might be groundless, might have no rational justification. We realize easily enough, however, that grounds soon give out—that we cannot go on giving reasons for our reasons. There arises from this realization the conception of a reason that is *self-justifying*—something whose credentials as a reason cannot be questioned.

This metaphysical conception makes its presence felt at many points—for example, as an explanation of how a person can tell what his mental image is *of*. We feel that the following remarks, imagined by Wittgenstein, are exactly right: " 'The image must be more similar to its object than any picture. For however similar I make the picture to what it is supposed to represent, it can always be the picture of something else. But it is essential to the image that it is the image of *this* and of nothing else' " (*PI*, 389). A pen and ink drawing represents the Eiffel Tower; but it could represent a mine shaft or a new type of automobile jack. Nothing prevents this drawing from being taken as a representation of something other than the Eiffel Tower. But my mental image of the Eiffel Tower is *necessarily* an image of the Eiffel Tower. Therefore it must be a "remarkable" kind of picture. As Wittgenstein observes: "Thus one might come to regard the image as a super-picture" (*ibid.*). Yet we have no intelligible conception of how a super-picture would differ from an ordinary picture. It would seem that it has to be a *super-likeness*—but what does this mean?

There is a familiar linguistic practice in which one person *tells* another what his image is of (or what he intends to do, or what he was about to say) and no question is raised of how the first one *knows* that what he says is true. This question is imposed from outside, artificially, by the philosophical craving for justification. We can see here the significance of these remarks: "It isn't a question of explaining a language-game by means of our experiences, but of noting a language-game" (*PI*, 655). "Look on the language-game as the *primary* thing" (*PI*, 656). Within a system of thinking and acting there occurs, *up to a point,* investigation and criticism of the reasons and justifications that are employed in that system. This inquiry into whether a reason is good or adequate cannot, as said, go on endlessly. We stop it. We bring it to an end. We come upon something that *satisfies* us. It is as if we made a decision or issued an edict: "*This* is an adequate reason!" (or explanation, or justification). Thereby we fix a boundary of our language-game.

There is nothing wrong with this. How else could we have disciplines, systems, games? But our fear of groundlessness makes us conceive that we are under some logical compulsion to terminate at *those particular* stopping points. We imagine that we have confronted the self-evident reason, the self-justifying explanation, the picture or symbol whose meaning cannot be questioned. This obscures from us the *human* aspect of our concepts—the fact that what we call "a reason," "evidence," "explanation," "justification," is what appeals to and satisfies *us*.

III

The desire to provide a rational foundation for a form of life is especially prominent in the philosophy of religion, where there is an intense preoccupation with purported proofs of the existence of God. In American universities there must be hundreds of courses in which these proofs are the main topic. We can be sure that nearly always the critical verdict is that the proofs are invalid and consequently that, up to the present time at least, religious belief has received no rational justification.

Well, of course not! The obsessive concern with the proofs reveals the assumption that in order for religious belief to be intellectually respectable it *ought* to have a rational justification. *That* is the misunderstanding. It is like the idea that we are not justified in relying on memory until memory has been proved reliable.

Roger Trigg makes the following remark: "To say that someone acts in a certain way because of his belief in God does seem to be more than a redescription of his action. . . . It is to give a *reason* for it. The belief is distinct from the commitment which may follow it, and is the justification for it." [2] It is evident from other remarks that by "belief in God" Trigg means "belief in the existence of God" or "belief that God exists". Presumably by the *acts* and *commitments* of a religious person Trigg refers to such things as prayer, worship, confession, thanksgiving, partaking of sacraments, and participation in the life of a religious group.

For myself I have great difficulty with the notion of belief in *the existence* of God, whereas the idea of belief *in* God is to me intelligible. If a man did not ever pray for help or forgiveness, or have any inclination toward it; nor ever felt that it is "a good and joyful thing" to thank God for the blessings of this life; nor was ever concerned about his failure to comply with divine commandments—then, it seems clear to me, he could not be said to believe in God. Belief in God is not an all or none thing; it can be more or less; it can wax and wane. But belief in God in any degree does require, as I understand the words, some religious action, some commitment, or if not, at least a bad conscience.

According to Trigg, if I take him correctly, a man who was entirely devoid of any inclination toward religious action or conscience, might believe in *the existence* of God. What would be the marks of this? Would it be that the man knows some theology, can recite the Creeds, is well-read in Scripture? Or is his belief in the existence of God something different from this? If so, what? What would be the difference between a man who knows some articles of faith, heresies, scriptural writings, and in addition believes in the existence of God, and one who knows these things but does not believe in the existence of God? I assume that both of them are indifferent to the acts and commitments of religious life.

2. *Reason and Commitment* (Cambridge, 1973), p. 75.

I do not comprehend this notion of belief in *the existence* of God which is thought to be distinct from belief *in* God. It seems to me to be an artificial construction of philosophy, another illustration of the craving for justification.

Religion is a form of life; it is language embedded in action— what Wittgenstein calls a "language-game." Science is another. Neither stands in need of justification, the one no more than the other.

Present-day academic philosophers are far more prone to challenge the credentials of religion than of science, probably for a number of reasons. One may be the illusion that science can justify its own framework. Another is the fact that science is a vastly greater force in our culture. Still another may be the fact that by and large religion is to university people an alien form of life. They do not participate in it and do not understand what it is all about.

Their nonunderstanding is of an interesting nature. It derives, at least in part, from the inclination of academics to suppose that their employment as scholars demands of them the most severe objectivity and dispassionateness. For an academic philosopher to become a religious believer would be a stain on his professional competence! Here I will quote from Nietzsche, who was commenting on the relation of the German scholar of his day to religious belief; yet his remarks continue to have a nice appropriateness for the American and British scholars of our own day:

Pious or even merely church-going people seldom realize *how much* good will, one might even say wilfulness, it requires nowadays for a German scholar to take the problem of religion seriously; his whole trade . . . disposes him to a superior, almost good-natured merriment in regard to religion, sometimes mixed with a mild contempt directed at the "uncleanliness" of spirit which he presupposes wherever one still belongs to the church. It is only with the aid of history (thus *not* from his personal experience) that the scholar succeeds in summoning up a reverent seriousness and a certain shy respect towards religion; but if he intensifies his feelings towards it even to the point of feeling grateful to it, he has still in his own person not got so much as a single step closer to that which still exists as church or piety; perhaps the reverse. The practical indifference to religious things in which he was born and raised is as a rule sublimated in him into a caution and clean-

liness which avoids contact with religious people and things; . . .
Every age has its own divine kind of naïvety for the invention of which
other ages may envy it—and how much naïvety, venerable, childlike
and boundlessly stupid naïvety there is in the scholar's belief in his su-
periority, in the good conscience of his tolerance, in the simple un-
suspecting certainty with which his instinct treats the religious man as
an inferior and lower type which he himself has grown beyond and
above.[3]

3. Friedrich Nietzsche, *Beyond Good and Evil*, trans. R. J. Hollingdale, para.
58.

8

The Groundlessness
of Religious Belief

COLIN LYAS

> We mind about the kind of expressions we use concerning these things; we do not understand them, however, but misinterpret them. When we do philosophy we are like savages, primitive people, who hear the expressions of civilised men, put a false interpretation on them, and then draw the strangest conclusions from it.
>
> —Ludwig Wittgenstein

A main conclusion of Malcolm's paper is that religion and religious belief are 'groundless' (p. 152) and do not stand 'in need of justification' (p. 156). That is to say they do not 'rise or fall on the basis of evidence or grounds' (p. 148). A failure to appreciate that religion is groundless is responsible for the 'obsessive concern' with proofs, and '*that*', Malcolm emphatically says, 'is the misunderstanding' (p. 154).

The first thing to be said of such a conclusion is that it *looks* counterintuitive. To begin with there seem to be clear examples of 'systems' (p. 146) that are, with no obvious impropriety, called 'religions' and that *are*, apparently, grounded upon beliefs for which evidence might be sought.[1] To take but one example, Christianity at least *seems* to be grounded upon beliefs to which evidence seems relevant, e.g., the beliefs that there in fact existed a person, Jesus bar Joseph, who said and did certain things and to whom certain things in fact happened. For this reason Saint Paul, to mention but one, clearly believed that Christianity would be unjustified were the falsity of these beliefs as to matters of fact to be discovered. For if there was in fact no person called Christ, then Christ did not die upon the

---

1. It has been argued that religions do in general have some historical strain in them. See R. N. Smart, *Mao* (London, 1974), pp. 83ff.

cross; and if Christ did not die, then he was not raised. And, then, as Paul wrote to the Corinthians, 'If Christ be not raised, then your faith is in vain'. We have here a clear statement from within religion of the dependence of a faith upon a matter of fact.

Malcolm's conclusions seem also to be at odds with the fact that there is in many theistic religions a rich apologetic tradition (by no means as yet exhausted).[2] That tradition, richer than I could here hope to instance, expresses the commitment of many believers to the opinion that reasons and grounds are relevant to the belief that there is a God. Thus, for example, early in a seminal work by Aquinas, itself part of the official doctrine of a major religion, we read, 'there are five ways in which one can prove that there is a God'.[3] This whole tradition of concern for proof is, we are now told, a 'misunderstanding'.[4]

Malcolm's claim that religious belief is groundless looks, then, to be at odds with known facts about religion and religious belief. That this should be so is likely to occasion further puzzlement. For this claim issues from a philosopher who, it is widely believed, supports his philosophical pronouncements by an appeal to what practitioners of language-games such as religion (p. 152) say and do. In this present case, it looks tempting to say that however Malcolm's conclusion that religious belief is groundless was reached, it could not have been arrived at by reflection upon what believers do and say.

Given that Malcolm's claims seem counterintuitive one needs then to ask why Malcolm should have said what he has said. For there is always the possibility that what he says is true and that traditional theistic religions do embody a massive misunderstanding. Even if that spectacular outcome does not emerge, we may well find that, despite appearances, what he says does not run counter to what occurs in religious practice but, on the contrary, constitutes a reminder of features of religion that are often overlooked.

2. See, e.g., Wallace I. Matson, *The Existence of God* (Ithaca, N.Y., 1965), for some up-to-date versions of the design argument.

3. *Summa Theologica*, 1a, 2, 3.

4. 'For a misunderstanding' the apologists might reply in conscious echo of a famous remark by Wittgenstein, 'that's too big'.

I

I would like to comment mainly upon the aspect of Malcolm's paper with which I am most unhappy, namely his treatment of the notion of groundlessness.

Sometimes when Malcolm calls a belief 'groundless' he clearly says that it is a belief for which we *do not in fact* seek grounds. Thus he tells us that children *'do not* ask for grounds' (my emphasis). A child 'does not' ask for evidence that the person feeding it is called 'Mama' (p. 143). Again we are told that the natural belief that things don't just cease to exist is something that we 'do not *try* to support with grounds' (p. 145). For 'the principle that material things do not cease to exist without physical cause is an unreflective part of the framework within which physical investigations are made' (p. 145). Even the analytically minded scientist makes the 'assumption' [5] that this principle holds. Malcolm writes: 'We are taught, or we absorb, the systems within which we raise doubts, make inquiries, draw conclusions. We grow into a framework. We *don't* question it. We accept it trustingly' (p. 147, my emphasis). In such passages emphasis appears to be laid on the fact that often we *do not* seek grounds for our beliefs. This emphasis is further stressed when Malcolm tells us that even where we *do* seek grounds our search will eventually come to rest in beliefs that we *do not* question: 'This inquiry into whether a reason is good or adequate cannot, as said, go on endlessly. We stop it. We bring it to an end. We come upon something that *satisfies* us' (p. 154).

I do not wish to deny any of these claims. In particular I do not wish to deny that people hold beliefs, often important ones, for which they do not seek grounds. Religious belief in God is often of this sort. Further I would not wish to deny that for many reasons, including the exigencies of action and sheer indolence, we often terminate our search for reasons by accepting something which satisfies us and for which we have no incli-

5. Even this word is fraught with peril. See the discussion of the difference between assumptions and presumptions in Stephen Toulmin, *The Philosophy of Science* (London, 1953), p. 144.

nation to seek grounds. Thus, suppose I ask a scientific col-
league why high-flying aircraft leave vapor trails. He replies by
telling me that aircraft engines emit warm, moist air, that air at
high altitudes is cold, and that warm, moist air condenses in
cold air. He cites the analogous cases of cloud formation and of
the condensation of breath on frosty mornings. His answer satisfies me. That is to say, I will have no inclination to ask, 'Is it
true (and if so why is it) that aircraft engines emit warm air,
that air at high altitudes is cold and that warm, moist air condenses in cold air?'.

If, then, Malcolm wishes merely to claim that there are many
beliefs, and many reasons given for beliefs, for which we *do not
in fact* seek grounds, what he says seems to me to be incon-
trovertible. And if he wishes to claim that religious belief is
groundless in that believers often in fact don't ask for reasons
for belief, then that, too, seems to be unarguable.

To admit all this, however, is to leave the theistic apologist
quite untouched. For such an apologist might well agree with
Malcolm that believers often *do not* in fact ask for grounds,
while asserting that there *are* grounds for such beliefs and that
these grounds *can* be, even if they *are not*, sought. So from the
fact upon which Malcolm lays such stress, i.e., that we seek no
grounds for a belief, it does not follow that there *are* no
grounds for a belief. Nor does it follow that to seek such
grounds is to display a misunderstanding.

II

If what I have said is true then more is needed in order to
show that the search for grounds for belief in God rests on a
misunderstanding.

Here it would be helpful to change the emphasis from the
claim that there are beliefs, including religious beliefs, for
which grounds *are not* sought to the claim that there is a type of
belief which can be shown to have no grounds and for which,
in consequence, grounds not merely *are not* but *could not* be
sought. To embark on a search for grounds for such beliefs
would display a misunderstanding of their nature. To show

that belief in God is of this type would then indeed be to show that the search for reasons for religious belief involves a misunderstanding.

There is some evidence that despite his apparent emphasis upon the point that in many cases we *do not* seek reasons for believing, Malcolm wishes rather to claim that we *cannot* seek grounds for religion and religious belief because there *can be* no grounds for beliefs of this type. Thus we have the remark that religious belief 'does not rise or fall on the basis of evidence and grounds: it is groundless' (p. 148). Here the term 'groundless' is so used as to suggest not merely that we *in fact* have not sought grounds for religious belief, but that since it can be demonstrated that there are none, it would *make no sense* to seek them. Again he writes, 'Grounds come to an end. Answers to How-do-we know? questions come to an end. Evidence comes to an end. We *must* speak, act, live, without evidence' (p. 151) (my emphasis). The word "must" is likely to suggest that there *could* be no grounds for certain of our beliefs.

Take finally this passage: '*Within* a language-game there is justification and lack of justification, evidence and proof, mistakes and groundless opinions. . . . One cannot properly apply these terms to a language-game itself. It may, however, be said to be "groundless," not in the sense of a groundless opinion' (p. 152). The point of the last sentence of this passage may be this: a man might believe, say, that an immigrant population has a higher crime rate than the native population of which he is a member. This belief may be called groundless opinion either if that man has sought no grounds for believing it, or if it is the case that although grounds could be imagined for the belief, there are in fact none. We might say that in such cases belief is groundless in a weaker sense. In this use of the term 'groundless' to say that a belief is groundless is to say that, since it is conceivable that the belief might have grounds, the search for these grounds, though it might be fruitless, at least makes sense. In the passage I have last quoted, however, Malcolm appears to contrast *this* notion of groundlessness with a stronger use of that term. According to that use to assert that a belief is 'groundless' is to assert that the search for grounds is senseless

since it can be established antecedently that there could be
none for that type of belief.

III

I have claimed that in order to show that there is a misunderstanding in seeking proofs or grounds for belief in God, one
needs to show not merely that we *do not* seek such proofs but
that we *could not*. One way to show this would be to establish,
prior to any search for proofs, that there are certain kinds of
beliefs, including religious beliefs, that are such as to have no
grounds. If someone were then to look for grounds for these
sorts of beliefs we would be in a position to say that he had not
understood what was involved in having a belief of that sort. I
wish now to ask whether Malcolm has established this sort of
case for saying that the search for proofs or grounds for belief
in God involves a misunderstanding.

Malcolm certainly gives some examples of beliefs that he is
prepared to assert to be groundless. They include the following: a child's belief that the person that feeds it is called
'Mama'; the belief that things don't just vanish; the scientific
belief that substance A always reacts to substance B in the same
way; a belief in the continuity of nature; one's knowledge that
one has an image of the Eiffel Tower; one's knowledge of what
one was about to say before being interrupted; one's knowledge of one's intentions; a chemist's belief in the Law of Induction (pp. 143, 144–145, 146, 148–149, 152–153).

In some of these cases Malcolm gives reasons for the claim
that there are no grounds and that there is something pointless
or 'circular' (p. 150) in the attempt to find grounds. I shall ask
shortly whether at least some of the examples that have been
cited *are* thus groundless. For the moment, however, suppose
that it could be shown that all these examples are examples of
beliefs for which it makes no sense to seek grounds. To have
shown that is to have shown at most that *some* beliefs are
groundless in such a way as to make it a misunderstanding to
seek to justify them. Since, however, the list does not include
any religious beliefs it has not as yet been shown that religious
belief in God is belief of this sort. For as the question at issue *is*

"Is it true that religious belief is groundless?", it will not do (as Malcolm does) first to outline various sorts of nonreligious groundless beliefs and then add the assertion that religious belief resembles them in being groundless. Thus even granted there *is* a demonstration that the beliefs I cited are such that the search for their grounds shows a misunderstanding, we still need a demonstration that *theistic religious belief,* too, is of this sort.

Although Malcolm does sometimes seem baldly to assert that religious belief is as groundless as some other beliefs that he mentions, it is possible to find potential arguments in the paper for this claim. I shall now look at one or two of these.

The first need not detain us long. There is some suggestion in Malcolm's paper that religious beliefs can be said to be groundless in that Malcolm (and, he suggests, Witgenstein) wishes to use the terms 'religious belief' and 'groundless belief' interchangeably. He writes: 'Wittgenstein remarks that 'a language-game is only possible if one trusts something.'' And he asks whether 'this trust or acceptance' isn't 'belief "in the sense of religious belief." He explicitly distinguishes it from *conjecture. . . .* I think this means that there is nothing tentative about it; it is not adopted as a hypothesis that might later be withdrawn in the light of new evidence. This also makes explicit an important feature of Wittgenstein's understanding of belief, in the sense of "religious belief," namely, that it does not rise or fall on the basis of evidence or grounds: it is "groundless" ' (p. 152). And he says: 'Wittgenstein observes that it would strike him as nonsense to say, "I know that the Law of Induction is true." . . . It would be more correct to say, "I believe in the Law of Induction." This way of putting it is better because it shows that the attitude toward induction is belief in the sense of "religious" belief—that is to say, an acceptance which is not conjecture or surmise and for which there is no reason—it is a groundless acceptance' (pp. 152–153).

Now if we decide to christen 'groundless acceptance' as 'religious belief' then it will, of course, be true that, in this sense of the term, religious belief is groundless. To make this move, however, is not to have shown that religious beliefs are groundless where 'religious belief' means 'central belief of a theistic religion'.

We must in this connection beware of the following line of thought. (1) Religious beliefs do not have grounds, (2) beliefs, such as the scientist has in the Law of Induction, do not have grounds, so (3) many beliefs, including many scientific beliefs, are religious beliefs. The move from (1) and (2) to (3) is fallacious. (Compare, Cats are animals, Dogs are animals, so, Cats are Dogs.) The most we can get from (1) and (2) is (3), Religious belief and belief in the Law of Induction have a feature in common, namely, they are groundless. Leaving aside the large question whether we *do* wish to say this of the Law of Induction, such a line of argument has the major drawback that it assumes in (1) what we wanted to have proved, namely that religious beliefs *are* groundless. (I should add that even if theistic religious belief and belief in the Law of Induction do have a feature, groundlessness, in common it seems to me to be stretching things to make this a reason for calling a belief in the Law of Induction a *religious* belief. In the same way, that cats and dogs have animality in common seems to me a poor reason for talking of the doggishness of cats.)

IV

I come now to the second and more important line of approach that Malcolm takes when claiming that religion and religious belief are groundless and that a search for proofs for a belief in God evidences a misunderstanding. Malcolm writes: 'Religion is a form of life; it is language embedded in action— what Wittgenstein calls a "language-game." Science is another. Neither stands in need of justification' (p. 156).

The claim involved here sometimes seems to be that what Malcolm calls 'systems' or 'frameworks' of belief, e.g., science, chemistry, calculation, and the like, can be shown to be groundless in such a way as to make the search for justification of them a misunderstanding. The claim that frameworks are as such groundless, together with the claim that religion is itself a system or a framework *do* generate the claim that religion is groundless.

Let us concede for the moment the claim Malcolm makes that religion is a system or framework of belief and turn first to the more general claim that systems (frameworks) such as, for example, science, are groundless in such a way as to render misconceived the attempt to justify them.

For Malcolm, a system or framework is, as these terms suggest, a set of fundamental beliefs and principles: 'Framework principles such as the continuity of nature or the assumption that material things do not cease to exist without physical cause, belong to what Wittgenstein calls a "system." . . . A "system" provides the boundaries within which we ask questions, carry out investigations, and make judgments (p. 146). Different sets of principles and beliefs give us different areas of human interest such as science, chemistry, mathematics, and religion.

What Malcolm stresses is that the principles making up the framework are groundless:

The framework propositions of the system are not put to the test, not backed up by evidence (p. 146).

We grow into a framework. We don't question it (p. 147).

Within a language-game there is justification and lack of justification, evidence and proof, mistakes and groundless opinions. . . . One cannot properly apply these terms to a language-game itself (p. 152).

Within the framework of each system there is criticism, explanation, justification. But we should not expect that there might be some sort of rational justification of the framework itself (p. 152).

Is the central assertion in these passages true? That is to say, is it true that what Malcolm calls 'framework principles' are, in general groundless?

One would expect at this point that Malcolm would tell us in some detail what the framework principles of religions are and would produce some considerations that would show us that they are groundless. This he does not do, beyond the hint that belief in God is a framework principle of religion. Rather his method seems more indirect. He specifies some scientific (and other) framework principles, suggests that these are groundless, and then claims that religious framework principles are like them in being groundless. What I wish to do in my turn is to show that some of Malcolm's favored scientific framework principles are arguably not groundless. This by itself will undermine the claim that belief in God is groundless just because it is a framework principle of religion. For, if my argument is right, a principle could be a framework principle and yet be one whose use we might seek to justify. Second, I wish to show that some framework principles in science *are* arguably groundless and that principles of this type may well occur in religious contexts. But I wish to claim that the existence of such groundless principles in science and religion gives no support to the claim that the attempt to prove the existence of God rests on a misunderstanding of the groundlessness of religious belief.

Let me start by observing that there seem to me to be two very different sorts of things that might be called the framework principles of science. The first sorts, which Malcolm touches on but does not make extensive use of, are the principles that are, so to speak, constitutive of scientific procedure. They include such roughly stated principles as, 'It is wrong to ignore the result of a properly conducted experiment', 'If there is a contradiction in a scientific theory it is worthless'. To spell out in detail the principles in terms of which we might define what it is to be scientific is a complex task. That there must be such a body of principles, however, if there is to be such a thing as science seems to me to be indubitable.

To spell out principles of the sort I have mentioned is to articulate what it means to engage in rational empirical inquiry, a mode of inquiry that in its more formalized versions gives us the various branches of science. Embodied in these principles, it should be noted, is formal logic, which is to say that inferences of various sorts are possible in science. Also included in science is mathematics (if that is different from logic). Hence scientific calculations are possible.

These sorts of principles which define rational empirical inquiry are *formal* principles. They tell us nothing about the world that is the subject matter of science. They tell us only how that world is to be approached if it is to be approached scientifically. I shall call these principles the *constitutive* principles of science, and I do so because I wish to suggest that without them there is nothing resembling what we know as science. To query these principles is to call science itself into question.

Although Malcolm mentions procedural principles of the sort that I have mentioned, he more often concentrates on principles like, 'Things don't just vanish' or "nature is continuous". Such principles, it seems to me, are not like the constitutive principles I have just mentioned. To call *those* into question is, as I have said, to call the possibility of science into question, and to change the principles is to undermine science as we understand that activity. But, as Malcolm himself allows, to imagine changes in the sort of principle upon which he focuses attention is not so much to change the meaning of the term 'science' as to produce a change in the scientific theories that occur *within* the framework of scientific inquiry. Thus, writing of people who *do* accept that things just vanish, he says: 'Generally, they would stand in a looser relation to the world than we do. . . . Of course, their scientific theories would be different' (p. 144). I shall call principles of the sort upon which Malcolm focuses attention *regulative* scientific principles. As Malcolm rightly stresses, scientists accept such principles and operate with them. They regulate their activities by them. What is not clear, as we shall see, is whether justifications for regulative principles are impossible.

The framework principles of science, then, are of two types, the constitutive and the regulative. Let us now ask whether and in what sense principles of each of these sorts might be said to be groundless.

Here I would say immediately that what I have called the constitutive rules of rational empirical inquiry seem to me to be arguably groundless and attempts to justify them are arguably pointless or circular. First they are groundless in that they include groundless laws of logic, such as the law of nonself-contradiction. Abiding by these laws is a *condition* of rational thought. It makes no sense to suppose we might set them aside until they are rationally proved.

The procedures constitutive of rational empirical inquiry

seem to me to be groundless in another way. Suppose someone queried these methods and asked us to justify them. We might ask him what 'justification' would mean here. If he replied, and it is difficult to see how he could avoid doing so, that he wishes to have them tested experimentally, wished them to be shown free of contradiction, and wished empirical evidence to be adduced in their support, then we would reply that in querying the methods of rational empirical inquiry (of which science is a formalized variety) it was these very test procedures he was questioning. It is therefore difficult to see why having queried them he should be content to accept results reached by them. These constitutive principles are groundless in that our only reply when asked to justify them is that without them justification makes no sense. They are what 'justification' means.

There is a sense, then, in which to seek to justify the methods of empirical inquiry displays a misunderstanding. (It is, however, not in the same way senseless to seek to justify the claim that these *are* those methods of empirical inquiry that we call 'science', nor is it senseless to seek to justify the use of those methods in this or that context.)

Although there is a sense in which the constitutive principles of rational empirical inquiry cannot be justified, the same is not so evidently true of what I have called 'regulative' principles, i.e., principles such as, 'Things do not suddenly vanish without explanation' or 'nature is continuous'. One reason I have for saying this is that there does seem to me to be such a thing as a fundamental change in theories in science. This change, it seems to me, sometimes amounts to a change in the sort of principles that I have called 'regulative'. This is, of course, a highly complex area in the history and philosophy of science and I must content myself with some, possibly, naive remarks on the subject.

I begin with some remarks on the possibility that there might be a change in the sorts of belief which Malcolm has mentioned, i.e., beliefs such as our natural belief that things don't just vanish or that nature is continuous. The possibility of changes in such framework beliefs seems to me to be more real than Malcolm allows. Thus, consider the problems which have

led scientists to worry about such apparently fundamental beliefs as that the speed of light cannot be exceeded or that
events cannot move backward in time or even that two events
in different places can happen simultaneously. Consider, too,
the problems which have led cosmologists to worry about the
principle that something cannot just come into existence, a
principle whose rejection might seem as much an affront to
common sense as would the rejection of Malcolm's principle
that things can't just cease to exist. Yet if I understand the matter, some cosmologists *do* talk of the continuous creation of
matter. In all these cases scientists come to question basic beliefs.

It is worth considering in this connection that even Malcolm's
belief in the principle that nature is continuous may not be as
well founded as he supposes. Consider the following:

> The tide has long been flowing strongly against continuous laws. From
> Dalton's atomic theory of chemistry, through the kinetic theory of
> matter, Mendel's particulate theory of heredity, Plank's theory of light
> and the belief in evolution through discontinuous variations to quan-
> tum mechanics the trend to 'quantization' is conspicuous. One is now
> tempted to say that discontinuous worlds are preferable to continuous
> ones. . . . Non uniformitarian principles are perfectly possible ways of
> explaining the facts.[6]

I have suggested then that principles of the sort that Malcolm cites as framework principles, principles scientists accept
and work within, can be changed. When such changes occur
they do not do so 'groundlessly'. Rather they are made for a
reason. They are made because in using the constitutive procedures of rational empirical inquiry (science) scientists discover
that a principle, hitherto unreflectively accepted, is less scientifically justified than another whose scientific credentials or
grounds are less suspect. What happens in these cases is, as is
well known, a matter of deep controversy in the philosophy of
science. The changes are not always entirely due to scientific

6. J. P. Day, "The Uniformity of Nature," *American Philosophical Quarterly*, 12
(1975), 4, 13. The whole of this article is relevant to the present discussion.

requirements.[7] Be that as it may, that we do apply what I have
called the constitutive principles of scientific inquiry to regulative principles of the kind Malcolm cites, and that we change
the regulative principles when that is scientifically appropriate,
gives some ground for saying that justification of regulative
principles can at least be envisaged. The regulative beliefs of
the scientists are not self-evidently beliefs for which no justification can be sought.

V

The upshot of the recent discussion is, I hope, that some case
has been made for saying that *some* framework principles, e.g.,
the constitutive principles of science, may be such as to make
the search for grounds for them an impossible undertaking
and that *some* framework principles, e.g., some of the regulative
principles of science, may be such as to give the search for their
justification some point. I wish now to apply these reflections in
the context of Malcolm's remarks about the groundlessness of
religion.

I have said that Malcolm appears to claim that scientific principles are groundless and that religious framework principles
are like them in this respect. In view of what I have said, the
following comments seem to be in order.

First, I have tried to show that it is arguable whether *all* scientific framework beliefs, and hence all framework beliefs, are
groundless in the sense that the attempt to seek justifications
for holding them is misbegotten. To that extent Malcolm's
claims for the groundlessness of religion are undermined. He
cannot now simply claim that religious framework beliefs are
groundless, giving as a reason for this claim the fact that a
framework belief is by definition so. Nor does it seem to me
that he can simply claim that if a religious belief functions as a
framework belief in the way in which a scientific belief functions as a framework belief, then it must be groundless. For

---

7. On which see the controversy surrounding the work of Thomas Kuhn in
The Structure of Scientific Revolutions (Chicago, 1962). On simplicity, explanatory
power, and possible truth as criteria in science, see Day, "Uniformity."

some of these religious beliefs, including the belief in God, might be like scientific framework beliefs, e.g., the belief in the continuity of nature, which I have said might, in certain circumstances, be the subject of scientific assessment.

It is not possible to avoid these difficulties by claiming that religious framework principles are groundless in that they are like the constitutive principles of science, principles that I *have* said to be groundless. Conceding this would not inconvenience anyone committed to the attempt to justify belief in God. For what I have allowed to be groundless in science is, so to speak, the rules of scientific proof. If the claim is that the groundless principles in religion are principles like these, then to concede this claim is to concede only that rules of proof that are used in religious contexts are groundless. Now, whether or not the rules of proof that are used in religious contexts are like those that are used in scientific contexts, I cannot see that any religious apologist has anything to lose by conceding that such rules of religious proof are groundless. For just as a scientist might accept that his procedures of proof are groundless while yet maintaining that other important scientific beliefs, e.g., the belief in the continuity of nature, might be the subject of inquiry by these procedures, so the religious apologist might accept that his procedures of proof are groundless while yet maintaining that other central religious beliefs, e.g., belief in God, might be the subject of those procedures of proof.

VI

At various points in his paper Malcolm asserts that religious belief is groundless. In view of what I have said so far, it will be obvious that I am in some doubt as to whether this conclusion has been proved. Nonetheless, whether there is, or is intended to be, a proof in Malcolm's paper that religious belief is, despite appearances, groundless, it is possible, without difficulty, to imagine arguments for some of the things that Malcolm says. I shall now try to show that this is so.

Suppose we were asked to demonstrate that if a belief is a religious belief then it not merely *does not*, but *could not*, rise or fall on the basis of grounds or evidence and *could not* later be withdrawn in the light of new evidence. (Note here that Malcolm does not say that religious belief cannot come to an end. He later remarks that it may 'wax or wane' [p. 155]. What he says is that it does not wax or wane as a result of changes in evidence.)

One way to demonstrate this would be to show that to come to understand what is involved in being *religious* is to come to see that a religious belief could not be one that rises or falls with the evidence. I shall now ask what aspects of the phenomenon of religion might lead one to this sort of claim. To ask this about religion is to seek what Malcolm elsewhere calls 'an understanding of the phenomena of human life that give rise to it'.[8] I shall try to show that if we investigate these phenomena we may come to see why it *might* be said that religious belief is not evidential belief.

There is, I think, ample evidence in the literature of the world's theistic religions (to say nothing of the nontheistic ones) that one spring of the religious impulse is an awareness that human beings are at the mercy of *what can happen*. That is, there is a human feeling that no matter how secure one might feel, or how healthy, or how rich, or how powerful, unfortunate things might happen, the chief of which is the unavoidable happening of one's own death.

Given, then, the sense that this world is an arena of things that may happen to our detriment there arises in some the desire, while living in the world, to be safe whatever happens in it. There is a desire to reach a state in which, although what happens to others may move us and although what happens to us may be hard to bear, still *whatever happens* we will remain secure.

I do not wish to say that people have to be religious in order to come to terms with the fact that what happens in the world may work to human ill. Some existentialists maintain, for example, that what is called 'authentic' existence may arise from a courage to face the situation we find ourselves in as inhabitants of this world and from an acceptance that we cannot be safe.

8. In his "Anselm's Ontological Arguments" in John Hick, ed., *The Existence of God* (New York, 1964), p. 66.

Others have managed in less theoretical ways to come to terms with the nature of human existence. Thus at the beginning of his autobiography Leonard Woolf writes:

> I resent the wasteful stupidity of a system which requires that human beings with great labour and pain should spend years in acquiring knowledge, experience and skill and then just when at last they might use all this in the service of mankind and for their own happiness, they lose their teeth and their hair and their wits and are hurriedly bundled, together with all they have learned, into the grave and nothingness.
>
> It is clear that if there is a purpose in the universe and a creator, both are unintelligible to us. But that does not provide them with an excuse or a defence. However, as I have said nothing can be done about it, and having made my protest, I must now think about my past.[9]

What characterizes a *religious* response, and hence a theistic religious response, is not merely that one who makes it thereby finds some way of coming to terms with the world's contingency. Rather it is that one who thus responds feels himself to have a source of security that does not come from him or from anything in the world. This sense of safety comes *to* him and not from him. It does not depend upon him, or anything that exists or might happen in the world around him. It makes him safe whatever happens in the world.

Many of the crucial texts of theistic religions seem to me to express the notions that I have been hinting at above. In Christianity there are such pronouncements as: 'Whatsoever is born of God overcometh the world', 'Not as the world gives give I unto you', 'Be not conformed to this world', 'Behold, what manner of love the Father hath bestowed on us, that we should be called the sons of God; therefore the world knoweth us not', 'The souls of the righteous are in the hands of God and there shall no torment touch them'.

From the source of religion that I have tried to indicate there arises also the requirement that the religious belief that is to sustain a person in need of it must not be a belief that depends on what may happen in the world or turn out to be the case. It is this that gives some sense to the claim that a *religious* belief

9. Leonard Woolf, *Sowing* (London, 1961), p. 12.

must not be one that depends upon and changes with *evidence*.

To understand this it is necessary to recall what it is to believe in the existence of something on the basis of evidence. An example may help. At one time people believed there to exist a planet (Pluto). They believed it existed, although they could not see it, because certain pieces of evidence, facts about the world, pointed to its existence.

Two features of this belief are relevant here. First, the belief was a belief in the probable existence of an object. To say this is to say that no matter how strong the evidence, still when direct inspection did become possible there might have turned out to be nothing there. (What is probably true is possibly false.) Second, there was always the possibility that more evidence might turn up that would undermine belief in the existence of the object. The belief could be affected by what might happen, namely the discovery of more evidence. Such beliefs, then, could, should, and probably would rise or fall with the evidence.

If this is what it is to be an evidenced belief in the existence of something, I hope it will be clear why it might be said that a belief in God, adequate to the needs from which I have said religion arises, could not be like that. For first a religiously adequate belief, a belief that will render one safe whatever could happen, could not be a belief in the *probable* existence of a God. Since what is probably true is possibly false a man who said to himself, 'God probably exists' should in consistency add, 'but possibly He does not,' or 'but it might turn out that there is no God'. Then, however, he has not found that sure and adequate basis for his life in the world that he seeks from religion. He is still at the mercy of what might happen. For he cannot but realize that to say, 'God probably exists' is to admit that it might happen that there is no God and no sure basis for his peace. Second, if his belief does rest upon evidence, he must admit that it could happen that other evidence might come to his attention and that this evidence could cause a change in the belief that gives him peace. If his belief thus depends on evidence, his peace is still at the mercy of what might happen. For other evidence could turn up. If, however he *is* still at the mercy of what might happen when he believes in God then that belief in God is not adequate to the religious need from which it arises. *That* sort of God is not a religiously adequate God. Belief in it cannot make us safe from what might happen.

VII

I have tried, then, to sketch a way in which the claim that religious belief in God does not rest upon evidence might be derived from reflection upon what is involved in being religious. The following comments might be made on such an attempt.

First, I wish to return to a point with which I began, namely the suggestion that conclusions in Malcolm's paper are at odds with what we know to be true about religion. That suggestion may also be made about what I have said.

Suppose someone said, when confronted with the sort of argument I have just sketched, 'There are many instances of religious people producing proofs that are designed to show the probability that there is a God. Hence your argument, as much as Malcolm's, is at odds with what happens in religion'. We now have the following sort of reply to this line of approach. We can say that if we have correctly characterized what we and believers think to be a characteristic of *religion,* then attempts by believers to produce evidence for the probable existence of God represent a misunderstanding of what by their own understanding believers think to be involved in religion. For they cannot both believe that what I have said about the springs of the religious impulse is true *and* think that producing probabilistic proofs for the existence of God is an appropriate activity.

I would, of course, concede that there *is* a sense of the term 'God' (possibly a residue from a time when religion may have been more intimately linked with science) [10] in which a God just is a superbeing. This is the sense in which one recent popular writer has suggested that God is or was an astronaut. In this sense of the term 'God' the question whether God exists just is

10. On which see, e.g., Robin Horton, "African Traditional Thought and Western Science," in B. Wilson, ed., *Rationality* (Oxford, 1974).

the empirical question, 'Is there evidence for the existence of superpersons *in* the universe who might take an interest in us? '

If this is the sense of 'God' with which believers operate then the religious significance of that God is unclear. Such a God, qua thing that happens to exist in the universe, is not self-evidently better off than we are vis-à-vis the problems of existence from which religious needs may arise.

VIII

I do not think, then, that it could be denied that people *do* use the term 'God' in nonreligious contexts. What philosophers in the Wittgensteinian tradition in the philosophy of religion seemed to me to have wished to stress, however, is that if one wishes to say that one has a *religiously adequate* God, then the use of the term 'religion' constrains what one can say about God. This claim is in no way circumvented by showing us that people *do* use the term 'God' without these constraints.

We can begin to see now how it might be claimed that the sorts of conclusions that Malcolm offers are derived from reflections on how *we* (including believers) use terms (in this case the term 'religion'). Malcolm's conclusion derives from the claim that as *we* use the term 'religion' evidencing procedures of the sort we use for establishing our right to believe in the probable existence of a thing *could* not be procedures that are used to establish the truth of a *religiously adequate* belief in God. If this conclusion is to be attacked it will not do, as I have said, merely to claim (even correctly to claim) that this or that person in fact *does* use such procedures in the name of religion. For the question is, 'Given our understanding of the term "religion" *could* anyone coherently try to establish the probable existence of a religiously adequate God?' If the conclusion is to be attacked it must be by an argument that shows that the account of religion in terms of which these methods of probable proof are shown to be incoherent in religious contexts is not a correct account of religion.

Such an attack will have to begin with the fact that the account I have offered takes the form, 'We, i.e., I and others with whom I speak (including believers), have these ideas in mind when they talk of religion'. I can imagine various sorts of criticisms of this. First, quite general problems *could* be raised about any philosophy that employs an appeal to 'what we say' as a part of its methodology. Second, although not denying the utility of appeals to what we say, problems might be raised about the right of philosophers to make claims about what we say without field surveys among language users. These are, of course, complex problems in the theory of philosophy the treatment of which would take me far beyond the confines of this paper.[11] Here I remark only that I have not yet seen an attack on post-Wittgensteinian philosophy of religion that undermines that philosophy by discovering serious flaws in its claim that an appeal to what we say is a relevant tool of philosophical inquiry.

Leaving these wider issues aside, I suppose that another line of attack would be to show that what I have said about our use of the term 'religion' is in error. An attack made along these lines would be an interesting one. Although I do not know of efforts in this direction I would look forward to seeing them for what they might tell me of religion. Here I should say that what I have said of religion, and of one of its sources, seems to me to be true and, moreover, if true to entail that certain ways of establishing beliefs are suspect when applied to the case of religious belief in God. That is why I say that as *we* use the term religion, a religious belief in God could not rise or fall with the evidence. I feel sure that the only way to undermine that entailment is to show that what I have said about religion is not true.

IX

There do seem to me to be difficulties in the account I have given of why someone might think that religious belief does not rise or fall with evidence and grounds, but they seem to me to come from directions other than those that I have so far mentioned.

First, the account of religious belief in God that is given in Malcolm's account is only negatively characterized. We are told that religious belief in God *is not* evidenced belief in the exis-

11. See the papers in my *Philosophy and Linguistics* (London, 1971).

tence of an object that we cannot observe. But we are told little of what religious belief *is*, other than that it entails such responses as prayer, thanksgiving, and fear of the judgment of God. Since, however, when we are puzzled about theistic religious belief we are puzzled about what it *is* to pray to, thank, or fear God, more is needed if the nature of religious belief is to be made clear. There is then little positive said about the nature of religious belief. Probably if we wish to find the sort of account of religious belief that might be given in the light of Malcolm's remarks we will have to go elsewhere, to Malcolm's other writings or to other writers on religion who have made use of Wittgenstein's work. It would involve too substantial a digression to undertake that task here. It seems to me, however, to be a work of great interest and importance to show what sort of belief in God as a religious object would be compatible with what I have said about the source of religion.

The second difficulty that I wish to mention concerns the connection between Malcolm's paper and what I have said in Section VI. There I tried to indicate a possible way of justifying the claim that religious belief might be groundless in that it does not rise or fall with evidence. What I have said would, if true, justify only the claim that religious belief is groundless where to call religious belief 'groundless' means that religious belief is not like an evidenced belief in the existence of a thing that cannot be directly perceived. As far as I can see, however, to show this is not to show that there is *no* sense in which one might talk of justifying or finding reasons for religious belief.[12] Yet this stronger claim that religion is wholly groundless is suggested by Malcolm's paper. I would like therefore to conclude by indicating one or two reasons why this stronger claim does not seem to me to be licensed by what *I* have said.

First, I have certainly said that there may be difficulties in treating religious belief in God like belief in the existence of things that we cannot directly perceive but for which we have evidence. That is, I have tried to suggest some difficulties in the

12. On which matter, John Wisdom's article "Gods," e.g., in Antony Flew, ed., *Logic and Language*, I (Oxford, 1951), is notably relevant.

notion that there might be indirect evidence for the probable existence of God.

I could, however, imagine someone asking whether it is possible that one might have a reason (ground) for belief in God by virtue of one's having *direct* evidence of the certain existence of God. (After all one might claim to have a reason for believing in the existence of the planet Pluto if one had made some direct observations of it.)

Nothing in what I have said so far rules out the possibility that one might have a direct acquaintance with and hence a ground for belief in God. On this matter I can say only that the notion of direct acquaintance with God is too complex for it to be entirely clear what this possibility amounts to.

Second, suppose that I and Malcolm had shown there to be drawbacks in the idea of finding grounds of *any* sort for theistic religious beliefs. There would then still remain nontheistic religions (e.g., varieties of Buddhism) to consider. And whatever one can show about the groundlessness of *theistic* religious belief one would have to look at these other varieties of religion before one could assert the more general proposition that religious belief as such is groundless.

9

Remarks

BASIL MITCHELL

As chairman I count myself very fortunate in my symposiasts. Lyas has not only addressed himself to the thesis advanced by Malcolm, but also concentrated upon what is most central and interesting in that thesis. We thus have before us a plainly recognizable topic to the discussion of which I am free to make a minor contribution.

There are, I think, two distinct stages in this discussion. The first concerns the alleged groundlessness of large-scale systems or frameworks of belief or of the central affirmations of such systems, and relates as much to scientific or metaphysical systems as to religious ones. The second concerns the need for a religious system (or perhaps, more specifically, a theistic system) to prove 'religiously adequate' and the extent to which this requirement rules out certain kinds of justification. Malcolm holds out for groundlessness at both stages; Lyas, only at the second stage and then only with careful qualifications.

I should like to suggest that something can be gained by considering how far the problem raised in stage 2 about religious belief arises also at stage 1 in relation to scientific and other systems. The problem is said to be that if belief in God is based at all upon evidence it will 'rise and fall' or 'wax and wane' with the evidence. But to be 'religiously adequate' it is not enough that God be probable. The question of 'religious adequacy' does not arise in science, but suppose we ask, as a question of interest in its own right, to what extent and in what way, science 'rises or falls with the evidence'. I have used the very general word 'science', although in this context it sounds distinctly odd, because we are in the habit of using the word 're-

181

ligion' in an equally undiscriminating way. Perhaps we should distinguish at least three cases (a) a particular scientific hypothesis, (b) a fundamental scientific law, (c) the whole body of a given science, say, chemistry. The scientific hypothesis is, let us suppose, still under test in various laboratories all over the world and, in a fairly straightforward sense, it 'riscs and falls with the evidence'. An expert in the field could say with reasonable confidence how it stands at the moment. The research is being conducted against a background of accepted theory and would be impossible otherwise. It is in this context, I suggest, that it is most natural to talk of 'evidence for and against', or of 'probability'. The fundamental scientific law is in a very different case. It is so firmly integrated into the system as a whole that nothing but a large-scale revolution could dislodge it. Does it 'rise and fall with the evidence'? I agree with Lyas in thinking that it is in principle revisable, however unlikely it is in fact to be revised; and, if it is revised, I should want to say that it is because it no longer accounts adequately, or *as* adequately as some rival theory, for the data of observation. So it is not entirely insensitive to the results of empirical research. Yet such is its centrality to the existing body of the science that it is to a large extent protected from the effects of changes at the periphery of the system. It does not 'rise and fall with the evidence' because it is buffered against the shocks which might otherwise cause it to do so. Or, to use a more colorful analogy, it resembles the mastermind at the center of a criminal network, who always manages to escape detection and punishment by sacrificing some of his less essential underlings unless or until, that is, the final day of reckoning comes and his whole empire collapses.

The entire body of a given science in a particular period is similarly liable to undergo change of so fundamental a character as to justify the claim that it has been superseded. But short of such a 'revolution' it experiences a continuous process of development designed to enable it to take account of the research findings which it has itself generated. It is obvious that difficult problems of identity arise, yet, as long as there is sufficient continuity of basic principles and concepts we are prepared to regard it as the *same* system, and this is compatible with a great deal of change in respect of what is less essential.

If this account is at all on the right lines the reason why scientists do not generally call into question the fundamental laws of their science as they are currently understood, let alone the entire system, is that there would be no point in doing so. There is, ex hypothesi, no effective alternative at present in sight, and their ability to continue with fruitful scientific work depends upon their *trusting* the existing framework, as Malcolm rightly insists. In the case of other, nonscientific systems and also, I should guess, very often in the case of the human sciences, the situation is different in the important respect that rival systems generally exist whose claims cannot be dismissed as negligible. But here too it is a condition of any thorough attempt to develop such a system and work out its theoretical and practical implications that it is adhered to with a considerable degree of tenacity. And where it is a system with moral and political implications, adherence to which may determine the whole cast of a man's mind and shape his character, this is even more obviously the case.

But—and here the discussion enters its second stage—it may be objected, and I think that both symposiasts do object, that such an account, even if it were to be allowed a certain plausibility in relation to nonreligious frameworks, cannot be true of religions, or at any rate of theistic ones. For any belief in God which rested, even in principle, upon evidence, could not be belief in a 'religiously adequate' God. (I have demurred from the use of the word 'evidence' in this context, because like 'hypothesis' it suggests that basic religious assertions are analogous to comparatively low-level scientific theories, but with that qualification I shall go on using it.) The reason for this, as set out by Lyas, is that one could not coherently try to establish the probable existence of a religiously adequate God. Lyas admits, of course, that philosophers have often tried to do this, but he suspects that the 'God of the philosophers' whose existence might conceivably thus be proved would not be the God of religion or, at any rate, not the God of the Judaeo-Christian tradition. He then insists, however, as against Malcolm, that an appeal to *evidence* of some kind might not be the only way in which one might justify or find reasons for belief in God. One might, for instance, claim direct acquaintance with him.

My first comment on this concession on Lyas's part to Malcolm is that it cancels one of his own initial arguments against Malcolm, viz. that at the very center of the Christian tradition an appeal is made to historical events in support of doctrinal claims. 'If Christ be not risen your faith is vain'. But historical evidence is a contingent matter and beliefs based upon it are, in principle, liable to rise and fall (though historical facts may be established beyond reasonable doubt). Nor can it be reasonably maintained that the doctrines so established are merely peripheral. The doctrine of the Incarnation affects our conception of the very nature of God. To the extent, then, that Lyas wants to press this point—and I think he should—he has an interest in allowing the appeal to evidence.

I wonder, in fact, whether the expression 'religiously adequate' is not being used in two different senses. In the first sense it may be maintained that the sort of God that might be established by a certain kind of proof, such as the design argument put forward by Cleanthes, would not be a 'religiously adequate God' because he would be a contingent God, an 'entity among other entities', not a transcendent Creator. In the second sense the religious inadequacy of a conception of God might consist in the impossibility of putting the existence of a God, so conceived, beyond all reasonable doubt, with the consequence that belief in such a God could not perform the essential religious function of safeguarding us from 'the changes and chances of this transitory life'. It is the second sense of 'religiously adequate' that Lyas seems to have chiefly in mind, judging from his excursus into the sources of religion.

But might a man not believe in a transcendent Creator 'in whom is no variableness or shadow of turning' in whose hands are the souls of the righteous and who loves them with a steadfast and unfailing love; and might he not believe that in some sense of the word 'necessarily' God necessarily has these attributes; and yet confess that the existence of such a Creator was not beyond all possible doubt; that he had good reasons to believe in him, indeed, and that among these reasons were certain historical events, but that it was conceivable that he did not, after all, exist? And, if he did believe in such a God, would he not be believing precisely in a God who would not fail him, because to do so was no part of his essential nature? This would be significantly different from believing in a God who might pass away or who might undergo eventual defeat or who might fail of his promises for some other reason, and who, therefore, could not be relied upon.

It may be argued that such a man's faith is not 'religiously adequate' because it cannot give him the reassurance he needs. If this is a psychological generalization about religious believers it is by no means obviously true. Some may crave logical guarantees of the truth of their beliefs; others may have no need of them. In any case, even if logical certainty were available, this cannot as a matter of psychology be relied upon to prevent the dryness of spirit in which even undoubted truths appear empty and unconsoling. If, on the other hand, the contention is that the believer *ought* not to be reassured, that his belief is in *this* sense, not religiously adequate, we can point out, as in stage 1 of the discussion, that he has, ex hypothesi, good reasons for believing as he does and sufficient reason for not allowing his belief continually to 'rise and fall with the evidence' and not letting himself be 'carried about with every wind of doctrine'.

But, says Lyas, as long as his belief to any extent depends upon evidence 'his peace is at the mercy of what might happen'. The question is in what sense this is true. He trusts in God and the God in whom he trusts he believes, and has reason to believe, is wholly trustworthy. In this trust his peace consists. Should there, after all, be no God, as remains for him logically possible, his peace will, indeed, have proved illusory; but it would not then follow that the God he believed in was not trustworthy, even necessarily trustworthy; only that the trustworthy God he believed in did not exist.

Postscript

NORMAN MALCOLM

Colin Lyas's paper may leave a misleading impression of what I was trying to do in my essay. He reminds us that in particular religions there are doctrinal beliefs based on evidence or to which evidence is relevant. This is indeed so. Some doctrinal beliefs about Jesus and the Holy Spirit, for example, are based on New Testament texts. Here is an area where evidence, interpretation, argument, are appropriate. Also there are doctrinal disputes between Christian sects (e.g., the controversy over the extent of the authority of the bishop of Rome), disputes to which textual evidences are relevant. All this is well known.

I was not talking about this or that doctrinal belief in my essay but, more generally, about *religious belief*. It would be convenient if I could substitute the words "belief in God" for the words "religious belief"; but I hesitate to do so because the Buddhists do not describe themselves as believing in God, and yet Buddhism is undoubtedly a religion. Religious belief as such, not particular creeds or doctrines, was my topic.

I think there can be evidence for the particular doctrines of a faith only within the framework or attitude of religious belief. Many people who read about incidents in the life of Jesus, as recounted in the Gospels, or events in the lives of Hebrew prophets, as recounted in the Old Testament, do not believe that the incidents actually occurred. But it is also possible to believe that they occurred without regarding them as *religiously significant*. That a man should die and then come to life again is not necessarily of religious significance. That the apparent motion of the sun should be interrupted, as it was for Joshua, does not have to be understood religiously. A well-known physicist

186

once remarked to me, only *half* humorously, that the empirical study of miracles could be a branch of applied physics! The miracles recounted in the Bible *can* be regarded as events of merely scientific interest. They can be looked at from either a scientific or a religious *Weltanschauung*. It is only from, or within, the framework of religious belief that they have religious import.

It is such a framework or (to use Wittgenstein's term) *Weltbild*, whether religious or scientific, that, in my paper, I say is "groundless." I am not saying that those different ways of picturing the world do not have *causes*. Education, culture, family upbringing, can create a way of seeing the world. A personal disaster can destroy, or produce, religious belief. Religious people often think of their own belief as God's gift.

But my interest is not in causes. What I am holding is that a religious viewpoint is not based on grounds or evidence, whether this is the Five Ways of Aquinas, the starry heavens, or whatever. Of course, some people *see* the wonders of nature as *manifestations* of God's loving presence. Someone might even be able to regard the Five Ways in that light. Anselm did thank God for His gift of the Ontological Proof. But seeing something as a manifestation of God's love or creative power is a very different matter from taking it either as evidence for an empirical hypothesis or as a kind of logical proof.

Lyas wants to know whether my position is that people do not *in fact* seek grounds for their religious belief, or whether, as a conceptual matter, there *could not* be grounds. I hold that both things are true, even though this may shock a well-trained analytic philosopher. When you are describing a language-game, a system of thought and action, you are describing concepts and also describing what certain people do—how they think, react, live. Wittgenstein points out that in doing mathematical calculations we do not worry about the figures changing their shape after being written down, and that scientists typically do not have doubts as to whether they are in their laboratories or not. That such doubts are rare is an empirical fact; yet if it were not for this kind of fact we *could not* have some of our concepts. Consider these remarks by Wittgenstein:

Mathematicians do not in general quarrel over the result of a calculation. (This is an important fact.)—If it were otherwise, if for instance,
one mathematician was convinced that a figure had altered unper-
ceived, or that memory had deceived either him or the other person,
and so on—then our concept of 'mathematical certainty' would not
exist (*PI,* p. 225).

If I am trying to mate someone in chess, I cannot be having doubts as
to whether the pieces are perhaps changing positions of themselves
and at the same time my memory is tricking me so that I don't notice it
(*OC,* 346).

Lyas feels that we need a "demonstration" that religious belief is groundless. I am not sure what would satisfy him, but let
me suggest this: It seems obvious that the wonders and horrors
of nature, the history of nations, great events in one's personal
experience, music, art, the Ontological Proof—can be re-
sponded to either religiously or nonreligiously. Suppose there
is a person who is hostile or indifferent to religious belief, and
another person who wants to present to him convincing
grounds for religious belief. Can he do it? I don't think so. The
first person can view the presented evidences as psycholog-
ically, historically, mythologically, or logically interesting. But
even if he has an "open mind," the presented phenomena or
observations cannot have personal religious import for him
unless he already has an inclination toward a religious *Weltbild.*
A religious way of responding to events and facts is the me-
dium, the atmosphere, in which those phenomena can have
religious significance. Wittgenstein's remarks about "the
language-game," namely that

It is not based on grounds.
It is not reasonable (or unreasonable).
It is there—like our life (*OC,* 559).

is meant to apply to all language-games, but seems to be true in
an especially obvious way of religious belief.

I won't attempt to follow Lyas's distinction between "constitutive" and "regulative" principles. A pie can be cut in many different shapes. In any case, I do not think the distinction applies
to religious belief, which is Lyas's main concern. Religious belief, as I understand it, is not composed of some set of framework principles. Belief in a God who creates, judges, and loves

humanity, is *one form* of religious belief. Belief in a mystical principle of causality according to which good produces good and evil produces evil, is *another form* of religious belief. Those perspectives on reality are not hypotheses for or against which evidence can be marshaled. You may invite someone to see the world as a heartless mechanism or, on the contrary, as throbbing with love. Once a person has the beginnings of such a vision you may strengthen it for him by means of luminous examples. But unless he already shares that vision to some degree, he will not take your examples in the way you want him to take them.

Finally, I want to say something on the question of whether the beliefs that (in Wittgenstein's words) "stand fast" for one, or are part of "the framework" of one's thought and language, are *empirical* beliefs. I am thinking of such beliefs of mine as that my name is N. M. (not Herman Münsterberg), or that I speak English (and not Chinese). First, these beliefs are *contingent;* they *could* have been false. It did not happen, but it *could* have happened that my parents removed me at an early age to China, and that I grew up speaking Chinese and not English. Second, these beliefs are based on my experience, taken in a broad sense to include both what I was taught and what I "picked up." These two points count in favor of saying that those beliefs are "empirical." At the same time, they are beliefs that I could not seriously consider as *possibly* being false. I could not, or would not, accept anything as *evidence against* them.

In philosophy there has been a tradition of understanding by an "empirical" belief a belief that is, first, contingent; second, based on experience; third, falsifiable by experience. This puts one in a quandary as to whether those framework beliefs that "stand fast" for a person, are or are not to be classified as "empirical." I think that in *On Certainty* Wittgenstein felt some difficulty on this point. This comes out in his saying that such beliefs have "the form" of empirical beliefs (*OC*, 96, 401, 402), apparently indicating some reluctance to say straight out that they *are* "empirical" beliefs.

I want to relate this point to some remarks by Lyas. He says that if a person's belief "Does rest upon evidence, he must admit that it could happen that other evidence might come to his attention and that this evidence could cause a change in the belief that gives him peace. If his belief thus depends on evidence, his peace is still at the mercy of what might happen. For other evidence could turn up." Here Lyas seems to be assuming that if a particular belief is based on evidence then the person whose belief it is, must admit that something could turn up that would be evidence against the belief. Lyas is talking here about belief in the existence of God. But I should like to relate his assumption to the doctrinal beliefs that, I admit, do rest on evidence. Consider the Christian doctrinal belief that Jesus rose from the dead. There is evidence for this belief in the New Testament. Saint Paul states that upwards of five hundred people saw Jesus alive after his death by crucifixion. Christianity is commonly said to be a "historical" religion. I should think this means, in part, that some of the Christian articles of faith are empirical beliefs.

Now I should suppose that there are people, indeed many people, who would cite evidence from the New Testament in support of their belief in the Resurrection, but would not regard anything as evidence *against* it. If we took the belief in the Resurrection as an "empirical" belief, in the full sense of the philosophical tradition, then we might be inclined to regard the attitude of those people as somewhat muddled and irrational.

I want to say that we do not *have* to regard the matter in that light. My belief that my name is N. M. is contingent and is based on experience; but it is not, *for me*, falsifiable by experience. Yet there is nothing confused or irrational in my attitude on this matter. This is indeed the attitude that any adult person normally has toward his own name.

I suggest that there need be nothing confused or irrational in a similar attitude taken toward some of the doctrinal beliefs of a particular religious faith. We should avoid the straitjacket of assuming, quite generally, that if a person's belief is broadly based on evidence or experience, and is contingent, then *logic* requires that person to admit that further evidence could disconfirm his belief.

PART FOUR

MEANING AND

RELIGIOUS LANGUAGE

10

Meaning and Religious Language

PETER WINCH

I

Contemporary discussions of meaning in connection with religious language commonly take as their starting point certain expressions which seem fundamental in the religious beliefs and theological doctrines of the sophisticated world religions of today and, very naturally, in Anglo-Saxon writings the examples concentrated on tend to be taken from the religions with which the authors are most familiar, roughly the Judaeo-Christian. Furthermore, philosophers are concerned today, as they have always been, with problems about the reference, if any, of the terms under discussion, with problems about the way in which predicates are attributed to these referential, or quasi-referential terms—whether the connection between subject and predicate is necessary or contingent, what kind of necessity or contingency is in question, and so on.

I shall, in the course of this essay, make some comments on aspects of some of these questions, but for the following reasons I shall not take them as my starting point. I am concerned with meaning and *religious language,* not the language characteristically used in this or that particular religion. I want to ask primarily: how do we identify a use of language as a religious use in the first place? If we *start* by asking questions about words like 'God,' and expressions like 'God is infinitely good and powerful', we are open to the objection that such expressions do not have analogues in all religions, so that what we say will miss the mark insofar as our aim is to arrive at a characterization of religious language as such; our remarks will be insufficiently general. It is, of course, possible that anything like a general account is after all impossible of achievement, but the approach I have indicated seems likely to *make* it impossible because of the very terms in which the question is raised.

A further reason for adopting a different approach is as follows. The treatment of questions about meaning, reference, predication, necessity, and the like, in Anglo-Saxon philosophy has concentrated very largely on the application of such terms within empirical discourse, scientific theory, and mathematics. But perhaps these provide misleading models. Such logical terminology does, of course, have application to religious discourse, but an application which might be more clearly illuminated by investigating it from a different point of view. There has in fact been a very strong tendency to construe the term 'God' on the analogy of names and descriptive phrases as they occur within empirical discourse and to seek analogies for expressions like 'God is infinitely loving and powerful' in the same area. It may turn out that such analogies are indeed the appropriate ones, but we should not assume at the outset that this is going to be so. I shall in fact suggest some limited analogy between certain aspects of some religious discourse and geometry, but I do not wish to *start* at this point. The helpfulness of such an analogy will depend on a good many prior considerations which I want to develop. There is much more to this question than I shall have space to discuss here. There are deep philosophical disagreements about the proper way to discuss issues concerning reference, sense, truth, etc., quite apart from disagreements specifically concerning religion. To those familiar with such issues it will no doubt be evident on which side of the fence I stand in such disagreements. But an attempt to justify my general position on these large matters cannot possibly be included in an essay of this scope.

Though it is true of all of us that we first become acquainted with religious uses of language in becoming familiar with a particular religious tradition (or pretty limited range of such traditions), in so doing we acquire some concepts which we feel able to apply outside the context provided by these particular traditions. I am thinking of concepts like *worship, reverence, religious awe, devoutness.* These are concepts which we apply to *human beings* in certain aspects of their lives, demeanor, and practice, and which we think of as characteristic of descriptions of the religious dimensions (or lack of such dimensions) of people's lives. It is a noteworthy fact that, being able to make something of the distinction between a man who is a devout Christian and one who is not, I do not feel at a loss when I hear such a distinction drawn within the context of Buddhism, even though I have very little understanding of Buddhist doctrine.[1] On the other hand, a term like Nirvana will mean absolutely nothing to me until I have learned a good deal about specifically Buddhist doctrine. The fact that, though ignorant of Buddhist doctrine, I can make some sense of the distinction between a devout and a nondevout Buddhist has a great deal to do with my recognition of Buddhism *as a religion.* I do not dispute, of course, that I am unlikely to get very far with recognition of the particular form which devoutness takes for a Buddhist without further understanding of the Buddhist tradition, its types of religious observance, and its doctrines. But if I can apply the concept to a Christian I already know a good deal about the direction in which I should look in applying it to a Buddhist.

It is noteworthy that the concepts of which I have given examples are concepts applicable to the lives and practices of human beings. This raises the important question of the relation between practice and belief in religious contexts.[2] Consider the following remarks by Wittgenstein.

When he [sc. Fraser] explains to us, for example, that the king must be killed in his prime because, according to the notions of the savages, his soul would not be kept fresh otherwise, we can only say: where that practice and these views go together, the practice does not spring from the view, but both of them are there.

It may happen, as it often does today, that someone will give up a practice when he has seen that something on which it depended is an error. But this happens only in cases where you can make a man

1. I owe this very important observation to a remark made by Rush Rhees in the course of a discussion at King's College, London.
2. The discussion which immediately follows again owes much to Rush Rhees: in this case to three lectures on "Ritual" which he gave at King's College; though I am not following the same direction as that taken by Rhees's lectures.

change his way of doing things simply by calling his attention to his error. This is not how it is in connection with the religious practices of a people and what we have here is *not* an error.[3]

'The practice does not spring from the view, but both of them are there'. Wittgenstein does *not*, of course, here claim any priority for the practice over the view, but I should like to examine *this* possibility further in a way which is suggested by other parts of his writings. My reason for this springs from questions about concept-formation. I want to suggest that what makes a belief a 'religious' belief can best be understood by investigating the roots in religious practice of the concepts at work in religious beliefs. The possibility of doing this seems to depend on our being able to identify a set of practices as 'religious' independently of any beliefs associated with them. This I shall attempt presently.

But first, to explain my remark about concept-formation, let me refer to a suggestion made by Wittgenstein in quite a different area.

How do words *refer* to sensations? . . . This question is the same as: how does a human being learn the meaning of the names of sensations?—of the word "pain". Here is one possibility: words are connected with the primitive, the natural, expressions of the sensation and used in their place. A child has hurt himself and he cries and then adults talk to him and teach him exclamations and, later, sentences. They teach the child new pain-behaviour.

"So you are saying that the word 'pain' really means crying?"—On the contrary: the verbal expression of pain replaces crying and does not describe it.[4]

Wittgenstein is here speaking, of course, of a society already possessing a complex language of sensations and of the transmission of this language from adults to children. But we might also think of the possibility that in the dawn of langage, a 'language of sensations' gradually grew up and developed out of *'primitive'* (nonlinguistic) expressions of sensations. *We* could (and indeed can) recognize people (babies—as well as animals)

3. Ludwig Wittgenstein, "Remarks on Frazer's *Golden Bough*," trans. A. C. Miles and Rush Rhees, *The Human World*, no. 3 (May 1971), p. 29.
    4. *Philosophical Investigations*, Part I, § 244.

as being in pain even though they have no *concept* of pain, in the sense that they have no 'pain language' and no beliefs *about* pain.

Is this case at all applicable in any analogy with religion? Let us imagine a tribe whose speech includes nothing that we want to identify as the expression of 'religious beliefs'. They have, however, certain striking practices. Let us suppose they live among mountains. When one of their number dies he is buried or burned with a certain ceremoniousness. The ceremony includes perhaps some moments of silent contemplation of the mountains, perhaps prostration of their bodies before the mountains. Similar things are done at other important moments in the life of the tribe—at a marriage, on the occasion of a birth, when an adolescent is initiated into adult life.

I want to consider something like this as having a certain analogy (in respect of its relation to religious belief) to *primitive* pain behavior (in respect of its relation to talk about pain). I think that in certain circumstances I should want to say that members of the tribe were expressing something like reverence and even religious awe. And I think I should already be able to recognize differences among individual tribesmen which I should want to call differences in their 'devoutness' in their conduct of these observances. For this reason I want to call such behavior *'primitive'* religious practice.

Of course, there are great differences between this imaginary case and *primitive* pain behavior, differences which might make it seem objectionable to use the word 'primitive' of both cases. So it is important to emphasize that in using this word of both cases I am wanting to stress mainly an analogy between the *relation* of such cases respectively to one in which there is a developed pain language or a developed religious language. One important difference between the cases is that in the case of the rituals which I am wanting to designate 'religious', we are already dealing with an established social practice rather than with the behavior of individuals considered separately. Other differences are connected with this. For instance, while the form of *primitive* human responses to pain is, I imagine, pretty well universally the same, there is no reason to suppose that

this must be (or is) so of primitive religious rituals. In my example I have supposed a certain gravity and solemnity, but rituals could equally well have a gay exuberant character. What I
think *is* necessary for us to be able to characterize behavior as
ritualistic is that it is in some way set apart from behavior associated with everyday practical concerns: not in the sense that
it has no connection at all with such concerns (on the contrary),
but in the sense that it is stylized, ruled by conventional forms
and perhaps thought of as stemming from long-standing traditions. I should also expect such rituals to be associated with a
sense of wonder and awe at the grandeur and beauty of aspects
of the tribe's environment and to be directed toward features
of that environment having particular importance in the tribe's
life (mountains, the sea, animals—consider the Cro-Magnon
cave paintings). This would help to provide connections between the ritualistic performances and other aspects of the
tribe's life and would doubtless be associated with differences of
attitude expressed on other occasions toward the objects of ritualistic reverence and other familiar objects (consider totems).
Last, one would expect differences in the degree of seriousness
with which the rituals were regarded as between individual
tribesmen: indeed, this would be important in finding an application for expressions like 'devoutness'.

I am suggesting, then, that such a context of behavior, even
in the absence of any recognizably religious talk or belief, may
already force the description 'religious' on us. Suppose, however, that we do now add such talk to the original picture; that
we think of such talk as growing out of the primitive ritualistic
observances. There might for instance be talk of the 'gods' who
inhabit the mountains—all sorts of elaborations of different
kinds are imaginable. And now the rituals are explicitly
regarded as showing reverence toward the mountain gods, concerning whom other stories come to be told and handed down
between generations.

It is important to the case I am trying to make that we should
not take for granted the introduction of a term such as that we
perhaps translate by our word 'gods.' I am suggesting that what
would make such a translation appropriate would be precisely

the connection of the talk in which it occurs with the rituals. The term acquires its sense from its connection with the rituals (which does not preclude the possibility of further elaborations of the talk of a kind in which the connection with the rituals is not explicit or obvious).

We should be wary at this point of supposing that the role of such talk is to 'explain' why the rituals are performed. The analogy with pain may help to make my point clearer. We may say of an individual, 'He is limping because he has a pain in his leg': this *does* give an explanation of this individual's limping. But if we say, 'People tend to limp when they have pains in their legs' the situation is different. Here we have something much more like a conceptual, or 'grammatical' observation pointing to the connection between phenomena like limping and the application of the term 'pain.' It is hard to imagine someone who understood the term 'pain' who would not already recognize that pains in the leg tend to go with limping; and, of course, if he did *not* already understand the term 'pain,' the remark 'People tend to limp when they have leg pains' could not explain anything.

Similarly, I am suggesting that to say of my tribesmen, 'They look to the mountains in order to show reverence to their gods', is not to *explain* why they look to the mountains, but to point to a conceptual connection between what they understand by their gods and their ritualistic practice. (*Of course*, this does not mean that what they understand by their gods will have no other conceptual connections.) We use the term 'gods' here because of its connection with their rituals. The case is quite different with, 'They look toward the mountains to seek animals to hunt'. This is explanatory and can be so because the term 'animals' can be given a sense quite independently of this habit of the tribesmen of looking toward the mountains.

What is the status of what I have been saying? [5] I do not, of course, want it to be taken as a sort of a priori history of the origin of religious belief. It is intended rather to suggest certain conceptual connections, rather in the manner of certain 'social

5. The immediately following remarks are a response to a question asked at the Lancaster Conference by Sydney Shoemaker, for which I am grateful.

contract' accounts of the state. It may be asked (as it was by Sydney Shoemaker) why the talk and the stories should not come first and only subsequently come to be associated with rituals of reverence and worship. My answer is that this could, of course, happen, but that *before* the connection of such talk with worship and the like, we should have no reason to attach any religious significance to it, and hence we should have no reason to say that such talk concerned 'gods'. This would not preclude such talk becoming associated with worship; but then, so I contend, its sense (its grammar) would have undergone a fundamental change.

At this point I am touching on issues concerning the nature of the 'reference' of certain religious expressions of the kind I mentioned at the beginning of this paper as being of particular interest to philosophers; and associated issues concerning the possibility of attributing 'existence' to what such expressions refer, or seem to refer to. Here I only want to remark that how a term refers has to be understood in the light of its *actual* application with its surrounding context in the lives of its users. I italicize *'actual'* by way of contrasting what I am talking about both with some ideal 'application' imagined by philosophers and also with what users of the term may be inclined to *say* about their application of it if asked. (Compare how people actually do use the verb 'to think' and what both philosophers and nonphilosophers may say about 'what thinking is'.) Notice that I am *not* saying the 'existence' of what is spoken of simply consists in the fact that people talk in a certain way; I am saying that what the 'existence' of whatever it is amounts to is expressed (shows itself) in the way people apply the language they speak.[6]

II

Against the background of the discussion in Section I, let me now address myself more directly to some of the issues constantly raised in the contemporary literature of philosophy of religion.

6. Most of the qualifications in this paragraph are designed to meet comments made by John Hick in discussion at Lancaster.

Much is made in this literature of the distinction between questions about truth and questions about meaning. Unfortunately, this by no means always reflects an adequate grasp of the relations between such questions. Commonly, questions about the meaning of religious language are conflated with questions about the possibility of verifying or falsifying theological claims, and questions about the rationality of religious belief are thought of as depending on the verifiability or falsifiability of the theological claims associated with particular forms of religious belief.

So we are presented with something like the following picture. The use of religious language is seen, by virtue of the meanings of the terms used, as committing the believer to certain 'existential' claims; these claims are articulated in theologies. Unless those theologies are verifiable or at least falsifiable, there is in principle no way of telling whether those existential presuppositions are warranted. Thus the believer's language has no clear meaning and his belief fails of rationality.

My aim is to undermine this position.

A man may be a very devout believer and have little understanding of, or interest in, the sophisticated arguments and doctrines of theologians. Perhaps he prays to the Lord Jesus Christ to intercede for him with God the Father; or he prays for the grace of the Holy Spirit. But perhaps too he is lost when it comes to learned discussions of the Trinity and of the sense in which Father, Son, and Holy Spirit are One God. Does this make his belief, religiously speaking, inferior to that of the theologian? The difference between them is not like that between a laboratory technician who sets up an experiment without having a clear idea of what he is doing and the scientist who directs him. That is to say, in respect of its scientific significance, the technician's activities differ from those of the scientist. There is no reason why the unsophisticate's belief should not be religiously deeper than that of the theologian.

Of course, the discussions of theologians affect the teachings of a church; and believers are brought up on those teachings which, in their turn, influence the forms of worship offered to the church's adherents. Thus the doctrine of Cathar theology that the world of matter is the work of the Devil was connected with the rejection of sacraments in the worship of the Cathar church.[7] The traffic, however, is not one way. Theological doctrines are not developed independently of their possibilities of application in the worship and religious lives of believers; and these latter have a certain, though not a complete, autonomy. I mean that if a doctrine were felt by believers to be hostile to their practices of prayer and worship, that would create a difficulty for the theological doctrine itself. I emphasize that the traffic goes in both directions and there is give and take. Believers' attitudes toward worship may be modified under the pressure of priests, for example, who in their turn are influenced by the theological doctrines in which they are trained in their church. But the attitudes of priests toward theological doctrines may also be affected by the resistances they encounter in the attitudes toward worship among their flocks. Of course, not all believers (or priests) will react in the same way, and thus arise possibilities of schism and heresy.

These jejune remarks are not absurdly intended as a contribution to ecclesiastical history or to the sociology of religion. They are meant to point to some of the complicated conceptual issues involved in the relation between theology and the language and practices of religion. In particular they are intended to raise questions about a pervasive view of such a relation: that the practices of believers are, at the most fundamental level, to be explained by the believers' 'belief in the truth' of certain theological doctrines. I have already suggested that worship (which may naturally take many forms) is a primitive human response to certain characteristic human situations and predicaments, that it is, to use a phrase of Wittgenstein's, part of the natural history of mankind. These practices will involve certain characteristic uses of language (again taking many different

7. See Fernand Niel, *Albigeois et Cathares, Que sais-je?*, No. 689 (Paris, 1974). What I say in this paragraph qualifies the discussion in section I of the primitive roots of religious belief; I am now discussing a developed religion with an articulated system of belief and a theology.

forms between which, however, analogies will be discernible). Given the existence of these practices and uses of language, theological doctrines will be elaborated which in their turn will react back on the practices and language of believers. In order to understand the sense of these doctrines (their 'relation to reality') we need to understand their application. This application takes place in contexts such as those of prayer and worship within which language is used according to a certain grammar. This grammar itself imposes limits on what will count as an acceptable theological doctrine, even though, as I have said, a doctrine may itself lead to modifications in the grammar of the language in which belief is expressed in worship.

The temptation to which we are subject in philosophizing about religion and theology is similar to temptations familiar enough in other areas of philosophy: that of seeming to see a quite different (and apparently more direct) kind of 'relation' between language and reality which is a result of disregarding the complexities of the *actual* application of that language. In succumbing to this temptation we are led to the view that, if someone uses religious language, he is committed to a theory about the nature of the world which this language somehow enshrines. To deny, as I wish to do, that this is so is not to deny that one whose thoughts are couched in the language of religion has in a sense a very different view of the world from one who does not think thus. It is to deny that the difference is one between men who accept opposing theories.

I have spoken of the uses of religious language in the lives of believers, and fairly clearly the context of belief is fundamental to the sense which such language has. But the distinction I have just drawn—between a man whose thoughts are and one whose thoughts are not couched in the language of religion—is not the same as the distinction between one who has religious faith and one who does not. A difficulty here is that this last phrase may mark various distinctions. Tolstoy's Father Sergius, at the climax of the story, has lost his religious faith. But this loss can only be expressed by him—or by Tolstoy or by us—in the language of religion. The case is very different from that, say, of a

Kai Nielsen, or of the 'sceptical young professor' who has a discussion with Sergius and who 'had agreed with him in everything as with someone who was mentally inferior. Father Sergius saw that the young man did not believe but yet was satisfied, tranquil and at ease, and the memory of that conversation now disquieted him.' [8] The difference is in some ways like that between the case of two music lovers who disagree on the relative merits of, say, Brahms and Wagner and the case of a music lover and one to whom music (and also what the music lover says), as we say, 'means nothing'. There are many to whom the language of religion means nothing. In trying to describe how they view life one would not need to use the language of religion. This is certainly *not* true of all those who 'do not believe' or who have 'lost their faith'.

The distinction between language and theory is obviously important to the way we approach the question of meaning in religion. It may be an important criticism of a theory that it has been made immune to falsification by the sandbagging of subsidiary hypotheses ('death by a thousand qualifications'). Sometimes a theory of which this is thought to be true may be said to have become 'meaningless'.

A theory requires a language in which it may be expressed. One theory may be opposed by another. Sometimes the opposition between the theories may be stated in a language which both share. In cases of very radical opposition this may not be possible in that the differences between the theories involve quite fundamental differences between some of the concepts expressed by shared verbal expressions, between the 'grammar', the mode of application, of those expressions. In such cases the opposition between the theories may not be satisfactorily stateable, but will make itself manifest, in the differences in modes of application.[9]

Philosophers often assume that the very use of certain forms of linguistic expression itself commits the speaker to something

8. Leo Tolstoy, *The Kreutzer Sonata and Other Tales* (Oxford, 1960), p. 339.
9. The formulation of this point owes much to some trenchant criticisms of an earlier version for which I am greatly indebted to Cora Diamond, though I am not confident that I have adequately met her criticisms. This would require a much more extended discussion than is possible here.

like a theory about the nature of things.[10] And it will certainly
be objected to what I have been saying that religious practices
and beliefs can be made no sense of without the thought that
their adherents make certain theoretical, theological presuppositions. 'Praying to God presupposes that there is a God to
pray to'. This treats the phrase 'praying to God' as if it were
analogous in a certain way to, say, 'writing to the Yugoslav ambassador at the Court of St James'. If I learn that Yugoslavia
has broken off diplomatic relations with the United Kingdom,
then obviously it would be mad of me to address letters to the
Yugoslav ambassador, because I know that no such person exists.

Compare this with the following: 'What if someone were to
say to me, "I am expecting three knocks at the door", and I
were to reply: "How do you know that *there are three knocks?*"
Wouldn't that be entirely analogous to the question, "How do
you know that there are six feet?", if someone had said, perhaps, he believed that A is six feet tall?' [11] Before asking which
of these cases is the better analogue for 'praying to God', let us
consider the nature of the differences between the cases. The
first and obvious difference is that while there is a clear sense to
'Does *x* exist?' where *x* = the Yugoslav ambassador, this is not so
where *x* = three knocks or six feet. At least, it seems obvious to
me, though some philosophers of mathematics talk as if they
thought there were sense in questions about the existence or
nonexistence of six feet. But I cannot go into such aberrations
here.

A second and connected difference is this. If someone were
to question the existence of a Yugoslav ambassador he would
be questioning the point of my sending letters addressed in this
particular way. My sending letters to other people—my wife,
say, or the U.S. ambassador—would not be in question. If it
were to be called in question it would have to be done so separately and new arguments would be needed. That is, the ra-

10. This assumption is one of the targets constantly under attack in Wittgenstein's writings. I discuss it more fully than I can here in "Language, Belief and
Relativism," in Hywel D. Lewis, ed., *Contemporary British Philosophy, Fourth Series*
(London, 1976).
11. Ludwig Wittgenstein, *Philosophische Bemerkungen*, III, § 36.

tionality of the *practice* of sending letters to people would not be in question. On the contrary, that would be presupposed by the arguments against my sending a letter in this particular case; it is precisely because we in general understand the point of sending letters to people that we are able to see the sense-lessness of addressing a letter to a nonexistent person. In the first of Wittgenstein's examples a case completely parallel to this would be one in which my expectation of three knocks at the door is criticized on the grounds that the person I am ex-pecting to knock does not exist or is not in the vicinity; again, such a criticism does not question, but presupposes, the point of knocking at doors. But that is not the case that Wittgenstein considers, or that is interesting. Insofar as we try to make sense of the question, 'How do you know that there are three knocks?' at all, I suppose we should have to construe it as a suggestion that the practice of knocking at doors (or knocking as much as three times at doors) has fallen into desuetude or has for some reason lost its point. This latter kind of suggestion would be easier to imagine in the case of the second example—perhaps the country has gone metric and nobody understands talk about 'feet' anymore.

Philosophers who say that praying to God makes sense only if it is presupposed that God exists seem to be offering the fol-lowing account. There is the practice of talking to people and making requests of them and the rationality of this practice is not in question. Particular instantiations of the practice may be criticized on the ground, for example, that the person ad-dressed does not exist, is in no position to hear what is said, or in no position to fulfill the request. Praying is a particular in-stantiation of this practice and can, therefore, be treated in a similar way. Perhaps the method of establishing God's existence or nonexistence, or his capabilities, is peculiar; but that is thought of as a distinct issue.

Against this I want to argue that there is a difference in grammar between 'asking something of God' and 'asking some-thing of the Yugoslav ambassador'. I mean that there is not merely a difference in the method it is appropriate to use in the two cases or in the nature of the requests it is appropriate

to make, though both these things are true. I mean that what
constitutes asking (and also answering) is different; or that the
point of prayer (presupposed in any discussion of the rationality of particular cases of prayer) can only be elucidated by
considering it in its religious context; that it cannot be elucidated by starting simply with the function 'making requests to
x', substituting 'God' for 'x', and then asking what difference is
made by the fact that God has different characteristics from
other x's. 'Making requests of x', that is, is not a function which
retains the same sense whether 'God' or some name or description of a human being is substituted for 'x'.

It would certainly be wrong to say that the existence of the
addressee is presupposed in the one case and not in the other.
But this does not mean that the existence of the addressee *is*
presupposed in both cases. It would be better to say that this
question of 'existence' cannot arise in the one case in the way it
can in the other, as the existence of six feet cannot arise in the
case of someone wondering how tall a certain person is (which
does not, of course, mean that the existence of six feet is 'presupposed' here). It is true that there would be something
wrong with a man who claimed to be praying to God while saying he did not believe in God's existence. But would the same
kind of thing be amiss as with a man who claimed to be writing
to the Yugoslav ambassador while saying that he did not believe
in the existence of such a person?

I feel inclined to say that, in the latter case, ceasing to see any
point in writing is a *consequence* of ceasing to believe in the ambassador's existence, whereas ceasing to see any point in praying is an *aspect* of ceasing to believe in God.[12] In other words
there are internal connections between ceasing to believe in
God's existence and ceasing to see any point in prayer of a sort

12. It is noteworthy that *this* is the phrase which comes naturally to mind
here, rather than 'believe in God's existence'. To this extent I agree with what
Norman Malcolm says about 'the existence of God' in his contribution to this
volume. It does seem to me, however, that the expression and discussion of
religious doubts can and sometimes does involve the 'questioning of God's existence'; only one has to see that what such questioning amounts to is quite different from what is involved in questioning the existence of a man and can only
be understood as an aspect of what, in general, is involved in 'religious doubts'.

which do not hold between ceasing to believe in the ambassador's existence and ceasing to see any point in addressing letters to him. This is not to say that seeing a point in praying is identical with believing in God's existence. For one thing, believing in God has many other aspects: thinking of one's life in terms of obedience to God's will, for instance, or regarding all men as God's creatures. And, on the other hand, a man may cease to see any point in (at least *his*) praying without ceasing to believe in God's existence (as in the case of Claudius in *Hamlet*). But ceasing to see any point in prayer is *one* form which ceasing to believe in God may take. A man who has had a religious upbringing and has prayed regularly as he was taught to do in childhood may someday realize that he is doing so quite mechanically and that it really 'means nothing to him'. He may express his realization in the thought: 'I don't believe that God exists'. But this will not necessarily mean that his attitude toward prayer is the *result* of his lack of belief.

But, it may be said, a man's belief in the nonexistence of the ambassador may also express itself, inter alia, in his no longer addressing letters to him; so can we not equally say that his attitude toward addressing letters thus is an 'aspect' of his not believing in the ambassador's existence? Yes, we can say this: there are internal connections *of a certain sort* here too. But in this case there is something that we can call 'discovering that the ambassador does not exist' which does not itself depend on any changed attitudes toward letter writing and the like. Here the changed attitudes are a consequence of the discovery, though we may also say that they express the fact that the discovery has been taken to heart. In religion, on the other hand, while there may be reflection on God's existence which may sometimes result in a cessation of belief, this reflection cannot itself be separated from reflection on prayer, worship, and the like. That is the form which reflection on God's existence takes.

When Michelangelo represented the creation of Adam, did he presuppose, or surmise, that there had been some event looking rather like this? And when we respond to his painting in a way which respects the religious ideas which it expresses, what sort of consideration is relevant? Well, one might speak

here of how the power of God the Father and Adam's dependence are, on both sides, inseparably linked with love. God's
power is not simply combined with his love; it *is* his love. And
likewise with Adam's dependence on and love for his Creator:
they are one. The point of this representation has to be seen in
relation to the way in which worship and love are connected in
the life of a believer. It is here that the picture is 'confronted
with reality'. The form of representation, the sort of connection with reality, involved are totally different from that in a
diagram of an accident presented with a claim on an insurance
company. That is shown by the difference between the questions it is appropriate to ask in the one case as contrasted with
the other.

The kind of philosopher I am arguing against rightly makes
much of the importance of being able to confront religious
beliefs with reality if we are not to end up with a set of practices
and beliefs hermetically sealed off from any relation to life or
to our understanding of the world. The position is sometimes
made to look by philosophers on both sides of the fence (and
perhaps I have not always been careful enough about this myself), as though religion is something people engage in part of
the time, taking care not to let it be confronted with what they
are doing and thinking the rest of the week: sealing the door
between the chapel and the laboratory to make sure there is no
intermingling of the incense and the hydrogen sulphide. Of
course, this is a travesty; and if it does characterize the lives of
some believers, that is an important criticism of them: a criticism as much of the depth and sincerity of their religious beliefs as of their general intellectual honesty.

My point, however, is not that there cannot or should not be
any confrontation between a man's religious convictions and
the understanding of the world which he has drawn from
sources other than religion. I am saying rather that the form
such a 'confrontation with reality' takes is very misleadingly
represented in terms of 'evidence for God's existence and nonexistence'. The point is quite analogous to that made by
Wittgenstein in his treatment of the attempt to explain the lack
of an application for the expression 'reddish-green' in terms of

the assertion that 'there is no such colour'. ('How do you know?', he asks.) ' "Yes, but has nature nothing to say here?" Indeed she has—but she makes herself audible in another way. "You'll surely run up against existence and non-existence somewhere." But that means against *facts*, not concepts.' [13] 'Nature' makes herself heard, both in the case discussed by Wittgenstein and in the case of religious language, by way of the factual circumstances in which language is applied. These are of different sorts, including both general facts of human existence—such as the complex conditions of dependence of men on the rest of nature and on each other described so well by Spinoza; and also the more 'internal' facts of human nature, such as the rich and varied responses (exemplified, for example, in Simone Weil's writing) which may be elicited when religious language is used in, say, encounter with affliction. This is not to say that the expression 'God' really *refers* to such facts; it is to say that the reality which it expresses is to be found in the conditions of its application. Simone Weil makes a similar point in a different way: 'The Gospel contains a conception of human life, not a theology.' And, astonishingly: 'Earthly things are the criterion of spiritual things. . . . Only spiritual things are of value, but only physical things have a verifiable existence. Therefore the value of the former can only be verified as an illumination projected on to the latter.' [14]

To say 'Earthly things are the criterion of spiritual things' is not to say they are *identical* any more than Wittgenstein was saying that 'inner processes' are identical with their 'outer criteria'. To think otherwise is to miss the crucial importance of the grammatical differences between the way we speak of the criteria and of that of which they are the criteria.

To say that expressions are used in accordance with different grammars is to say, among other things, that the kind of consideration which would count for or against one use would not do so in the case of the other; it is not to say that there are no relations between the two cases or even that the one is conceivable apart from the other. (Compare, 'Then I murdered her',

13. *Zettel*, § 364.
14. Simone Weil, *First and Last Notebooks* (Oxford, 1970), p. 147.

(a) in a report of what I did and (b) in a report of my dream.) Thus the grammar of the function 'x loves his children' is altered when 'my brother' or 'God' respectively are substituted for 'x'. What would go into an explanation of the sense of the one is of a different kind from what would go into an explanation of the sense of the other. And what, e.g., would be relevant to the genesis of a doubt about the one is different from what would support a doubt about the other. This is so even though the two uses of 'loves' are connected: one would hardly be able to speak of God's love for his children if one could not also speak of the love of human fathers for their children; and conversely, the way in which we think about human love will be different if the notion of God as a loving father occupies a central place in our thought.

One might compare this situation with the relation between the way we use expressions like 'triangle', 'circle', etc., in our descriptions of spatial objects and the way we use these expressions in geometry. A man would hardly be in a position to grasp the proof of Pythagoras's Theorem if he were not able to recognize triangular and square figures when he saw them. But, having grasped the proof, he will be able to think about such figures differently. I shall return to this comparison. But let me first consider some remarks by Michael Durrant [15] which seem to me to betray confusions—by no means peculiar to Durrant—about what is involved in speaking of 'differences in grammar' between the uses of expressions in religious and other contexts.

Durrant objects to the claim that sentences of the form 'God is F' (e.g., 'God is infinitely good') 'have the function of determining what is possible within such a [e.g., Christian] system of discourse'. In particular Durrant discusses the claim that to say 'God is infinitely good' is to insist on the senselessness of saying that God's goodness might sometimes 'fail to operate' and thus to point to a contrast between the grammar of 'good' as predicated of God and as predicated of some human agent. He develops an argument of A. G. N. Flew's (part of Flew's polemic against 'death by a thousand qualifications') which

15. *The Logical Status of 'God'* (London, 1974), chap. 4.

relies on the assertion that if, in a given context, it makes no sense to speak of x's goodness 'failing to operate', then it can make no sense, in that context, to speak of x's goodness 'operating' either. Such a conclusion, Durrant says, no doubt rightly, must be unacceptable to a believer who wishes to speak of God's goodness.

The argument is presented as a general logical thesis which must be accepted independently of any individual peculiarities of context in which the expressions in question are being used. The thesis is that expressions like 'operating' and 'failing to operate' are 'necessarily correlatives, irrespective of context' and that this can be denied only

at the cost of ignoring an important logical point. Granted, it is possible that in various 'universes of discourse' (language games) what constitutes X operating or failing to operate will be different as between those language games, but this concession does not mitigate against [sic] the above argument—rather it supposes that in such areas of discourse the distinction between 'operating' and 'failing to operate' is itself in operation, which has to be denied on the construction of 'God is infinitely F' as remarks of grammar concerning God.[16]

Durrant here commits an error similar to one of which the philosophers he is criticizing are often accused: that of treating the uses of expressions in religious contexts as if they are independent of their uses elsewhere. This leads him to overlook the possibility that when a believer speaks of God's goodness operating in the world, a contrast is indeed presupposed with cases in which goodness fails to operate in the world (cases, e.g., in which a human agent falls short of his usually high standards). But the contrast in this case is *itself a grammatical contrast*. The contrast *shows itself* in the different *applications* of the term 'goodness' by someone who talks of man's goodness and a believer who talks of God's goodness. If it is said that my account treats 'God is infinitely good' as saying nothing about the world, my reply is that this is so only if one takes as one's model an expression like 'Saint Francis was a good man'. Does 'red is darker than pink' say anything about the world? Not in the way

16. Ibid., p. 83.

that 'this material is darker than that' does (said of two pieces of material one of which is red and the other pink). 'Red is darker than pink' draws our attention to relations between the ways in which we use the 'red/pink' and the 'dark/light' distinctions respectively. 'God is infinitely good' draws attention to the difference in the way we use 'good' of God and the way we use it of human beings. This difference, as I shall try to illustrate in Section III, affects the way we speak about things, people, and events in the world. So 'God is infinitely good' does reflect important things about the way we regard the world. To call it a 'grammatical' observation is not to cut it off from any relation with the real world.[17]

A believer who says that God's goodness cannot fail to operate is not in the position of being unable to attach any sense to talk of 'goodness failing to operate'. Indeed, the force of talking of God's infinite goodness does depend on an understanding that (in the case of man) goodness may, and frequently does, fail to operate. Such talk is largely a response to such an understanding—a response which in its turn provides a point of view from which the frequent failure of human goodness may be understood and treated differently than would otherwise be possible. In a similar way the force of speaking of the interior angles of a Euclidean triangle as necessarily equal to two right angles lies in the way such talk enters into our treatment of empirical triangles whose interior angles are found not to be equal to two right angles.

The following is an adaptation of a sentence on page 82 of Durrant's book, in which I have substituted geometrical expressions for the original references to God and his goodness.

If it is part of the 'grammar' of the interior angles of the triangle, or follows from that 'grammar' that nothing can possibly constitute the triangle's interior angles failing to be equal to two right angles, then it must also follow from that 'grammar' that nothing can constitute those interior angles being equal to two right angles either and if nothing can possibly constitute this then the notion of the triangle's interior

17. I have amplified my original presentation of this point as a result of a very valuable private discussion with Michael Durrant at the Lancaster Conference.

angles being equal to two right angles is itself a nonsensical one, for the sense of 'being equal to two right angles' is dependent upon the sense of 'failing to be equal to two right angles'; they are correlatives.

As far as I can see, Durrant has given no reason for thinking that his argument, if good against the grammatical construction of 'God is infinitely good' is not equally valid against such a construction of 'the interior angles of the triangle are equal to two right angles'. Of course, he might want to reject such a construction of geometry too—and I cannot defend it here. But what seems initially clear is that his own mode of argument is going to face him with the formidable task of showing that sense *can* be attached to the idea that the Euclidean triangle might fail to have interior angles equal to two right angles.

III

I have already noted that while geometry does not describe the properties of empirical structures, it does have an application in such descriptions and makes possible ways of thinking and techniques (e.g., of measurement) in dealing with them which would not otherwise be possible. *This* is its 'relation to reality', which does not lie in its being a description of some other 'realm of reality' distinct from that to which empirical structures belong. (This expression, 'realm of reality', is a sticky one which I shall come back to later.) Religious uses of language equally, I want to say, are not descriptions of an 'order of reality' distinct from the earthly life with which we are familiar. (Cf. the passage from Simone Weil which I cited in Section II.) These uses of language do, however, have an application in what religious people say and do in the course of their life on earth; and this is where their 'relation to reality' is to be sought.

Earlier I discussed Michelangelo's representation of the creation of Adam and remarked that, in it, God's power and love are combined into a single whole: God's power here *is* his love. And similarly for Adam's dependence on, and love for, his Creator. In Plato's *Symposium* Agathon says, 'Whatever Love may suffer, it cannot be by violence—which, indeed, cannot so much as touch him; nor does he need to go to work by force, for the world asks no compulsion, but is glad to serve him'. The model for God's power in Michelangelo's representation (which corresponds to and enriches an important strand in Christian—and not only Christian—religious belief) is the love that moves the human heart by *consent*. What it elicits in those who have a sense of it is not mere external compliance but gladly willing compliance.

Without any explicit reference to religious ideas we do sometimes speak of the limits of the kind of power which operates through force. We may perhaps say that there is something in a man which force cannot reach. If we speak thus, we are making the kind of remark Wittgenstein might have called 'grammatical'. *Consent* (and especially loving consent) has to be *given*. If it seems to be exacted by force this is an illusion; what is so exacted is something different.

A test case for the application of this grammatical observation might be the position of Winston Smith at the end of George Orwell's *1984*, where the final triumph of the Party is expressed by saying that Winston 'loved' Big Brother. And this is, of course, presented as the ultimate outrage: a violation, as it were, of that which of all things we had believed cannot be violated. People may react in different ways to this part of the story and these differences may correspond to acceptance or rejection of the grammar of 'love' and 'consent', suggested in my remarks in the previous paragraph. I express no opinion on who would be 'right' in the case of such a disagreement. I am not sure that there *is* any answer to such a question, though it may certainly give rise to searching inquiries into 'the nature of the human condition'—as the works of Simone Weil, among those of many other writers, testify. This is characteristic of the kind of grammatical question which goes deep: the kind which interests philosophers.

It is possible to speak as Orwell seems, despairingly, to be speaking. But it is also possible (which does not mean easy) to maintain our conceptual limit. We may want to say that Winston's is not 'true' consent. And I think there are few who would want to say, or who would not at least feel a twinge about saying, that what Winston felt for Big Brother was genuine love. 'Love isn't *like* that', we want to protest. And we may go on to say that Big Brother is deluding himself if he thinks that his power is at last able to breach this conceptual barrier.

This issue is, of course, closely connected with the discussion between Swinburne and Phillips in this volume. To think that 'God is Love' and at the same time to think of him as 'all-powerful' is not to *conjoin* the thoughts of someone as both loving and powerful, as we might in thinking of some benevolent human despot, and then to raise the qualities of love and power to the nth degree ($n = $ infinity). Any more than to think (geometrically) of the perfect sphere is to think of ball bearings manufactured with such perfect precision that no margin of error at all is presupposed in our thought of their sphericity. We have no clear idea of what this could mean in either case. We are making a conceptual, or grammatical, move in speaking of the power and love of God in the way we do; just as we are making a conceptual, or grammatical, move when we treat the idea of sphericity (which we may indeed have originally formed in connection with our observation of things like ball bearings) in a system such as Euclidean geometry. These moves will have their repercussions on what we say, and the ways in which we act in connection with, the power of men or the sphericity of ball bearings, but they are not mere extrapolations from these cases. The way in which notions like infinity and perfection are here introduced makes the idea of any mere extrapolation unintelligible.

I can do no more than sketchily illustrate the kind of repercussion which the conceptual amalgamation of love and power as predicated of God may have on what we say and do in the course of our lives. The conception of God as all-powerful and all-good carries with it the idea that we owe him absolute obedience—'absolute' not merely as concerns external compliance, but, much more important, as concerns the spirit in which one obeys, i.e., with reciprocal love as expressed on the face of Michelangelo's Adam. When we are dealing with a benevolent despot—let us call him the duke of Omnium—we can raise questions like: 'Is he really as powerful as we think?', 'Or as good?'. Connectedly we can raise the further question: 'Do we really owe him such absolute obedience?'; perhaps he is not as

good as we thought and is demanding actions of us which we
have no right to commit; or perhaps, though very powerful,
there is the chance that he will sometimes be unable to detect
or punish acts of disobedience. Such doubts will be relevant to
our decision whether or not to obey him. In this case too, the
doubts about the duke's power or about his goodness may well
be quite independent of each other.

On the other hand, because God *is* Love and because here
Love cannot be distinguished from Power, the situation is quite
different. We cannot ask whether his love may not sometimes
fail. (How can Love's power of love fail?) Or, if we *do* find ourselves forced to a question expressible in some such terms, it
will not be the same kind of question as we ask of the duke of
Omnium; we shall be wondering rather whether we can continue to think in such terms at all; and I should think it could
be only a rather shallow believer, or one whose life had been *extremely* sheltered, who never had to face such a doubt. Equally,
because of the way power and love are conceptually linked in
the case of God, we cannot ask whether our lapses of obedience
might sometimes escape his notice or whether it is always true
that vengeance is his and he will repay. This is because, if we
are thinking in these terms at all, we are judging ourselves and
our lives against a certain conception of the power of love.
(Here I am touching on issues aspects of which receive fuller
treatment in my essay 'Ethical Reward and Punishment'.) [18]
Once again, if we find ourselves led, forced, to frame questions
in these words, they will not be the questions we wanted to ask
about the duke of Omnium, but questions about whether we
can find it in us to continue to think in such terms.

How are these ways of thinking to be applied to earthly situations? If we think that absolute obedience is due only to absolute love, we shall have a standard against which we can judge
the extent of the obedience due to earthly authorities. (I am
not suggesting that this is the *only* source of such a standard,
but it will be connected in different ways with our thinking and
acting in other aspects of our lives from standards which do not
involve the idea of such a God.) We may say, for instance, 'I

18. Peter Winch, *Ethics and Action* (London, 1972), pp. 210ff.

owe obedience to the duke of Omnium's will only insofar as it is God's will that I obey him'; and this is a way, one way, of measuring the duke of Omnium's will against some higher standard.

But the notion of obedience to God's will goes far beyond questions about the attitude to be taken toward the will of earthly authorities. (It also *connects* such questions with these further issues in characteristic ways.) Religious people will talk of 'obedience to God's will' when the question of obeying or not obeying temporal authorities is not an issue at all. To think in such a way is to approach moral questions from an entirely different point of view from that expressed, for example, in a utilitarian outlook, where actions are judged against the standard of what the agent achieves, or at least intends to achieve. Where an act has the character of 'obedience' on the other hand, care for the good rests with the will of the one who commands, not with the will of the one who obeys. And while this would sound like an abdication of moral responsibility of an objectionable sort where the will of a temporal authority is in question, the case is not so obvious where obedience is to love itself. The sense of such an attitude toward moral questions lies in its connections with very many different aspects of human existence. For instance, a man often will not be in a position to know whether he will have the strength or the favorable circumstances to carry his action through to the achievement of the good he aims at; and he will, arguably, *never* be in a position to know with certainty that what his action results in will be good in the way he had hoped, or to know that, even if it is, this good will not be outweighed by other future circumstances which he will be in no position to foresee or evaluate. Such considerations are familiar enough in criticisms of utilitarian morality. The point about action which has the character of 'obedience' is that it may be thought of as retaining its sense and value nevertheless.

Consider a stock case from the literature on utilitarianism. A man is threatened by a horrible death which I have the power to prevent. I know him perhaps to be an evil man whose continued existence is far more likely to result in more evil in the world than would his death, however horrible. (Though: how far can a man judge such things?) I may feel, however, that I cannot, that it is impossible for me, simply to leave him to his fate; and, if I am a religious man, this impossibility may present itself in the form that it is God's will that I should save him. Against this, I may feel that balancing the probabilities of good and evil involved in the alternatives open to me count for nothing. 'These are in the hands of God.'

I am not, of course, claiming that no objections can be mounted against such a way of thinking, that the arguments are all in favor of the believer and against, in this case, the utilitarian. I am not advocating the attitude of the believer, but trying to understand what it is. And my purpose in doing this is to suggest that it is in the discussion of questions like this, about the *application* of notions like the infinite power and goodness of God, that the character of 'necessity' with which such notions are predicated of God is to be sought. We have to see the *point* of such predications as necessary and that can only be done by seeing what their application looks like, not by trying to press them into prefabricated logician's pigeonholes.

Finally I return, as I promised earlier, to the notion of 'different realms of reality'. My line of argument throughout has been that, if we want to understand the way in which a system of ideas is related to reality, we had best proceed by examining the actual application in life of those ideas, rather than, as it were, fastening our attention on the peculiar nature of the 'entities referred to' by them. Philosophers who speak (either for or against) the notion of 'different realities' often give the impression that they conceive the matter as if they were discussing the differences between various planets.[19] But when talk of 'different realities' is introduced *into philosophical discussion,* the issue is nearly always one involving the differences in grammar and the differences in application of different ways of speaking. And we only land ourselves in confusion if we treat it as one about the differences in the natures or properties of things referred to.

19. Cf. D. Z. Phillips's remarks on this subject in his contribution to this volume.

I italicized the phrase 'into philosophical discussion' just now. My reason for doing this was that it seems to me that expressions like 'a different reality', 'a higher order', may perfectly well be used by a religious believer, as part of the expression of his belief, without confusion. Similarly, I do not think any confusion is involved when someone, say, who cannot understand what is the attitude toward him of a woman he loves, says: 'I wonder what is going on in her head'; whereas someone who, in the course of philosophizing about the nature of thought, speaks about it as 'something which goes on in the head' (or anywhere else for that matter), *is* confused. The problem for the philosopher in all such cases is to understand the grammar, the proper application, of such expressions within the sort of discourse to which they belong.

There are features of religious belief and practice which seem to me to make it very natural, and not at all objectionable, for believers—and I do not mean only Christian believers—to find a use for expressions like 'not of this world'. This is connected with what I said in Section I about the importance of ritualistic practices for our understanding of what religious belief is. A feature of such practices is that they characteristically involve a demeanor which *sets them apart* from everyday, practical ways of behaving. I hope that my discussion has made it clear that I do not at all mean by this that such ritualistic practices (and the 'beliefs' which may be associated with them) *have no connection* with what the practitioners do, say, and think at other times in the course of their lives. On the contrary, were this the case, I should be inclined to think the rituals could only with very great difficulty be interpreted as having religious significance. Nevertheless, I think that such rituals do have the sense of expressing a contrast with the order (or, as Phillips says in his paper in this volume, 'the lack of such an order') in the lives of human beings. And I think too that this is connected with the ways in which expressions used in religious contexts differ importantly in their grammar and application from the same or similar expressions used in contexts where religious belief is not being explicitly emphasized. It is connected with the ways in which expressions used with a religious emphasis may serve to articulate a standard from the point of view of which the disorder and wretchedness which so largely characterize human life in its fundamental aspects may be assessed and come to terms with. Though what sort of 'coming to terms with' this is, I have neither the space nor the comprehension to say more about.*

* This essay is a considerably enlarged, and completely recast, version of the paper originally circulated among the participants at the Lancaster Conference. The modifications owe much to comments made by my fellow symposiast, Stuart Brown, and I should like to express my thanks to him for helping me to say better what I wanted to say.

11

Some Comments on "Meaning and Religious Language"

MICHAEL DURRANT

Peter Winch accuses me of committing an error—that of treating the uses of expressions in religious contexts as if they were independent of their uses elsewhere.[1] This, he claims, leads me to overlook the possibility that when a believer speaks of God's goodness operating in the world a contrast is indeed presupposed with cases in which goodness fails to operate in the world, cases, e.g., in which a human agent falls short of his usually high standards. *But,* he emphasizes, the contrast in this case is *itself a grammatical contrast.* Thus the contrast required for sense is indeed present but not 'internal' to religious language but as between it and our talk of human agents as good. In the human case we may sensibly speak of the agent's goodness failing; in the case of God we may not so sensibly speak: but the believer who says that God's goodness cannot fail to operate is not in the position of being unable to attach any sense to the talk of 'goodness failing to operate' precisely because the force of talking of God's infinite goodness does depend on our understanding that (in the case of man) goodness may and often does fail to operate.

As I see it the kernel of Winch's case depends upon whether it is a *sufficient* condition of sensibly speaking of God's goodness operating that we can understand what it is for human

1. I am greatly indebted to Renford Bambrough, Stuart Brown and Peter Winch for affording me the opportunity of making these comments. I should also point out that at a later stage I was invited to write a separate contribution; I regret that time did not permit me to undertake this task. I should also like to say that I have benefited from private discussion and correspondence with Winch.

goodness to fail. So I raise the question: Is it? How does or could Winch establish this? As far as I can see there is no explicit attempt to establish this and so I will consider some possibilities. *One* answer might be that Winch is implicitly introducing the idea of 'goodness as such' (per se), which is exemplified in different 'forms of life' and then inferring that one can attach sense to 'God's goodness not failing to operate' since we can attach sense to the *general* idea of goodness operating and failing to operate. But in spite of his invocation of the phrase 'goodness "failing to operate" ' and 'goodness' (p. 212), to accuse him of such a move would be unfair since (a) he nowhere explicitly invokes it, (b) to so invoke it would be inconsistent with his known philosophical position, (c) in any case there are strong arguments in favor of the thesis that to speak of goodness per se is an error.[2] So I turn to a possible alternative account—that we have a sufficient condition in that either God *is* a human being or 'sufficiently like' a human being to make any difference for these purposes irrelevant.

At this point it may be contended that far from God's being either a human being or sufficiently like a human being to make any differences for these purposes irrelevant, God could not possibly be a human being or 'sufficiently like'. That is, far from it being a sufficient condition of sensibly speaking of God's goodness operating that we should be able to speak of and understand what it is for human goodness to fail, this is not possibly a sufficient condition. The case in favor of this contention would be as follows. The predicates which specify God's essence, i.e., what it is for something *to be* God (sometimes put as God's 'inalienable properties'—cf. Stuart Brown's paper, p. 237), e.g., necessary existence, necessary eternity, necessary aspatiality, necessary incorruptibility (to consider a few), formally exclude the possibility that God is a human being and also rule out God's being 'sufficiently like' a human being to permit it to be a possible sufficient condition of understanding what it is to speak of God's goodness not failing to operate that we can understand what it is for human goodness so to do. For something to be God, that thing must be such that it necessarily

2. Cf. *The Logical Status of 'God'* (London, 1973), pp. 73–76.

makes no sense to say, e.g., (a) that it might not have existed (as opposed to merely saying that it might be false that it does exist), whereas for something to be human it necessarily does make sense to say that it might not have existed (as opposed to merely saying that it is contingently false that it does not); (b) that it might be in time, i.e., have continued existence through a period of time (as opposed to merely saying that it might be false that it has existence in time), whereas for something to be human it necessarily does make sense to say that it has continued existence through a period of time (as opposed to merely saying that it is contingently true that it does). On this contention the crunch of the issue between Winch and the contender is the very error of which I am accused. For this position is indeed denying that any contrast is *possible* between speaking of human goodness and God's goodness. Someone who advocates such a position will justify his position by saying that a contrast supposes that what is to be contrasted falls under at least some one general category. We may, for example, contrast a particular human being's love for his wife with that of his neighbor's love for his (own) wife since both fall under the category of 'being a husband'. At a more general level we may contrast paternal love with filial love since both fathers and sons fall under the category of 'human beings'. There is, however, no possibility of a category under which both God and human beings fall such that a contrast can be made since nothing can be such that, e.g., $(a)_1$ it necessarily makes no sense to speak of it as possibly not-existing, $(b)_1$ it necessarily does make sense to speak of it as possibly not-existing; $(a)_2$ it necessarily makes no sense to speak of it as having the possibility of extension in space, $(b)_2$ it necessarily does make sense to speak of it as having the possibility of extension in space. To introduce 'being' as such a category is an error, for as Aristotle saw, and as Peter Geach has developed the point, there is no such class of things as the class of things which simply *are*. Such an advocate may continue that he would agree with Winch's implied criticism that it is an error to hold that in general 'language-games', 'forms of life' [3] are independent of

3. Winch noticeably and purposively steers clear of this jargon; I introduce it simply to cut down on verbiage.

each other, but in the case of the language-games of 'human goodness' and 'divine goodness' there is no alternative to saying that they necessarily are. For that reason such an advocate will have to say that Winch's condition not only could not be sufficient, but could not even be necessary. He will press that the situation concerning God is very much akin to the situation regarding Plato's 'Forms' as admirably discussed at *Parmenides* 133 C 10—134 C 1.

To advocate such a position, however, is indeed a two-edged sword, for if valid not only does it cut Winch's throat but also the throat of anyone else who holds that in some sense it must be possible to speak of God. My position, too, as advocated in *Logical Status,* would also be hewn by this sword, for as Plato points out, if the Forms are necessarily and absolutely 'separate' then there is no *possibility* of *our* being able to say anything about them or to know them. It might be counteracted that the situation is different in the case of God since while human beings are necessarily not able to say anything about God as thus conceived (the 'transcendent') of their own nature, they are not left in the position Plato might impute to them since Christ has been present among us and he presents us with a 'faithful and true image' of God. But now the problem arises as to in what sense Christ can be said to be an image of God.[4] Such a position as that just advocated seems to me to land one in all the difficulties Plato raised concerning the Forms in that part of the *Parmenides* referred to.

One may submit, however, that in order to show that Winch has not supplied us with a sufficient condition one need not argue the case that what he supplies us with could not possibly be a sufficient condition; all we need contend is that it simply is not a sufficient condition. We may argue: 'It is not a sufficient condition since in order so to be it must be assumed that God either is a human being or in some sense a species of human being. God, however, is not a human being since some predicates which hold true of human beings, e.g., "—— is subject to whims and fancies", "—— is mortal", "—— is liable to change his mind for no good reason", "—— is governed by emotions" do not hold true of God. Further, since whatever holds true of

4. Cf. my paper "God and Analogy," *Sophia* 8 (1969), 11–24.

the genus in the genus-species relation must also hold true of the species, God is not, in some sense, a species of human being'. This argument too lands its advocate in difficulties, for if we say that God is not a human being (or a species thereof), since some predicates which hold true of human beings do not hold true of God, we are putting the matter in a misleading, even deceptive manner. Rather we should say that such predicates chosen (and note the examples) cannot hold true of God: it is of the essence of human beings that they are subject to whims and fancies, are mortal, are liable to change their minds without good reason, etc., whereas it is of the essence of God that whatever is God is necessarily not subject to whims and fancies, being mortal, etc. But if such predicates logically cannot hold true of God then one cannot speak simply in terms of God not being a human being, but one is forced to speak in terms of God not possibly being such. Granted this, then indeed Winch has not his sufficient condition, but if it is not possible to speak of God in such ways and not merely false, then the 'traditionalist' is equally in difficulties when he claims that it is possible to speak of God as infinitely good by analogy with speaking of human beings as good.

The difficulty is that Winch's thesis requires that God either be a human being or species of human being in order for it to be a sufficient condition of our understanding what it is to speak of God's goodness not failing to operate. But objections to Winch in either of the above forms bring excruciating difficulties for a 'traditionalist'. This having been admitted, however, it still remains true that Winch himself has not shown that it *is* a sufficient condition of our understanding the notion of God's goodness not failing that we should understand what it is for human goodness so to do. All he can reasonably be said to have indicated is that it is a *necessary* condition (cf. 'Indeed, the force of talking of God's infinite goodness does depend on our understanding that (in the case of man) goodness may, and frequently does fail to operate' (p. 213) and 'one would hardly be able to speak of God's love for his children if one could not also speak of the love of human fathers for their children' (p. 211)), yet he requires a sufficient condition.

It might now be commented that the above arguments and my way of expressing the difficulty I conceive Winch to be in are in any case unfair to him since they still treat of God as an entity whereas he does not wish to; indeed he regards it as a misunderstanding to so regard God. This in turn is to misunderstand Winch's position; what he denies is that God is a *separate* entity (cf. p. 210, 'To say "Earthly things are the criterion of spiritual things" is not to say they are *identical* any more than Wittgenstein was saying that "inner processes" are identical with their "outer criteria". To think otherwise is to miss the crucial importance of the grammatical differences between the way we speak of the criteria and of that of which they are the criteria'.). In my discussion above I *have,* as is traditionally the case, treated God as a separate entity. How fair (or unfair) the above discussion and charge against Winch is depends on how far it can be claimed that he has established the case that God does not stand in an 'external' relation to the believer but in an 'internal' one, as maintained in his earlier discussion of prayer and the contrast he draws between believing in God and believing in the existence of the Yugoslavian ambassador (pp. 205–208). To discuss his case would take me too far afield, but if his earlier arguments are conclusive then the above arguments and my charge are unfair.[5] Even so to advance such arguments and such a charge is of worth since (a) they represent a possible—indeed a probable—'traditionalist' response; (b) in that they bring excruciating difficulties in their train for a 'traditionalist's' case they add grist to Winch's mill; grist from considerations other than those presented by Winch. As concerns the quotation from p. 210 mentioned above, however, I hold that the previous arguments and charge are not unfair since *here* it is not clear how Winch shows, as opposed to suggests, that earthly things are the criterion of spiritual things. Indeed there is a problem concerning the phrase 'spiritual things' in the sentence, 'Earthly things are the criterion of spiritual things' and in the subsequent premise in the quote from

5. I have attempted to keep my comments roughly within the bounds of Winch's criticism of me save for my three reflections on his position introduced later.

Simone Weil, 'Only spiritual things are of value'. She may mean by the phrase, 'Things of the spirit', things of which, for example, Saint Paul speaks, or she may simply mean 'spiritual things'. God may come under the latter but not under the former yet I surmise that on Winch's reading God comes under the former. Now whereas I think it can be held with some degree of plausibility that the value of the 'things of the spirit' can be verified only as an illumination projected on physical things, i.e., that to speak of the things of the spirit (Love, Joy, Hope, Peace) is an illuminating way of speaking of, of viewing, the activities of men in this world, it is *not* clear to say if a Christian holds that God is spirit he holds that God is a 'thing of the spirit'. It is to be noted that Winch later on (p. 217) equates 'Love' and 'God', but it is not necessary so to do. 'God is Love' need not be construed as an identity proposition; indeed to do so leads to a number of difficulties; [6] 'God is Love' may be construed as 'God is the paradigm instance of love'—an interpretation Winch does not consider. (In connection with the passage from Simone Weil one might have pressed the objection: 'Why does "inability to be verified in this world" entail "inability to be verified at all"?'. To press this objection does not get us very far; the notion of 'eschatological verification' presents us with a mass of difficulties.)

Winch is quite right to castigate me by substituting geometrical expressions for the originals in the sentence from page 82 of *Logical Status,* for I am wrong to claim that for *any* context whatever, if it makes no sense to introduce not-F (where 'F' is some predicate), then it makes no sense to introduce F. I should have expressed my original thesis in terms of 'For any context in which something is said concerning how things are then if it makes no sense to introduce not-F . . .' and my original answer to Winch would be, as Brown suggested in his original paper, that 'The interior angles of a Euclidean triangle are equal to two right angles' does *not* say anything about how things are. The underlying worry that 'traditionalists' have about saying that 'God is infinitely good' is a 'grammatical remark' is that such remarks do not say anything about how

6. Cf. *Logical Status,* p. 72.

things are, yet, they hold, 'God is infinitely good' *does*. Now, however, Winch has helpfully expanded on the notion of 'grammatical remark' and tries to develop a sense in which such remarks do 'say something about the world' (cf. p. 212)—they reflect the way we speak. I think Winch's further point is that *in that* they so reflect, they reflect the way things are. This point I consider lies behind his invocation of the remark, 'red is darker than pink'. So, Winch seems to claim, just as 'red is darker than pink' reflects important things about the world—reflects how the world is for those who use the language, so 'God is infinitely good' reflects important things about the way those who use the language regard the world, how the world is for them. Thus, on the 'grammatical account', theological sentences have the role of expressing a point of view from which the world may be seen and judged and which forms a contrast with another or other points of view (cf. p. 213, 'Such talk is largely a response . . . would otherwise be possible'). This account ties in with what Winch says in the first part of his paper and with what he says at the end (p. 220, 'It is connected with the ways in which expressions used with a religious emphasis may serve to articulate a standard from the point of view of which the disorder and wretchedness which so largely characterize human life in its fundamental aspects may be assessed and come to terms with'.). 'God is infinitely good' therefore does *not* give us a description of some other 'realm of reality' distinct from the earthly life with which we are familiar, but rather *shows* something, shows something about the way Christians view this world. In the language of the *Tractatus* the 'traditionalists' have misconstrued 'God is infinitely good' as a sentence which *says* something, i.e., a proposition, when properly understood it is to be seen as a sentence which *shows* something. How then is it to be demonstrated that when properly understood it is a sentence which shows something? This is properly the purview of Brown's essay, but I shall avail myself of the opportunity of offering some three reflections on Winch's position.

Winch would reply, by considering 'its *actual* application with its surrounding context in the lives of its users' (cf. p. 200 and at various stages throughout his paper). My worry is what ex-

actly is to be covered by 'its actual application with its surrounding context in the lives of its users'? From the fact that there is
no detailed reference to specifically religious contexts, e.g., no
reference to prayers or to the actual rituals of Christianity, I
take it that these are excluded; indeed Winch seems to be con-
tending that we can only understand these uses in the light of
the uses covered by 'its actual application with its surrounding
contexts in the lives of its users'—a position which I suspect
causes him some embarrassment.[7] To understand such applications we must investigate the roots in religious practice of concepts such as reverence, religious awe, devoutness, hence the
account offered in the first part of the paper. But from the fact
that in a primitive situation (a 'conceptually primitive situation',
that is) religious language can be seen to have a certain role,
i.e., that of expressing reverence or awe toward some natural
object, why should it follow that there is some kind of a misunderstanding in thinking that religious language could do anything other than express an attitude toward the world? Winch
uses Wittgenstein's comments about how a language of sensations develops, or might be seen to develop, but Wittgenstein
does not deny that in certain contexts pain language may be
descriptive and not merely a verbal expression which replaces
the crying.[8] That is, a consideration of how certain expressions
may come to be learned and the role which they have in so
being learned does not, as far as I can see, entail that they cannot be used in any other way.

Winch stresses the point about 'factual circumstances in
which language is applied' again on page 210 with reference to
passages from both Wittgenstein and Simone Weil. I quote:
'These [factual circumstances] are of different sorts, including
both general facts of human existence . . . and also the more
'internal" facts of human nature, such as the rich and varied
responses (exemplified, for example, in Simone Weil's writing)
which may be elicited when religious language is used in, say,

7. Cf. his wishing to accent the point that he does not wish to say that
religious practices, which set the religious man apart, have no connection with
what religious people do in the ordinary course of their lives (cf. p. 209).
   8. Cf. *PI*, II, ix, p. 189.

encounter with affliction'. I may have misunderstood Winch here, but from the consideration that rich and varied responses may be elicited when religious language is used in encounter with affliction, why does it follow either (a) that it is the function of religious language to elicit such responses or (b) that it is the sole function of religious language to be a response to a situation? [9] If (a) is being held then someone with an Austinian frame of mind will accuse Winch of confusing the perlocutionary force of an expression with its illocutionary force; if (b) then we must ask for a fuller defense of the case in the light of the difficulty I raised in my first reflection above. It would have greatly helped if Winch had produced some specific examples from Simone Weil's writing at this point to enable us to see the actual cases relied on.

Finally, one brief comment on a point Winch makes on p. 216—'We are making a conceptual, or grammatical, move in speaking of the power and love of God in the way we do; just as we are making a conceptual, or grammatical, move when we treat the idea of sphericity . . . in a system such as Euclidean geometry'. Winch *seems* to be arguing here that since we could have no clear idea of what it would mean to say that God were like a human person who possessed the qualities of love and power to infinity, we must be making a grammatical remark in speaking of the power and love of God in the way we do. This is, as it were, 'the only way out'. A nasty critic might object that (a) from the fact that the notion of an infinitely good F is not clearly intelligible, it does not follow that the notion is distinctly unintelligible, whereas the alleged parallel notion in geometry is; (b) Winch's case (if correctly understood) relies on the assumption that in that a sentence has a use in a system of discourse it must have meaning, but why assume this? Why not accept the possibility that religious sentences might be meaningless after all? To pursue criticisms would clearly take me beyond the scope of my brief and in any case I am not now happy about such forms of criticism. At least one nasty taste in the mind remains in spite of Winch's illuminating case that we

9. I find Winch's point unclear here and therefore consider both possibilities.

cannot think of God as we think of the duke of Omnium, namely, he holds that we *cannot* ask whether God's love might fail (or if we *do* it will not be the same kind of question we ask of the duke of Omnium)—how then does he cope with the truth that there is no forgiveness for those who sin against the Holy Spirit, either in this life or in the world to come?

It should be obvious from the above comments that while I am not yet persuaded of Winch's account of religious language I have found his paper extremely illuminating and persuasive and am grateful for his critical comments and indeed for those of Stuart Brown.

12

Religion and the Limits of Language

STUART C. BROWN

My discussion is divided into three parts. First, I address myself to the criticisms made by Michael Durrant of Peter Winch's paper. I do not think these criticisms altogether hit their target, although there is, I suggest, some substance in the difficulties Durrant raises. In Section II, I attempt to articulate these difficulties in terms which are close to those in which Winch conducts his own discussion. I suggest that Winch's view involves an antimetaphysical and, more tentatively, what might be called an 'anthropological' conception of religion. Someone who, like Durrant, wants to uphold a 'traditional' conception of religion will want to allow sense to such utterances as 'God *really* is merciful'. I suggest that, for Winch, the tendency of religious persons to express themselves in this way should be seen as a tendency, in Wittgenstein's phrase, to run their heads against 'the limits of language'.[1] To acknowledge this is not, however, to deny that 'God is merciful' has, for reasons Winch gives, a 'relation to reality'. But it is to deny that such expressions have any sense except in relation to human life.

To refer to Winch's account as 'anthropological' is not to suggest that it is yet another of those facile accounts which reduce religion to ethics or, like Ludwig Feuerbach's, take

1. The phrase occurs in *Philosophical Investigations*. I, § 119. Wittgenstein is not, in that context, writing about religious language. There is, if what I say in section II is right, less reason than is generally supposed for thinking that Wittgenstein abandoned the view expressed in his "Lecture on Ethics" that the attempt to make claims in religion leads to utterances that are, strictly, nonsensical. He never thought, of course, that such utterances were 'plain nonsense'.

statements about God to be oblique ways of talking about man.
A merit of Winch's account is that it can do justice to the depth
of religious experience. Here I consider Winch's emphasis on
the primacy of religious practice over the articulation of religious beliefs to be a most fruitful one. In Section III, I discuss
his suggestion that there might be 'primitive' religious practices
which do not find linguistic expression but in relation to which
subsequent developments in religious language are an elaboration.

I

The disagreement between Winch and Durrant is a pro-
found one, and indeed I find it difficult to identify enough
common ground between them to see what would be acceptable as a resolution of it. Symptomatic of the depth of philosophical disparity between them is Durrant's belief (pp. 222f.)
that Winch ought to have argued for, rather than assumed,
that 'it is a *sufficient* condition of sensibly speaking of God's goodness operating that we can understand what it is for human
goodness to fail'. Winch does not, in fact, claim this. Nor, as far
as I can see, is he committed to this view. Why then should
Durrant have supposed that he was? Perhaps it is because
Winch denies that it is necessary to sensible talk about divine
goodness that something should count as God's failing to be
good. That might have led to the view Durrant regards him as
committed to defending if his problem had been to show that it
is possible to talk sensibly of divine goodness. But that is not
something which, from Winch's point of view, needs to be
shown. What Winch says is that 'the force of talking of God's
infinite goodness does depend on our understanding that (in
the case of man) goodness may and often does fail to operate'
(p. 213). That might commit him to the view that it is a *necessary*
condition of understanding what it means to say 'God is infinitely good' that one should understand what it is for human
goodness to fail. But I cannot see any basis in this remark, or in
other remarks Winch makes, for Durrant's suggestion that 'the
kernel of Winch's case' depends upon this being a *sufficient* condition.

The roots of this misunderstanding lie, I suggest, in the way in which Winch replies to the difficulties raised by Durrant for 'grammatical' constructions of 'God is F', in his book, *The Logical Status of 'God'*. As Durrant's reply in this volume makes clear, he had wanted to say that, for any context in which something is said concerning how things are, if it makes no sense to introduce not-F (where "F" is some predicate) then it makes no sense to introduce F (p. 228). Durrant wishes to construe statements like 'God is infinitely good' as 'concerning how things are' and therefore objects to such statements being construed as 'grammatical' on the ground that, so construed, they fail to meet this requirement. Winch took the requirement to state a necessary condition of *any* utterance's having meaning. So understood, as Durrant now agrees, those who impose the requirement are indeed faced with 'the formidable task of showing that sense *can* be attached to the idea that the Euclidean triangle might fail to have interior angles equal to two right angles' (p. 214). Durrant has now clarified the requirement so that he is no longer faced with this embarrassment. Geometrical propositions do *not*, he may now say, tell us about how things are. Durrant can now restate his difficulty: 'The underlying worry that "traditionalists" have about saying that "God is infinitely good" is a "grammatical remark" is that such remarks do not say anything about how things are, yet, they hold, "God is infinitely good" *does*' (pp. 228–229).

This clarification may make it look as if the issue is not, after all, about meaningfulness but about the conditions under which a remark can be 'about how things are'. But this is not so. For Durrant, if I understand him right, is also concerned with what it is to sensibly speak-about-how-things-are. I think he wants to insist that we can only make sense of 'As are F' as a remark-about-how-things-are if we know what it would be for As not to be F. That, I think, is why he considers the question as to what genus God and man might equally fall under. For our knowing what it is for Bs to be not-F might seem to help our understanding of the claim 'As are F' if As are Bs or, at least, As and Bs are all Cs. Durrant holds, however, that there is 'no possibility of a category under which both God and human beings fall' and that therefore it is not enough to know what it is for human goodness to fail to operate to understand what it is for God to be infinitely good. I think it is because this is the kernel of his objection to Winch that he takes the denial of this conclusion to be 'the kernel of Winch's case'. But this would be right only if Winch were trying to *meet* Durrant's requirement. It may well be that Winch would agree that we should not have such concepts as 'love' and so on unless we knew when to apply and when to refrain from applying them. But it does not follow from this that we cannot understand 'God's love is infinite' unless we knew what it would be like for God's love not to 'operate'.

Durrant's remarks in the first half of his reply are, I think, addressed to the case he thinks Winch *ought* to be arguing rather than to his actual case. But even if Winch ought to be arguing that 'it is a *sufficient* condition of sensibly speaking of God's goodness operating that we can understand what it is for human goodness to fail', Durrant's objection does not seem to me altogether convincing. I shall attempt to rebut it by means of an analogy. It is sometimes said that computers are 'infallible' and in that spirit the 'cannot' in 'Computers cannot make mistakes' is a grammatical and not a causal 'cannot'. That it is not a causal 'cannot' is evident from that fact that, if it were, it would make sense to say of a computer that it had made a 'mistake'. But this is precisely what is being denied by those who say that computers are 'infallible'. It is not that errors do not emerge from computers. It is, rather, that such errors are due to faults in programming, maintenance, or whatever, and not due to a 'mistake' on the part of the computers. We understand quite well what it is for a human being to make a mistake or not to make a mistake. Do computers have to be a species of human being, or computers and humans species of a common genus, for us to understand what is meant by 'Computers are infallible' or 'Computers cannot make mistakes'? I do not think so.

II

Nonetheless, there seems to me to be some substance in Durrant's criticisms of Winch. On what Durrant refers to as the 'traditional' view, there are what are claimed to be factual propositions in which the word 'God' appears as the subject-term. According to the 'traditional' view, some such propositions as 'God is merciful' must be put forward as substantive truths. Like Durrant I think Winch is committed to rejecting this view entirely. I do not find this consequence quite as intolerable as Durrant does. But it does seem to me to be a consequence, as I shall now try to bring out.

According to the traditional view, what is said about God concerns, in Anthony Kenny's inviting phrase, 'real existence'.[2] There is, or there is supposed to be, a fact, or set of facts, corresponding to 'God is just' and another fact, or set of facts, corresponding to 'God is merciful'. In Durrant's terms, if someone says that God is just and God is merciful, he might be taken as holding that there is some eternal, aspatiotemporal individual who is God and, further, that this individual is both just and merciful. If what he holds is true then it is true at all times. But he could conceivably be wrong in a number of ways. He could be wrong about there being a God at all, or right about that and wrong about there being a just God, or right about there being a just God but wrong in thinking him merciful. And so on. Of course, some properties may be taken as properties an individual must have to be God. Such properties are, one might say, 'inalienable' in the sense that God cannot be thought not to have them. While Durrant wishes to say that all God's properties are necessary, i.e., they are such that, if he has them he has them eternally, he does not think that all such properties are in this sense 'inalienable'. On the contrary he evidently thinks that God would still be God even if he were not good, that we can or should be able to specify what would count as God's goodness failing, even if it is not possible for that state of affairs to come about. Such 'alienable' properties are, it might be thought, ones which must be ascribed to God if anything is to be *said* about God. The apparent ascription of 'inalienable'

2. Kenny attempts to defend, within a traditional view, an interpretation of 'necessary' in which it can be said that all propositions about God are necessary propositions. See "God and Necessity" in Bernard Williams and Alan Montefiore, eds., *British Analytical Philosophy* (London, 1966), p. 147. Durrant follows Kenny at this point in his *The Logical Status of 'God'*, referred to by Winch in his paper.

properties, which appear to say something about the essence of God, shows something about the use of the word 'God'.

Now, if it is once conceded that God does have alienable properties, there seems no way to avoid embracing the standard conception. For example, if it is said that God is merciful though he would still be God if he were not, then the relation between the belief that God is merciful and a range of religious practices would be that supposed in the standard conception. It would be appropriate to ask what reason there is to believe that God is merciful and, in the absence of a satisfactory answer, to call in question the point of praying for forgiveness. Moreover, it would be difficult, once one alienable property is admitted, to hold the line at that. The way would then be open to reflections on the existence and nature of God which are designed to provide some independent justification for the practice of religion. This is just what Winch does not wish to concede any validity to. And I think that, to avoid that concession, he has to deny that God has *any* alienable properties.[3]

It seems, for these reasons, that Winch cannot depart from the 'traditional' view without departing radically, without holding that all statements about God are 'grammatical'. What does such a thesis involve? I think that, in the first place, Winch is taking over the term 'grammatical' from its use in Wittgenstein's later writings. Moreover, Winch evidently wishes to say, in the sense in which Wittgenstein said it, that the rules of grammar are 'arbitrary'. He wishes, accordingly, to reject the

---

3. Perhaps such a denial is indeed hinted at by Wittgenstein's remark 'Theology as grammar' in *Philosophical Investigations*, I, §373. The context gives some substance to such a suggestion:

> *Essence* is expressed by grammar.

> Consider: "The only correlate in language to an intrinsic necessity is an arbitrary rule. It is the only thing which one can milk out of this intrinsic necessity into a proposition."

> Grammar tells what kind of object anything is. (Theology as grammar.)

> The great difficulty here is not to represent the matter as if there were something one *couldn't* do. As if there really were an object, from which I derive its description, but I were unable to shew it to anyone.

idea that such a conviction as that God is merciful is to be measured against evidence. On pages 209–210 he suggests that the kind of confrontation between religious convictions and reality is 'quite analogous' to that of our color system, as discussed by Wittgenstein. He is concerned with the positive aspect of this analogy as well as its negative aspect. And so, indeed, was Wittgenstein. Having asked whether our color system and our number system 'reside in *our* nature or in the nature of things', Wittgenstein goes on: 'How are we to put it?—*Not* in the nature of numbers or colours' (*Zettel*, § 357). Having emphasized this negative aspect of the view he wished to accept, Wittgenstein poses and responds to a question it immediately raises: 'Then is there something arbitrary about this system? Yes and no. It is akin both to what is arbitrary and to what is non-arbitrary' (*Zettel*, § 358). A sentence such as 'There is no such thing as reddish green' neither states an intrinsic necessity nor does it state a fact about the nature of colors. The same can be said, on Wittgenstein's view, of the sentence, 'You can't hear God speak to someone else, you can hear him only if you are being addressed'. Both of these are, for Wittgenstein, 'grammatical remarks' (see *Zettel*, §§ 346 and 717). And I see no reason why, on his view, a system of implicit theology—the 'grammar' of a particular religion—should not equally be said to be 'akin both to what is arbitrary and to what is non-arbitrary'. I think this may be seen as part of the analogy Winch makes use of, provided we acknowledge that there is no more necessity for an explicit theology attached to a religion than there is for making such remarks as, 'There is no such thing as reddish green', apropos of our color system.

I shall consider first the negative implications of this analogy. If we accept sentences such as 'God is merciful' as rules of grammar, parity of reasoning seems to require our being prepared to substitute 'But God really is merciful' (and so on) for 'But there really are four primary colours' in the following statements: 'One is tempted to justify rules of grammar by sentences like "But there really are four primary colours". And the saying that rules of grammar are arbitrary is directed against the possibility of this justification, which is constructed on the

model of justifying a sentence by pointing to what verifies it'
(*Zettel* §331).

There is, Wittgenstein thought, a particular kind of nonsense
which is produced 'by trying to express by the use of language
what ought to be embodied in the grammar'.[4] What 'I can't feel
his toothache' means, to give his example, is ' "I feel his toothache" makes no sense.' If someone tried to insist, however, that
he *really* could not feel the toothache of another, his saying 'I
can't feel his toothache' would acquire a metaphysical inflection. It would be nonsense to treat this 'can't' as though it were
like that in 'I can't play chess'. The same, on a grammatical construction of 'God is good', would be true of 'God cannot do
evil', which philosophers have also been tempted to construe in
a metaphysical way. In holding that the rules of grammar are
'arbitrary' Wittgenstein was, as I understand him, ruling out as
nonsensical any construction of them which represented such
rules as substantive truths.

If this view about the arbitrariness of grammar is coupled
with the view that *all* remarks about God are 'grammatical' it
seems to yield a radically antimetaphysical conception of religion, at least as far as concerns God-centered religions. In a
curious way, then, I think that Winch is committed on his own
terms to accepting Durrant's diagnosis, namely, that on a grammatical construction of them, no affirmations about God make
substantive claims about how things are. What is 'curious' about
this is that, if I am right, Winch is committed to making a virtue out of what Durrant regards as a defect. Contrariwise, Durrant's criticism will appear itself to be founded on just that urge
to transgress the limits of language that, on Wittgenstein's view,
will lead to nonsense. In other words, Durrant sees the loss of a
metaphysical element in what is said about God as the loss of
something essential to religion. That is why he emphasizes, in
the name of 'traditionalists', that 'God is infinitely good' *does* say
something about how things are.

At this point the yawning gulf between the philosophical traditions from which Winch and Durrant write will be evident

4. G. E. Moore reports Wittgenstein as having said this in his lectures in
1932–1933. See *Philosophical Papers* (London, 1959), p. 311.

enough. They do, I think, have fundamentally different views about meaning. These differences imply further differences in the kind of theology they think possible. Where, on a traditionalist conception of religion, the arguments of natural theology quite properly occupy a prominent place in philosophical thinking about it, such arguments, from Winch's point of view, can be no more than a catalogue of errors. The only one of the traditional arguments which, from such a point of view, is at least tempting is the Ontological Argument. For that argument alone is consistent with regarding all God's properties as inalienable, i.e., ones which are essential to his being God. For its conclusion, 'God exists', is put forward as an intrinsically necessary proposition. Given its metaphysical inflection, 'God cannot but exist' is, from Wittgenstein's point of view, nonsensical. It is an attempt to 'milk' an intrinsic necessity out of an 'arbitrary' rule.

It is noteworthy, therefore, that such a distinguished student of Wittgenstein's as Norman Malcolm should have sought to defend a version of the Ontological Argument. Malcolm indeed expresses an inclination 'to hold the "modern" view that logically necessary truth "merely reflects our use of words".' [5] And that 'modern' view is at least consistent with what I take to be Wittgenstein's view about the 'arbitrariness' of grammar. This means he cannot consistently have put forward his conclusion as a substantive claim about how things are. It has been suggested [6] that Malcolm was not attempting to prove a metaphysical conclusion. On my reading, however, he was. In order to reach such a conclusion, it would be necessary to resist the inclination to accept the 'modern' view of logically necessary propositions at some point. Malcolm does this when he writes: 'That God is omniscient and omnipotent . . . . are requirements of our conception of Him. They are internal properties of the concept, although they are also rightly said to be properties of God'.[7] The implication of the 'although . . . also' is that it is not the same thing to say that these are 'internal properties

5. *Knowledge and Certainty* (Englewood Cliffs, N.J., 1963), p. 155.
6. By D. Z. Phillips in *The Concept of Prayer* (London, 1965), p. 18.
7. Malcolm, *Knowledge and Certainty*, p. 150.

of the concept' as it is to say they are properties of God. The problem is, how the argument can proceed if it does not assume that properties in God can be inferred from 'internal properties of the concept'. If it does assume it, then it constitutes just that kind of attempt to milk intrinsic necessities out of 'arbitrary' grammatical rules, which leads to metaphysical nonsense. The grammatical modality of 'God must be omnipotent' ('God cannot be other than omnipotent') is given a metaphysical inflection by such an inference. It is, I think, an example where, as Wittgenstein put it: 'We predicate of the thing what lies in the method of representing it' (*Philosophical Investigations*, I, §104). The remark, 'What looks as if it *had* to exist, is part of the language' (I, 50) seems as apposite to talk to God as it is to talk about universals, numbers, and so on.

So far I have emphasized the antimetaphysical implications of Winch's remarks. I want now to turn to the positive aspect of the analogy he draws between religious convictions and those which are manifested by utterances like 'There is no such thing as reddish-green'. There is, as I noted earlier, a sense in which, according to Wittgenstein, rules of grammar are 'non-arbitrary'. There is, then, *a* relation to reality which such convictions as that 'God is merciful' have. Only it is not, according to Winch, the relation required by Durrant and others. Nature, as Wittgenstein puts it in relation to the analogous case, 'makes herself audible in another way' (*Zettel*, § 364). This, Winch claims, is also true of religious convictions.

There is, I think, a difficulty for an account such as Winch's in finding a route between the Scylla of metaphysics and the Charybdis of anthropocentrism. There is no easy route, if there is one at all, for a radical 'internalist' in religion to take, if he wishes to avoid regressing into metaphysics, on the one hand, or reducing religion to its anthropological dimension, on the other. The most severe part of the route, it seems to me, is just where the question is raised as to how religious convictions can be true or how they relate to reality. It is not uninstructive to note the mishaps which have befallen earlier attempts at pioneering such a route. Consider, for instance, the case of Paul Tillich's Neo-Kantian Existentialist theology. Tillich regarded the predicates traditionally ascribed as properties to God as symbols. The utterance 'God is merciful' is not a categorical attribution but an expression of acceptance of a 'symbol'. Tillich concedes to his inhibitions about metaphysics that 'The criterion of truth of a symbol naturally cannot be the comparison of it with the reality to which it refers, just because this reality is absolutely beyond human comprehension.' Tillich draws his inspiration for an alternative account of the 'truth' of religious symbols from existentialism. The suggestion he makes is that the truth of a symbol depends on 'its inner necessity for the symbol-creating consciousness'.[8] He is very impressed by the fact that such symbols cannot merely be invented. Their 'inner necessity' consists in their ability to keep a hold on how people look at things. Symbols may not be adequate to new situations. Those which are 'true' are those which can retain their hold whatever new situations men are confronted with.

There would undoubtedly be something far from arbitrary about symbols which can have such power. At the same time, if their being true consists in their having such power—consists in their 'inner necessity for the symbol-creating consciousness'—the account of truth does seem to have become entirely anthropocentric. Tillich did, perhaps, recognize that he had gone too far in this direction. For he later suggested that a symbol is 'true' to the extent that it 'reaches the referent of all religious symbols'.[9] With that rather violent heave on the tiller, however, Tillich seems to have overreacted to his tendency to anthropocentrism. Far from finding a route between the Scylla of metaphysics and the Charybdis of anthropocentrism, he seems to have run his craft aground on both sides. It would be rather short shrift to suggest that Tillich's theology is shipwrecked on both sides. But such are the hazards that even that is possible.

D. Z. Phillips's 'internalism', like Tillich's, is indebted to Kierkegaard. They, and Winch, are substantially in agreement in rejecting causal views about such connections as between for-

8. In Sidney Hook, ed., *Religious Experience and Truth* (New York, 1961, and Edinburgh, 1962), p. 316.
   9. Ibid., p. 10.

giving and being forgiven oneself, between sinning and being subject to divine punishment, and between praying and being given an answer to one's prayer.[10] They all depart from what Durrant refers to as the 'traditional' view, on which such connections are of independent events which, though they may be eternally and infallibly connected, may at least be *thought of* as disconnected. It is, as I suggested in Section I, the need for consistency which polarizes the dispute between these two positions. What I have called 'internalism' is thus a label for an extreme position. It is not, however, a mere caricature. For if someone were to concede, for example, that something counts as unpunished sin, but then elsewhere wanted to insist that nothing counts as unanswered prayer, it would be difficult to see this as an expression of a coherent theological position. For why should the existence or nonexistence of unpunished sins be a matter of evidence and the existence or nonexistence of unanswered prayers not also be? There would need, I think, to be some special reason which gave the nonexistence of unanswered prayers a kind of definitional status like God's being omnipotent. In the absence of such a special reason, the pressure to give a consistent account forces a choice between two radically and systematically different positions. There is no scope for an intermediate position.

Where Tillich takes belief in divine judgment as involving acceptance of a 'symbol', Phillips adopts one of Wittgenstein's uses of the word 'picture'. What he has to say about such 'pictures', however, is strikingly similar to what Tillich has to say about 'symbols'. In *Death and Immortality*, Phillips writes:

From a consideration of the kind of force which characteristic religious pictures have, we can see that to ask whether they are true as if they were would-be empirical propositions is to ask the wrong kind of question. It is of the utmost philosophical importance to recognise that for the believers these pictures constitute truths, truths which form the essence of life's meaning for them. To ask someone whether he thinks

10. See, for example, Tillich's *Systematic Theology* (Chicago and London, 1953), I, 315, and elsewhere: Kierkegaard's *Concluding Unscientific Postscript*, 1st ed., 1846 (Princeton, 1941), pp. 201ff.; Phillips, *The Concept of Prayer*. See also Winch's "Can a Good Man Be Harmed?" *Proceedings of the Aristotelian Society* 66 (1965–66), 55–70.

these beliefs are true is not to ask him to produce evidence for them, but rather to ask him whether he can live by them, whether he can digest them, whether they constitute food for him.[11]

Unlike Tillich, however, Phillips steadfastly rejects the idea of a transcendent order of facts to which religious 'pictures' may or may not correspond. He thus agrees that, in one sense, they cannot be said to be 'true'. At the same time he recognizes—a point insisted upon by Durrant—that believers regard what they believe as 'true'. He does not take this as evidence of an urge characteristic in religion to run one's head up against the limits of language. Rather, he credits the believer with a particular construction on this use of the word 'true', with using it in a different sense. His thesis is that a believer, asked whether he thinks the 'pictures' he adheres to are 'true' or not, will take the question in one way rather than another. This seems to be an empirically vulnerable claim. But supposing it to be true, the question arises as to how, on this account, such 'pictures' can be embedded in anything more than facts to do with human nature, the conditions of human life, and the diverse social relationships which people can enter into. Expressed more generally, that question is as to whether an internalist is committed to a merely 'anthropological' account of religion once he turns his back on metaphysics. It is open to an internalist to put a metaphysical construction on the statements of internal relation, as Spinoza did. But if these are taken as 'grammatical', in Wittgenstein's sense, that option is closed, as we have seen.

The difficulty I express here is related to a characteristic which David Pears identifies in Wittgenstein's later thought.[12] It is one which needs a rather sharper expression than I have given it before one would be entitled to complain that Phillips had failed to answer it. And here Section III of Winch's paper is particularly relevant. For he is aware that there is, from his standpoint, a problem about the kind of 'relation to reality' religious uses of language have. It is to be sought, he suggests, in the application such uses of language have 'in what religious people say and do in the course of their life on earth' (p. 214).

11. Phillips, *Death and Immortality* (London, 1970), p. 71.
12. In his *Ludwig Wittgenstein* (New York, 1969), chap. IX.

In his remarks about *how* 'Nature' makes herself heard, both in Wittgenstein's examples and in the case of religious language, Winch alludes to 'general facts of human existence'. He makes it clear, however, that talk of God is by no means just a roundabout way of referring to such facts (p. 210). If earthly things are, in Simone Weil's phrase, 'the criterion of spiritual things', this relation is not therefore one of identity.

If there is a sense, then, in which Winch's account is 'anthropological', the diagnosis implied by using that word must be distinguished from that implied by its use in relation to certain other writers. Ludwig Feuerbach, for example, expressly sought to *reduce* theology to anthropology, to identify the true meaning of statements about God with statements about man.[13] Neither Winch nor Phillips has the slightest inclination or commitment to such a project. Nor should they be taken as denying that religious beliefs are, properly, beliefs. This is one respect in which their accounts are to be distinguished from positivist-inspired attempts to construe affirmations of religious 'belief' as expressions of intention or feeling.[14]

I am inclined to think, nonetheless, that Winch's account is 'anthropological'. That it is so is due, I think, to his rejection of the idea that religious claims can be true or false in an impersonal way. That the earth is (roughly) round is an impersonal truth in that its being true (as opposed to its being recognized as true) is independent of there being people who are capable of believing it and to whose lives such a belief would have a relevance. The Christian religion has been presented as embodying such impersonal truth. The existentialist theologies of Kierkegaard and Tillich represent, in part, a reaction against just this traditional mode of presentation. And such a reaction has, no doubt, some point. If, however, that traditional understanding of the Christian religion is rejected outright, those who reject it seem committed to making the truth of religious beliefs dependent on there being people who are able to hold

13. In his *The Essence of Christianity,* 1st ed. 1841. Trans. George Eliot (New York, 1957).
14. Such as Richard B. Braithwaite's *An Empiricist's View of the Nature of Religious Belief* (Cambridge, 1955).

them and to whose lives such a belief would have a relevance. Phillips indeed seems to think that the truth of such beliefs consists in people being able to 'live by them'. It is, on this account, the grounding of such beliefs in human lives that constitutes their 'relation to reality'. They are not true whether or not they have such a grounding. If I understand him rightly, that is Winch's view. That is the sense in which I suggest his view is 'anthropological'.

III

One of the emphases in Winch's paper is on the primacy of religious practice over religious belief. I do not think that Winch wishes to deny that religious practices are often informed by, and in that way are therefore often secondary to, beliefs. That a Muslim, for example, prays facing in one direction rather than any other is because of a belief he holds. His practice is, to that extent, informed by his belief that Mecca lies in a particular direction. What Winch wants to oppose is the idea that *all* religious practice is like this. He wants to suggest, moreover, that, in its most basic features, religious practice is *not* like this. This leads him, in the earlier part of his paper, to consider what it would be for a religious practice to involve a 'primitive' (nonlinguistic) response of people to their environment. Such a 'primitive' response will have some points of analogy with what Wittgenstein referred to as the 'natural' expressions of being in pain. What Winch wants mainly to stress is 'an analogy between the *relation* of such cases respectively to one in which there is a developed pain language or a developed religious language' (p. 197). There are, as Winch points out, significant points of disanalogy, e.g., in that the religious response is not that of an individual but is a matter of 'an established social practice'. Hence there is not the uniformity of religious responses which there is, by and large, in human pain behavior.

There are, it seems to me, too many points of difference between the supposed primitive expressions of religious reverence which Winch discusses and the primitive expressions of pain for the analogy as it stands to be more than tenuous. I

shall proceed, in discussing this part of Winch's paper, by trying to eliminate some of the grosser points of difference between expressions of pain and expressions of religious reverence. My hope is that a closer approximation of the
nonreligious analogue will make the issues clearer. I shall consider then whether the main points of analogy on which Winch
wishes to insist are retained.

In the first place, the responses expressive of religious awe,
reverence, or wonder are expressions of emotion. As Winch
points out, it is always possible to distinguish varying degrees of
devoutness in religious practices. There are those who, on the
one hand, seem only to be going through the motions and
those who, on the other hand, are very much caught up in
what they are doing. The behavior of such devout people is
expressive of emotions—adoration, gratitude, repentance—
which are appropriate to the ritual. When they say: 'Praise be
to God!' they *mean* it. Pain, by contrast, is not an emotion. Neither the feeling of pain nor the behavior expressive of pain is
directed toward anything. It may, of course, be natural for a
being to kick or bite whatever caused it pain. But in this case
the pain is accompanied by an emotion, namely, anger.

The case for saying that there are 'primitive' (natural, nonlinguistic) expressions of emotion is, however, almost as secure
as the case for saying it of pain. Emotions, however, vary
greatly in their complexity. Some, like fear, can be attributed as
confidently to nonlanguage-using animals as can pain. There is
no threat to Winch's analogy if it is made closer by substituting
for the case of pain that of an emotion like fear. Other emotions, like resentment, indignation, gratitude, and pique, are a
good deal more complicated. It is less clear, in such cases,
whether they could be felt and expressed at all if there were no
linguistic expression of them. It is not clear that, if I do not
have the language in which to say 'You ought not to have done
that!' I could be credited with being indignant about something. Of course, there are always other ways of expressing
emotions than by using language. But Winch's claim is that
there can be religious emotions which are *never* given verbal

expression. Not all emotions are like that. Nor is Winch claiming even that all *religious* emotions are like that.

There is a second way in which we can make the analogy closer. That is by recognizing that, unlike fear, many human emotions have symbolic as well as natural expressions. Grief, for instance, can be expressed by weeping but also by symbolic acts such as wearing black clothes. Symbolic acts also affirm or confirm social relationships. There are various natural expressions of hostility, all of which involve physical postures such as keeping one's eyes on the foe and the arms positioned for attack or defense. A symbolic act of hostility, such as shaking one's fist and glaring at someone, affirms an enmity. There are also natural expressions of submission, involving the adoption of vulnerable postures such as, in the case of dogs, exposing the underside of the throat. *Symbolic* acts of submission—such as bowing, handing over one's sword, or, in extreme cases, prostrating oneself before someone with arms outstretched and face down—are not unconnected with such *natural* expressions of submission. What makes them 'symbolic' is not that they are merely artificial or conventional. It is, rather, that they are a way of acknowledging and thus confirming a situation which already exists. The general who ceremonially hands over his sword is acknowledging defeat but is already beaten. The subject who bows and kneels before his king thereby acknowledges and confirms the relationship between them. There need have been no hostility expressed by the king. Other familiar symbolic or ritual acts, shaking hands, exchanging rings, taking off hats, and touching the forelock, seem equally to be in token of established human relationships. They are ritualized expressions of friendship, or various kinds of respect owing by gentlemen to ladies or serfs to landowners. Many ritual acts express respect. They can be done in a respectful manner, as a mere token or even, in a mocking manner, to show disrespect.

I mention these ordinary cases of ritualistic behavior because Winch mars his account by taking features of religious ritual as features of ritual in general and by overstressing the conventional aspects of ritual. He writes: 'What I think *is* necessary for us to be able to characterize behavior as ritualistic is that it is in some way set apart from behavior associated with everyday practical concerns: not in the sense that it has no connection at all with such concerns (on the contrary), but in the sense that it is stylized, ruled by conventional forms and perhaps thought of as stemming from long-standing traditions (p. 198). It is clear that Winch is only concerned with religious rituals which, I agree, are set apart in some way from ordinary behavior. But this 'setting apart' is not a feature of the ritual, as such. It derives from how the object of the ritual is regarded, namely, as what we would call 'sacred'. It is because the mountains, ancestors, or whatever are set apart in this way that the ritual becomes 'religious'. The burial of the dead, for instance, is a ritual which, among other things, marks a respect which is commonly regarded as due in such circumstances. A nonreligious man may bury a complete stranger rather than leave his body to the vultures. Burial of the dead begins to acquire something of a religious character when it is expressive of a continuing relationship to the dead person (e.g., putting flowers on the grave) or has to do with the relation of that person to other 'spirits', such as the ancestors. It may be assumed without question that death only transforms the relations between people. There is no reason why such a belief should find a verbal expression among a people to whom it had never occurred that death might simply bring relations to an end. The existence, then, of religious rituals directed toward the dead could be a kind of extension of rituals which have to do with preserving ordinary social relationships.

It is not in dispute that such rituals do characteristically involve the use of words. Phillips, just before a passage I referred to earlier,[15] quotes a song from a Ho dirge whose singing constitutes part of such a ritual: 'We ever loved and cherished you; and have lived long together under the same roof; Desert it not now! . . . Come to your home! It is swept for you and clean; and we are there who loved you ever; and there is rice put for you; and water; Come home, come home, come to us

15. *Death and Immortality*, pp. 70f. Phillips's source is E. B. Tylor's *Primitive Culture* (London, 1920), p. 33.

again'. Phillips suggests that as long as people can sing such a
song the dead have not deserted them. 'The song is an expression of that truth'. Some light may be thrown on the character
of such a ritual, and on the way in which the dead are 'set
apart', by imagining this song addressed to a living warrior
whose return is long overdue. The meaning of the song is altogether changed if it is read in this way. The words 'Desert it
not now! Come to your home!' acquire the character of a peti-
tion whose outcome is uncertain. It expresses a wish that a sep-
aration should be brought to an end. The way in which the absent warrior is 'set apart' from his family is, quite simply,
through his being absent. That is not the way in which the dead
are 'set apart'. They are set apart by the way in which they are
continually present to those from whom death has separated
them. The sense of that continual presence is expressed in the
ritual. It does not require a doctrinal expression and indeed I
make no apology for the fact that my 'statement' of the way the
dead are set apart is paradoxical and, in a way, nonsense. For
the ritual is not rendered pointless by the problems of articulat-
ing what someone who engages in it might offer as his belief.
On the contrary, the practice provides a measure of the adequacy of such articulations.

  I agree with Winch that the practice of religion is, in this
sense, prior—at least in its elemental forms—to the verbal expression of religious beliefs. This is indeed a matter of considerable importance for the study of religion. I think, however,
that Winch overreacts to the widespread tendency to look first
at articulations of belief and to see the practice of religion as informed by beliefs. For he sets himself two objectives, neither of
which needs to be secured in order to defend his main point.
(1) He attempts to show that it is possible to 'identify a set of
practices as "religious" independently of any beliefs associated
with them' (p. 196). (2) He attempts to describe a social group
'whose speech includes nothing that we want to identify as the
expression of "religious beliefs" ' (p. 197).

  I think it is possible that Winch confuses these two objectives,
i.e., takes the absence of any *expression* of 'religious beliefs' as
showing, without more ado, that no such beliefs are associated

with a practice. But it does not follow from the fact that a tribe has no occasion to *express* belief in their ancestors that they do not believe in them. They would have no occasion if, as I suggested, it has not occurred to them that death might simply bring personal relations to an end. If some European came along and poured scorn on their practices, the tribe might then find some point in affirming such beliefs. They need not doubt them, since they may think only a fool would say in his heart that the ancestors did not exist.

I am inclined to think that it may be necessary, in identifying a practice as a 'religious' one, to mention beliefs. This does seem to be necessary in the case I have mentioned of practices showing reverence for ancestors. Winch's own case makes much of other religious emotions, such as awe and wonder. While I do not doubt the prevalence of awe and wonder, they seem to me too general for there to be particual rituals expressive of them. What is sacred may indeed be awe-inspiring and wondersome. But so indeed is the Niagara Falls. To be awestruck by or to marvel at the grandeur of such a place is not eo ipso to regard it with a religious attention. The tribe whose ceremonies Winch describes as including 'perhaps moments of silent contemplation of the mountains', whose rituals are associated with 'a sense of wonder and awe at the grandeur and beauty of aspects of the tribe's environment' presumably do give religious attention to such places. This part of Winch's example seems to me insufficiently described. Any such tribe I have tried to imagine has turned out to be a group of nineteenth-century Englishmen in disguise. What is needed is a clue as to what the mountains mean to these people. The difficulty is to do this without mentioning beliefs.

I have confined myself to rituals expressive of reverence as involving something like submissive respect. Many religious rituals relate to objects or actions which are set apart as 'unclean'. It would be implausible to suggest, therefore, that all religious rituals affirm or confirm quasi-social relationships. My reasons for emphasizing the connection of *some* religious rituals with rituals which confirm ordinary social relationships have partly to do with the way in which reverence strikes me as at once

closely related to respect and at the same time a development
from it. The nature of that development is bound up with the
way in which what is regarded as sacred is 'set apart'. We can
imagine a tribe in which rituals are performed out of respect
for the elders. Being the object of such tokens of respect is part
of what it is to be an elder. But there is an asymmetry about the
way in which the ancestors are regarded which there is not
about the way in which the elders are regarded if the ancestors
become the object of tokens of reverence. For, without the
tribe, the elders are as nothing. The elders may then be said to
need the tribe, at least qua elders. The ancestors, by contrast,
are characteristically not regarded as needing the tribe. The
need is wholly one way. If the ancestors were not paid the tribute due to them, a harm is indeed done, but not to the ancestors. The harm of a sacrilegious act can be turned back only on
he who commits it. If their rituals are to be 'religious', those
who perform the acts have to have *some* sense of this. Moreover, if, to be religious, that 'can' has to be a grammatical 'can',
that sense of how the ancestors are set part would have to have
a verbal expression. There would need, that is to say, to be a
grammar of religious talk.

At this point I think that Winch's position is not obviously
consistent. For he seems to want to say that a religious use of
language ('God is merciful', 'The ancestors have not forgotten
us', and so on) involves a change of grammar (pp. 210ff.). Yet
he wants to deny that anything analogous is needed to identify
a ritual as 'religious'. But if the sense of how the dead are set
apart which is embodied in the practice of certain rites needs
no language at all, it seems to follow that the 'cannot' in 'The
ancestors cannot be harmed' does not need to be a grammatical
one. Winch's concern with finding a case where there are no
linguistic expressions of beliefs which are associated with a religious ritual seems to commit him to denying that there is the
clear-cut distinction between the religious and the nonreligious
he elsewhere argues for. If, in other words, the contrast between respect and reverence is a grammatical one—you can insult the elders but God is not mocked—then a sense of that distinction requires a mastery of a religious use of language.

Conversely, if no such mastery is required, the contrast between respect and reverence cannot be a grammatical one.

One obvious kind of case where the borderline between respect and reverence is in doubt is in the rituals performed by a people in relation to their king. Writers on religion commonly distinguish cases where kings are regarded as divine and where they are regarded as less than divine. It may be that these form a spectrum of cases with a borderline which is not determined by any sharp criterion. If that were so, it would, I believe, be subversive of any program to construe theology as having entirely to do with 'grammar'. It would follow that the characterization of theology as grammar is not correct as a general account of religion but at best for particular traditions. The dispute in relation to a particular tradition as between those who hold such an 'internalist' view and those who hold a 'traditional' view would then itself be a theological one.

It may be open for Winch (or others who are faced with a like problem) to say that religious practices in which there are no verbal expressions of belief are not to be sharply distinguished from other practices. Or perhaps it may be held that there is a conception of how the ancestors (or whatever) are set apart which can only be adequately expressed by grammatical remarks like 'The ancestors cannot be harmed by us'. In the first case, the addition of a grammar would have to be accepted as an improvement, as a clarification of the understanding of those who engage in the rituals. The difficulty in the second case would be in justifying the claim that there can be pre-linguistic attitudes which can be given adequate verbal expression only by grammatical remarks.

These difficulties, if they are real ones, do not detract from Winch's main point that religious practices are not, at bottom, informed by beliefs. Ancestor worship does not stand in relation to such beliefs as it may involve as my running toward the station stands to my belief that a train is due. In the religious case the beliefs in question are implicit in the practices rather than opinions or theories on which the practices are founded. So while, of course, people do give up belief in the ancestors this is not, I think, the result of coming to admit a mistake.

This raises questions which were the subject of the preceding symposium on the rationality of religious belief. My arrival at the boundary with this related topic I take as my cue to bring my incomplete discussion to a halt.

PART FIVE
IMMORTALITY

13

Immortality and Dualism

SYDNEY SHOEMAKER

I

Someone who believes in immortality is not thereby committed, logically, to believing in dualism and in the possibility of
disembodied existence. Nevertheless, any antidualist who believes in immortality is committed to believing things which
most antidualists would find even less plausible than dualism.
Observe that if at some future time I die and then undergo
bodily resurrection, or if I arrange to have myself deep-frozen
and then thawed a few millennia later,[1] or if I have my brain
transferred to a younger and heathier body, or if I have my
brainstates transferred to a younger and healthier brain, or if I
undergo rejuvenation at the hands of the microsurgeons, then
no matter how much my bodily existence will have been extended beyond threescore years and ten, I will still have an
eternity ahead of me. None of the imagined life-prolonging (or
life-restoring) episodes would, by itself, bring one immortality,
as opposed to mere increased longevity. If someone believes
that he is (will be?) immortal, but rejects dualism and the possibility of disembodied existence, he is committed to believing either (a) that beginning now or later he will live forever embodied in a body of the sort he currently has, one subject to all of
the ills flesh is heir to, or (b) that at some future time his body
will be transformed into, or replaced by, one that is imperish-
able and indestructible (by natural means), in which he will
then be embodied forever, or (c) that he will undergo and survive an unending series of life-prolonging episodes (resurrec-

1. See Robert C. W. Ettinger, *The Prospect of Immortality* (New York, 1966).

tions, brain transplants, rejuvenations, etc.). Even if none of these beliefs can be faulted on logical or conceptual grounds, most people would agree that there are overwhelming empirical grounds for rejecting all of them.

For anyone who wants to believe in personal immortality, dualism seems to offer obvious advantages over antidualism. A dualist can believe in immortality without clashing head-on with science and with the fund of experience which has made "All men are mortal" a truism. While we have abundant empirical evidence of the perishability and impermanence of material substances, especially organic ones, we have none at all of the perishability and impermanence of immaterial substances. To be sure, we also have no empirical evidence of the *im*perishability and permanence of immaterial substances. But to many philosophers it has seemed that we are guaranteed the latter on a priori grounds. An undoubted attraction of the idea that persons are immaterial substances is the idea that such substances, being simple and without parts (a supposed consequence of their lacking spatial extension), will be incapable of going out of existence through dissolution of parts, and so will be "incorruptible" by natural means. Nowadays, of course, such ideas do not have the following they once had. There are few who subscribe to the sort of "rational psychology" attacked by Kant in the Paralogisms. But the effects of such ideas linger on, and the view persists that belief in dualism is appreciably more compatible with belief in immortality than is belief in materialism. One of my objects in this paper is to undermine this view.

II

Recent philosophers who reject dualism and deny the possibility of disembodied existence of persons tend to fall into one of two groups. Those in one group seek to show that the falsity of dualism can be demonstrated on conceptual grounds.[2] Those in the other group maintain that dualism is an intelligi-

2. I have not been able to find a unequivocal and unqualified statement of this view in the literature; but it is implicit in my own book *Self-Knowledge and Self-Identity* (Ithaca, N.Y., 1963), and in the writings of other philosophers who have attacked dualism on conceptual (or logical) rather than empirical grounds.

ble and logically coherent doctrine, but that we have overwhelming empirical grounds for rejecting it as false.[3] On the
first view there is no possible world in which dualism is true.
On the second view dualism is true in some possible worlds, but
not in the actual world.

I think that there is an element of truth in each of these
views; roughly, they are true of different versions of dualism.
There is a version of dualism, and one that implies that disembodied existence of persons is possible, to which there is, as far
as I can see, no decisive logical or conceptual objection. This it
seems reasonable to regard as a doctrine to be accepted or
rejected (I opt for the latter) on empirical grounds. Once it is
clearly distinguished from other versions, this version turns out
not to be of much help to believers in immortality, and it is not,
I think, the doctrine that such believers have ordinarily held.
There is another version of dualism which at least some believers in immortality have held, and which seems in harmony
with the doctrine of immortality. I believe that this second version is conceptually incoherent, but I shall content myself here
with arguing that there is, and could be, no reason to believe it
true.

Presumably any dualist who believes that it is possible for
him to exist in disembodied form believes that there is an immaterial substance such that (a) what mental states he has depends on what states the immaterial substance has, (b) all causal
connections involving mental states between his sensory "input"
and his behavioral "output" are mediated by states of this immaterial substance, and (c) it is possible for him to exist, as a
subject of mental states, without having a body, as long as the
immaterial substance exists and has the appropriate states. Let
us say that anyone of whom all of this is true has a minimally
dualistic nature. I shall use the term "Minimal Dualism" for the
doctrine that all persons have minimally dualistic natures—but
it is worth noting that there is no evident incoherence involved
in holding that some persons have minimally dualistic natures
while others are purely material creatures.

3. See David M. Armstrong, *A Materialist Theory of Mind* (London, 1968),
p. 19.

Notice that Minimal Dualism does not say either (a) that the immaterial substance associated with a person *is* the person, or (b) that the states of the immaterial substance *are* the mental states of the person. Neither does it deny that (a) and (b) are true. So two versions of Minimal Dualism can be distinguished. Both of these hold that the person is something distinct from (nonidentical with) his body, and that physical states (height, weight, etc.) belong to a person only derivatively—so, for example, a person has a certain weight in virtue of having (rather than being) a body having that weight. And both hold that the mental states of a person belong to him nonderivatively—that a person's being angry, for example, is not a matter of his being related in a certain way to something (nonidentical to himself) that is angry. But one version affirms what the other denies, that a person is identical with an immaterial substance, the states of which are the mental states of the person. I shall call the version that says that persons are immaterial substances Cartesian Dualism, and shall call the other Non-Cartesian Dualism. But these are only suggestive names, and I do not claim that Descartes consistently adhered to the doctrine I call Cartesian Dualism.

It is worth noting that what Minimal Dualism says about immaterial substances is the same as what many contemporary philosophers are prepared to say about *brains*. Many philosophers would hold that for each person there exists a brain such that (a) what mental states the person has depends on what states the brain has, (b) all causal connections involving mental states between the person's sensory input and behavioral output are mediated by states of the brain, and (c) it is possible for the person to exist, as a subject of mental states, as long as the brain exists and has the appropriate states. The only part of this that would ordinarily be regarded as at all controversial is (c), which is affirmed by those who think that a person could survive the destruction of his body if his brain were detached and kept alive "in vitro." Now this view about brains does not seem to imply that persons *are* brains (and so weigh only a few pounds, are greyish in color, and so on), and that the mental states of persons just *are* states of their brains. And no more does Minimal Dualism seem to imply Cartesian Dualism. It seems compatible with Minimal Dualism that an immaterial substance should be related to a person in much the way we ordinarily think of a person's brain as related to him—that it should be, in effect, a ghostly brain.[4] And this is what I shall take Non-Cartesian Dualism to hold.

It should come as no surprise that the version of dualism I regard as conceptually coherent (although empirically very implausible) is Non-Cartesian Dualism, while that which I believe to be conceptually incoherent is Cartesian Dualism.

III

Before I can go on I must explain some terminology and state some assumptions.

A substance, as I shall use the term, is a "continuant" in W. E. Johnson's sense—something that can persist through time, and can have different properties at different times. A material substance I take to be a substance whose nonderivative and nonrelational properties are necessarily limited to (a) physical properties and (b) properties it has in virtue of what physical properties it has (in the way a machine can have a certain computational capacity in virtue of having a particular physical structure, even though things having very different physical structures, and perhaps even immaterial things, could have the same computational capacity).[5] And I take it that physical properties can belong, nonderivatively, only to material substances. Beyond this I shall not attempt to define the terms "material" and "physical." I shall simply assume, for the sake of this discussion, that the correct definitions of these terms (if there are such), or the ways in which their references are fixed, are not such as to make it self-contradictory to suppose that there might be properties and states that are not physical and substances that are not material.

It is misleading to treat the terms "material substance" and "immaterial substance" on a par. The relationship between

4. See my paper "Embodiment and Behavior," in Amelie Rorty, ed., *The Identities of Persons* (Berkeley and Los Angeles, 1976).
5. I owe this example to Richard Boyd.

them should be thought of as analogous, not to that between "iron" and "copper," but to that between "iron" and "nonferrous metal." If there can be immaterial substances at all, presumably there can be different kinds of immaterial substances, these being as different from one another as they are from material substances. For each possible kind of immaterial substances there will be a kind of properties which are essential to those substances in the way physical properties are essential to material substances. Just as physical properties can belong (nonderivatively) only to material substances, so immaterial properties of one of these kinds will be capable of belonging (nonderivatively) only to immaterial substances of the corresponding kind; and, conversely, the nonderivative and nonrelational properties of immaterial substances of a given kind will be necessarily limited to (a) immaterial properties of the corresponding kind and (b) properties they have in virtue of what immaterial properties of that kind they have.

A term that purports to refer to a kind of immaterial substances, and to be on a par with "material substance," is "spiritual substance." Spiritual substances are what Cartesian Dualists believe persons to be. They are (or would be if they existed) substances whose nonderivative and nonrelational properties are necessarily mental properties (if you like, modes of consciousness); and anyone who holds that there can be such substances is committed to holding that mental properties can belong (nonderivatively) *only* to such substances.

It might be supposed that "immaterial substance" could be defined as meaning simply "substance that is not a material substance." A reason for not so defining it (one that would not, however, impress a Cartesian Dualist) is that this would make Non-Cartesian Dualism logically incoherent. Persons are certainly substances in the broad sense I have defined; they are "continuants." Now Non-Cartesian Dualism denies that persons are material substances, and so would be committed, by the proposed definition of "immaterial substance," to holding that they are immaterial substances. But I have characterized Non-Cartesian Dualism as the version of Minimal Dualism which denies that a person *is* the immaterial substance on which his mental states depend; and if a person is not that immaterial substance, what immaterial substance could he be? No answer seems forthcoming.

But there is another reason, and one that even a Cartesian Dualist should appreciate, for rejecting the proposed definition. On any version of dualism which allows for the possibility of causal interaction between material and immaterial substances (and only such versions are under consideration here) there can exist systems which consist of one or more immaterial substances interacting causally with one or more material substances. Such systems (I will call them "partly physical systems") will be continuants, and so substances in the broad sense. And such systems will have properties—dispositional properties at least—which they possess in virtue of what properties their material and immaterial components have, and of how these components are related to one another; something's having such a property will be a "partly physical" state of it. Clearly such a system will not be a material substance. Yet it will not do to characterize such systems as immaterial substances; for obviously a system which has material as well as immaterial components cannot be immaterial in the same sense in which its immaterial components are immaterial.

Immaterial substances, if there are any, will be substances whose nonrelational and nonderivative properties are neither physical nor partly physical. What we have just seen is that if we admit the possibility of there being immaterial substances as well as material substances, we must admit the possibility of there also being substances, or at any rate continuants, which are themselves neither material substances nor immaterial substances but whose existence in some way consists in the existence of material and immaterial substances. We cannot, I think, rule out a priori the possibility that persons, or even minds, will turn out to be such entities.[6]

6. Even on the assumption that there are no immaterial substances, and that the existence of everything in some way consists in the existence of material substances, there may be a sense in which persons are neither material nor immaterial substances. For even on materialist assumptions, it is natural to hold that stones, trees, and automobiles are material substances in a sense in which corporations, nations, and political parties are not. If such a narrow sense of

IV

I shall follow tradition by assuming that immaterial substances lack spatial properties, and so are not spatially extended, and that they do not have spatial location in their own
right. Some philosophers have held that the nonspatiality of
immaterial substances makes the very idea of an immaterial
substance incoherent. Their argument has been that there
could be no satisfactory way of individuating such entities;
since immaterial substances are supposed to be particulars,
rather than abstract entities, they could not be individuated by
their nonrelational properties (for it ought to be possible
for two particulars to share all of their nonrelational properties), and since they are supposed to be nonspatial they could
not be individuated by spatial relations. Likewise, it has been
objected that there is no way in which the notion of identity
through time could be applied to entities to which the notion of
spatiotemporal continuity is inapplicable.

Those who make such objections usually assume, as do most
philosophers who write about dualism, that immaterial substances would be spiritual substances. It does seem logically
possible that two numerically different persons should be exactly similar with respect to their mental or psychological attributes. And it may seem to follow that the notion of a spiritual
substance, a substance having only mental (psychological) properties and states, is not a coherent notion.

Even if this constituted a valid objection against Cartesian
Dualism, which takes persons to be spiritual substances, it
would not refute Non-Cartesian Dualism, which is not committed to the existence of spiritual substances. And in fact it
does not seem to me a convincing objection to Cartesian Dualism.

Both Cartesian Dualism and Non-Cartesian Dualism are ver-

"material substance" can be defined (and I shall not attempt to define it here),
it may be that even a materialist should deny that persons are material substances in the narrow sense—for one thing, the identity conditions for persons
seem to differ importantly from those for paradigmatic "material objects," but
not in ways that call materialism into question.

sions of what I have called Minimal Dualism. And Minimal Dualism is committed to the claim that immaterial substances are such that they can interact causally with material substances; for it is essential to Minimal Dualism that the states of immaterial substances mediate the causal connections between the sensory input and the behavioral output of the bodies of living persons.[7] Now immaterial substances are usually thought to lack spatial position, and spatial relations, as well as spatial extension. And this makes it difficult to understand how there can be causal connections of the required sorts between immaterial substances (and their states) and material substances (and their states). There can be no spatial relationship, such as spatial contiguity, which relates the immaterial substance which is my mind, soul, or ghostly brain to *my* body and not to any other, and which relates my body to *my* mind (soul, ghostly brain) and not to any other immaterial substance. Why, then, do the states of my mind affect only the states of my body, and why is it only my mind that is directly affected by sensory stimulation of my body? Since I am supposing that Minimal Dualism is coherent, I must suppose that this difficulty can be overcome. And to suppose this we must suppose, I think, that there could be nonspatial relationships between immaterial substances ("minds") and material substances ("bodies") which play a role in determining what causal relationships can hold between these substances which is analogous to the role which spatial relationships play in determining what causal relationships can hold between material substances. Let us speak of these as "quasi-spatial relationships." Now there seems no reason why a Non-Cartesian Dualist cannot hold that immaterial substances are, or can be, related to material substances by such relationships; there seems to be no conflict between this claim and the essentially negative characterization of immaterial substances given by Non-Cartesian Dualism. If it is incompatible with the notion of a spiritual substance that such a substance

7. So I am not discussing Occasionalism, and other versions of dualism that deny interaction between material and immaterial substances. I believe, but have not the space to argue here, that interactionism is the only coherent form of dualism.

should stand in quasi-spatial relationships to material substances, then Cartesian Dualism cannot make intelligible the
possibility of interaction between mind and body, and can be
rejected on that account. But it is not clear that this is incompatible with the notion of a spiritual substance. What we know
from the notion of a spiritual substance, beyond the fact that
spiritual substances are immaterial, is that the *non*relational
properties of spiritual substances are mental properties. Off-
hand, this implies nothing about what relations such substances
can enter into, except (perhaps) that they cannot enter into
spatial relationships. But, and here is the point, if it is intelligible to suppose that immaterial substances can be related to material substances by such quasi-spatial relationships, there seems
no reason why we should not suppose that they stand in quasi-
spatial relationships to one another. And then their quasi-spatial relationships could play the role in their individuation, and
in their identity through time, which spatial relationships play
in the case of material substances. It seems that this could be
held by Cartesian Dualists as well as by Non-Cartesian Dualists.[8]

8. Despite what I have said here, something must be conceded to the objection that there is no satisfactory principle of individuation for immaterial substances. In the sense in which we have a conception of material substance,
which includes, as central to it, a partial specification of the identity conditions
for material objects, we do not have a conception of immaterial substances, or
of any particular kind of immaterial substances. The definition I have given of
"spiritual substance" does not specify such a conception, for it says nothing positive about what relationships would hold between spiritual substances (to say
that some of these relationships would be "quasi-spatial" is not to say what they
would be). So it is in a rather thin sense that it is "conceivable" that there
should be immaterial substances. It is not that we have a determinate conception of some kind of immaterial substance, and can conceive of there being
things that satisfy this conception. It is rather that we can conceive of having
(or acquiring) such a determinate notion, and of believing, intelligibly and consistently, that there are things that satisfy it. However, in the remainder of this
essay I shall write as if we do have a determinate conception of immaterial substance; this can be thought of as a concession to my opponents.

One other common objection to dualism should be mentioned here. It is
sometimes urged that there are intimate conceptual, or logical, connections between mental states and their behavioral manifestations or expressions, and
that because of these connections it is logically incoherent to suppose that a
person might exist in disembodied form. In order to assess this objection we
must consider in what sense, if any, mental states and behavior are "concep-

V

Immaterial substances have traditionally been supposed to be "simple," in the sense of being indivisible and without separable parts, and this supposition has figured prominently in a priori arguments for immortality. One basis for this view has been the view that *persons* are simple and indivisible, this being based on considerations which we can lump together under the heading "the unity of consciousness." Given the premise that persons are simple and indivisible, that properly speaking nothing can be a *part* of a person, plus the premise that persons must be either material substances or immaterial substances, plus the obvious fact that material substances are *not* simple and indivisible, we can derive both the conclusion that persons are immaterial substances and the conclusion that at least some immaterial substances (namely those that are persons) are simple and indivisible. In order to reject this argument I do not need to dispute the claim that persons are (in some sense) simple and indivisible. For I have already rejected the second premise of the argument, namely that persons must be either material substances or immaterial substances. A Non-Cartesian Dualist, who denies that persons *are* immaterial substances, cannot conclude from the (alleged) simplicity of persons that immaterial substances are simple, and cannot cite the simplicity of persons as proof that there are immaterial substances.

It may be objected that even if persons are not identical with either material or immaterial substances, their existence must in some sense consist in the existence of substances of one, or both, of these kinds. With this I agree. And it might further be held that if something is simple and indivisible, its existence cannot consist in the existence of substances that are not themselves simple and indivisible. But this further claim seems to me unwarranted. I can imagine someone arguing that the United States Supreme Court, for example, is in some important sense

---

tually connected." I cannot discuss this complex issue here; but I have argued elsewhere that what seems to me the most defensible version of the "conceptual connection thesis" is compatible with the view that disembodied existence is possible—see my "Embodiment and Behavior."

without parts and indivisible, and that the relationship of the individual justices to the court is not that of part of whole (since, arguably, the court would continue to exist even if all of the justices were simultaneously to die or resign and since, presumably, the question, "How much does the Supreme Court weigh?" is one we should reject rather than answer by summing the weights of the individual justices). But nothing that could plausibly be meant by this would persuade a materialist that he must choose between denying the existence of the Supreme Court and abandoning his materialist view that the things that exist in the world are either material substances or things whose existence consists in the existence of material substances and their relationships to one another.

There is, however, a traditional reason for thinking that immaterial substances would have to be simple and indivisible which does not rest on the claim that persons are simple and indivisible. For it is taken for granted (as I do here) that an immaterial substance cannot be spatially extended, and from this it is concluded that immaterial substances, if there be such, are necessarily indivisible and without parts. No doubt this consideration and those leading directly to the conclusion that persons are simple have tended to reinforce each other—if someone has been persuaded on independent grounds that (a) persons are simple and (b) immaterial substances are simple, it will not be surprising if he concludes that immaterial substances are just the right sorts of things for persons to be.

But this second reason for thinking immaterial substances to be simple is undermined by the points made in Section IV. We saw there that in order to make intelligible the possibility of causal interaction between immaterial substances and material bodies (as is required by both forms of Minimal Dualism) we must suppose that there are "quasi-spatial" relationships which immaterial substances can stand in which constrain what causal relationships they can stand in to material substances, and do so in a way analogous to that in which spatial relationships constrain what causal relationships can hold between different material substances. Moreover, we saw that in order to answer the "individuation" objection to dualism we must suppose that there are "quasi-spatial" relationships that hold between different immaterial substances. But given all this, it is surely intelligible (if talk about immaterial substances is intelligible at all) to suppose that immaterial substances can interact causally with one another, as well as with material substances, the causal connections between them being constrained by quasi-spatial relationships holding between them. And if there could be causal interaction between different immaterial substances, surely there could exist, in virtue of the holding of causal connections, *systems* of immaterial substances which constitute causal units in much the way a (physical) machine is a causal unit in virtue of the causal connections that hold between its parts. And such systems would have parts, or at any rate components, some of these being subsystems and some (perhaps) being "atomic" immaterial substances which are simple and without parts. Presumably such systems could have a quasi-spatial unity which goes with their causal unity in much the way that the spatial unity of material bodies goes with their causal unity.

Someone might allow that there could be such systems of immaterial substances, but deny that such systems would themselves be immaterial substances. If this denial stems from a stipulation that a substance, of whatever sort, must be simple and without parts, we can point out that this stipulation rules out talk of material substances (or at any rate excludes human bodies, and other macroscopic material things, from being substances). But there is no need for us to quibble here about the word "substance"; if need be, we can abandon it in favor of "thing," "entity," or "continuant." The point is that if there can be immaterial substances at all, of the sort required by Minimal Dualism, there seems no reason why there should not be immaterial entities that have parts. More specifically, if Non-Cartesian Dualism is coherent, there seems no reason why the "ghostly brain" of a person should not be a composite immaterial thing, a system of immaterial things which are so related as to constitute a causal unit, rather than an "atomic" immaterial substance. Certainly the view that we have immaterial brains that are such systems is no less intelligible than the view that we have immaterial brains that are immaterial atoms.

Finally, and this is, of course, the point of all this, if it is possible for immaterial substances (or things) to have parts or components, then there seems no reason to suppose that immaterial substances are not subject to destruction through the dissolution of their parts. Clearly we have no empirical evidence of the indestructibility of immaterial substances. Let us suspend, for a moment, our skepticism about purported cases of communication with the dead, "out-of-body experiences," and other spiritualistic phenomena. Even if such cases were evidence that there are immaterial substances, it is clear that they would provide no evidence that these substances are simple and indivisible, or that they are for any other reason indestructible. Likewise, if we discovered evidence that the structure of the human brain and nervous system is insufficiently complex to account for all aspects of human behavior, then while this might be evidence that there exist immaterial substances which function as the "ghostly brains" of persons, or which are the immaterial components of partly physical systems which function as "partly ghostly brains," it clearly would not be evidence that these immaterial substances are simple and indestructible.

It is plain that support for Non-Cartesian Dualism, if we had it, would not as such be support for the doctrine of immortality. Moreover, it seems (and I shall argue later) that whatever empirical evidence we can imagine having for the truth of Minimal Dualism would be compatible with Non-Cartesian Dualism—assuming, of course, that Non-Cartesian Dualism is a coherent position. If so, dualism can be used to buttress the plausibility of the doctrine of immortality only if it can be shown on a priori grounds that Non-Cartesian Dualism is not coherent and that Cartesian Dualism is—in other words, that Cartesian Dualism is the only coherent form of dualism. It will turn out that in order to maintain this one must maintain that it can be established a priori not merely that Cartesian Dualism is the only coherent form of dualism, but that it is the only coherent philosophy of mind. In other words, one must maintain that it can be established a priori that persons are spiritual substances and that mental states are immaterial states of such substances. As will become clear in the following sections, I think that there are no sound a priori reasons for believing this to be true, and that there are strong a priori reasons for believing it to be false.

VI

Let us consider what the status of mental states would be if Non-Cartesian Dualism were true. The brief answer, I think, is that their status would be much the same as it would be (or is) if materialism were (or is) true—where by "materialism" is meant the view that whatever exists (apart from "abstract entities" such as numbers) is either a material substance or something whose existence consists in the existence of material substances, their states, and their relations to one another.

Materialists sometimes assert that mental states are neurophysiological states of the brain. Now on one understanding of this, it implies something which many materialists would want to deny (and which, I think, any materialist *should* want to deny). Suppose that pain is said to be the firing of C-fibers. This might mean that the mental property, or attribute, *being in pain* is identical with the neurophysiological attribute *has its C-fibers firing*. Now this ought to imply, not merely that in all actual cases, whatever has the mental attribute has the neurophysiological one, and vice versa, but also that this holds in all possible cases as well—for it is a principle of modal logic that if *a* is identical with *b*, *a* is *necessarily* identical with *b*.[9] And if every mental attribute were thus identical with some physical feature of human brains, it would follow (a) that disembodied existence of subjects of mental states is not even a possibility, and (b) that other physical creatures (e.g., the inhabitants of remote planets) cannot be subjects of mental states unless they have brains capable of having the relevant physical features, e.g., brains containing C-fibers. But many materialists would reject (a), and most would reject (b). There is, however, another way of taking the claim that mental states are neurophysiological states of the brain. To say that pain is the firing of C-fibers might mean that in the case of human beings (but not,

9. See Saul Kripke, "Identity and Necessity," in Milton Munitz, ed., *Identity and Individuation* (New York, 1971), pp. 135–164.

necessarily, in the case of all possible creatures) being in pain "consists in," and "is nothing over and above," the firing of C-fibers. Or as it might be put, in human beings the attribute of being in pain is "realized in" the firing of C-fibers—which is compatible with its being realized in other ways in other creatures. It is even possible to hold that in the case of human beings a given mental state sometimes has one physical "realization" and sometimes another. Of course, it needs to be explained what this relationship of "being realized in," or "existing in virtue of," amounts to. I think that this can best be understood if we adopt a causal, or functional, analysis of mental concepts. Roughly, to say that in a certain person at a certain time the attribute of being in pain is realized in the firing of C-fibers is to say that in that person at that time the firing of C-fibers plays the causal role which is definitive of pain.[10]

Now a Non-Cartesian Dualist will not hold that mental attributes are identical to immaterial attributes of immaterial substances. Just as it seems possible that there should be creatures which, given their behavior, we would want to count as having mental states despite the fact that the physical makeup of their brains or "control systems" is very different from ours, so it seems possible (assuming the coherence of Minimal Dualism) that there should be creatures to which we would be willing to assign the same mental states despite the fact that they have "ghostly brains" having very different immaterial states. What the Non-Cartesian Dualist will hold is that the mental states of a person are realized in, that they exist in virtue of, immaterial states of an immaterial substance that functions as the person's "ghostly brain," and that it is possible (in principle, anyhow) for the same mental attribute to be realized in different immaterial states on different occasions or in different persons. Indeed, just as a materialist can hold that there *could* be creatures (though in fact there aren't) whose mental states are realized in immaterial states, so a Non-Cartesian Dualist could hold that

10. See Armstrong, *A Materialist Theory of Mind,* and David Lewis, "An Argument for the Identity Theory," in D. M. Rosenthal, ed., *Materialism and the Mind-Body Problem* (Englewood Cliffs, N.J., 1971), and "Psychophysical and Theoretical Identifications," in *Australasian Journal of Philosophy,* 50 (1972), 249–257.

there could be creatures (though in fact there aren't) whose mental states are realized in physical states. And somebody could hold, although I doubt if anyone ever has, that the mental states of some creatures are realized in physical states of brains, while those of other creatures are realized in immaterial states of "ghostly brains."

While the Non-Cartesian Dualist holds that mental states are "realized in" states of immaterial substances, he does not hold that they are themselves states of immaterial substances. They are states of persons; and just as a sensible materialist does not hold that persons *are* their brains, a Non-Cartesian Dualist does not hold that persons *are* the immaterial substances which function as their "ghostly brains." A person, according to Non-Cartesian Dualism, is an entity which normally exists, and has the properties it has, in virtue of the existence of a "mind" and a "body" which are related in a certain way and have certain properties, but which can exist in virtue of the existence of the mind (immaterial substance) alone. Perhaps the Non-Cartesian Dualist can say, harking back to the discussion in Section III, that a normal, i.e., embodied, person is a "partly physical system," but one whose identity conditions permit it to survive the loss of its physical components. But if he says this he must avoid saying that in becoming disembodied a person would become an immaterial substance; for immaterial substances are essentially immaterial, and nothing can become one or cease to be one. Likewise, a materialist who thinks that mental states are "realized" in physical states of the brain will not think (or should not think) that mental states are themselves states of the brain; for he will know that they are states of a person, and that a person is not identical with his brain (for one thing, the size, shape, weight, etc., of a person are not normally the size, shape, weight, etc. of his brain).[11]

11. It may be thought that if a person's brain is kept alive in vitro, and is all that physically remains of him, then (on materialist assumptions) he will be identical with it—and, likewise, that if all that is left of a person is an immaterial brain, he will be identical with it. But this cannot be so if, as I believe, it is impossible for entities X and Y to be numerically different at one time and numerically identical at another (or if, what would seem to come to the same thing, identical entities must have identical histories).

VII

Now let us turn our attention to Cartesian Dualism. The Cartesian Dualist holds that mental attributes *are,* in the sense of being identical with rather than in the sense of being realized in, immaterial states of spiritual substances. This means that he must hold, not merely that neither materialism nor Non-Cartesian Dualism *is* true, but that neither of these positions *could be,* or *could have been,* true. If being in pain (say) were merely realized in some immaterial attribute (rather than being identical with it), this would not rule out the possibility of its also being realized (in other creatures, or in other possible worlds) in some physical attribute of a material substance. But if being in pain is *identical with* an immaterial attribute, it is plainly impossible that it should be realized in a physical attribute of a material substance. Likewise, if it is identical with an immaterial attribute (an attribute which can belong only to immaterial substances), it cannot belong to something which is *not* an immaterial substance (e.g., a person as conceived by Non-Cartesian Dualism), and so cannot do so in virtue of some immaterial substance (someone's ghostly brain) having some *other* immaterial attribute (one that is not mental).

This is not yet to say that the Cartesian Dualist is committed to holding that it can be established a priori that both Non-Cartesian Dualism and materialism are false or incoherent. For while he is committed to holding that neither of these positions could possibly be true (that neither is true in any possible world), this would be compatible with his holding that the truth of his own position, and the falsity of these others, is necessary a posteriori (in Kripke's sense) rather than necessary a priori.[12] Just as an identity like "Hesperus is Phosphorus" is established empirically, despite the fact that if true it is necessarily so in the sense that it could not have been false (is false in no possible world), so it might be held that identities between immaterial

12. See Kripke's "Identity and Necessity," and his "Naming and Necessity," in Donald Davidson and Gilbert Harman, eds., *Semantics of Natural Language* (Dordrecht, 1972), pp. 253–355.

attributes and mental attributes are (like all identities) necessary in this sense, but are known to hold a posteriori.

But this view has no plausibility at all. For suppose, first of all, that we wished to establish empirically an identity statement of the form "Mental state M is immaterial state I." Clearly we would need, to begin with, to have some way of identifying or picking out state I which guarantees that it is an immaterial state but which leaves it an open question, to be settled empirically, whether it is identical with M. In fact, of course, we lack any such way (or any way at all) of picking out immaterial states. But even if we had such a way of picking out immaterial states, what could we discover empirically that would show that a mental state M is identical with an immaterial state I, as opposed to being merely correlated with it, or being realized in it? We could rule out *mere* correlation if we could establish that effects (e.g., behavioral ones) which we confidently attribute to M are in fact due to I. But this would no more establish that M is identical to I than the discovery that pain behavior is produced by the firing of C-fibers would establish that the attribute *is in pain* is identical (and so identical in all possible worlds) to the physical attribute *has its C-fibers firing*. At best such a discovery would establish that, in the creatures investigated, state M is realized in state I; and this in no way rules out the possibility that there should be creatures in which it is realized in some other state, either immaterial or physical (i.e., that there should be creatures in which behavioral and other effects which would correctly be regarded as manifestations of M are due to some state other than I). Yet if this would not establish that M and I are identical, it seems to me that no empirical discovery would establish this.

Of course, someone might maintain that we could establish empirically that mental states are immaterial states without establishing identities of the form "Mental state M is immaterial state I" (just as many materialists would hold that we can establish that mental states are [realized in] physical states without establishing any statements of the form "Mental state M is [realized in] physical state P"). But essentially the same difficulty arises about this. For in the absence of an a priori argument against the possibility of Non-Cartesian Dualism being true, it seems that any conceivable evidence that might be thought to show that mental states *are* immaterial states would be compatible with the claim that they are merely realized in them, and that the same mental state could (in principle) be realized in more than one way. This is true, for example, of the (perhaps) imaginable discovery that we need to posit the existence of immaterial substances in order to explain the behavior that is attributed to mental states.

VIII

Let us turn, then, to the question of whether the Cartesian Dualist has any hope of establishing his position a priori.

The a priori arguments for dualism that I know of simply assume, and make no attempt to show, that Cartesian Dualism is the only viable form of dualism. I do not myself think that any of these arguments are sound. But what is relevant to our present concerns is that even if some of them were sound, and did establish Minimal Dualism, they would not establish Cartesian Dualism. For example, one typical argument goes (fallaciously, I believe) from the (alleged) fact that I can conceive of myself existing in disembodied form to the claim that it is possible for me to exist in disembodied form, where this is taken as a statement of de re modality to the effect that I am something that can exist in disembodied form,[13] from which in turn it is concluded (validly) that I am not a material substance. But even if this conclusion were established, we could not legitimately go from it to the conclusion that I am a spiritual substance (or, more generally, that persons are spiritual substances), for nothing in the argument excludes the possibility that I am (that persons are) as Non-Cartesian Dualism represents persons as

13. The fallacy in this, I think, involves a confusion of a certain sort of epistemic possibility with metaphysical possibility. In the sense in which it is true that I can conceive of myself existing in disembodied form, this comes to the fact that it is compatible with what I know about my essential nature (supposing that I do not know that I am an essentially material being) that I should exist in disembodied form. From this it does not follow that my essential nature is in fact such as to permit me to exist in disembodied form.

being. Or consider the arguments that purport to show that mental states are not physical states. If the conclusion means simply that mental attributes are not identical with physical attributes (and that it is therefore possible for them to be realized nonphysically), then even a materialist can accept it. If it means that mental attributes cannot be realized in physical states (that the having of a mental attribute cannot be "nothing over and above" the having of certain physical attributes), then I do not think it can be established a priori. But even if it could be, this would not establish Cartesian Dualism, for it would be compatible with the truth of Non-Cartesian Dualism. Still another argument is from the alleged "simplicity" of persons; we have already seen that this fails to establish Cartesian Dualism.

Moreover, I think we can see that there *could* be no sound a priori argument for Cartesian Dualism. For suppose (per impossibile) I had such an argument, and knew a priori that all mental states are identical with immaterial states of spiritual substances. And suppose that, having this knowledge, I am faced with what looks like someone who is, with great ingenuity and resourcefulness, repairing a complicated machine; that is, I am faced with what, as things are, I would take without question to be a person having certain mental states. On our supposition, I could not be entitled to regard what is before me as a person having these mental states unless I were entitled to believe that the body before me is animated by a spiritual substance. Someone might argue that since I would be entitled to believe that there is a conscious person before me, and since, ex hypothesi, I would know that all mental states are identical with immaterial states, I would ipso facto be entitled to believe that the body before me is animated by a spiritual substance having the appropriate immaterial states. But here it seems more appropriate to argue backward, and to say that since one *cannot* be justified on empirical grounds in believing that something is animated by a spiritual substance, and since, ex hypothesi, I would know that all mental states are immaterial states of spiritual substances, I could not be entitled to believe that what was before me was (or was the embodiment of) a person having those (or any) mental states.

To elaborate this, suppose that I am confronted with *two* creatures, one from Venus and one from Mars, both of which are exhibiting behavior which one would ordinarily take to show the existence of certain mental states. And suppose, what seems compatible with this, that the physical makeups of these two creatures are entirely different (their evolutionary histories having been different), and that I know this. There are two possibilities here; either the causes of the observed behavior are entirely physical, or they are at least partly immaterial. If I had good reason to believe the former, and was guaranteed on a priori grounds that mental states are immaterial states, I certainly could not be entitled to take the observed behavior as evidence of the existence of mental states. So let us suppose that I have good reason to believe that the causes of the behavior are at least partly immaterial. Now, given that the physical makeups of these creatures are entirely different, it seems reasonable to suppose that they would have to be acted on by different sorts of immaterial states or events in order to yield the same output of behavior (roughly, that there would have to be immaterial differences to compensate for the physical differences).[14] Moreover, if we can investigate immaterial substances empirically at all, it ought to make sense to suppose that we have investigated the immaterial substances that animate our Martian and Venusian and discovered that they have very different immaterial states. So let us suppose that I have discovered this. I would therefore know, given our supposition that I am guaranteed a priori that mental states are immaterial states of spiritual substances, that at least one of the creatures was not the subject of the mental states which seem to be manifested in the behavior of both. And this would be true *no matter what* the behavior was, and no matter how extensive it was. Moreover, given what I argued in Section VII, nothing I could establish empirically would show *which* creature, if either, is a subject of those (or any) mental states—that is, there is nothing that would show which body, if either, is animated by a *spiritual* substance. More generally, on the supposition that we are guaranteed a priori that mental states are immaterial states of spiritual

14. See my "Embodiment and Behavior," for an elaboration of this.

substances, the behavioral evidence we would ordinarily take as establishing that a creature is a subject of certain mental states does not establish this, and there is no empirical data which in conjunction with this evidence would establish it. In other words, on this supposition mental states are unknowable. And this seems to me a reductio ad absurdum of the supposition.

It seems, then, that we could have neither good empirical grounds nor good a priori grounds for believing Cartesian Dualism to be true. It does not follow from this, perhaps, that Cartesian Dualism could not be true—that it is logically or conceptually incoherent. We could establish this stronger conclusion if we could establish that either materialism or Non-Cartesian Dualism *could* be true. For as we have seen, if it is so much as logically possible that either of these positions is true, Cartesian Dualism cannot be true. And if the falsity of Cartesian Dualism follows from a true statement of logical possibility, then it is not even logically possible that Cartesian Dualism should be true. We could establish the logical possibility of materialism or Non-Cartesian Dualism being true if we could establish a causal or functional account of what mental states are—for such an account would allow for the possibility of mental states being realized in a variety of physical states or a variety of immaterial states. I believe myself that only such an account makes sense of our ability to have knowledge of mental states (our own as well as those of others). But I have not the space to argue this here. If, however, I have succeeded in showing that there is and could be no good reason for believing in Cartesian Dualism, then, given what I argued earlier, I have shown that there is and could be no good reason for believing in a form of dualism that would make belief in immortality significantly more plausible than it is on antidualist assumptions.

14

Immortality and Dualism

HYWEL LEWIS

I am in entire agreement with Sydney Shoemaker on one main point. This is the point with which he begins, namely that we are reduced to desperate straits, in seeking to make any case for immortality, unless we can first make out a case for dualism on the mind-body problem. I would indeed go further. I do not think that any case for immortality can begin to get off the ground if we fail to make a case for dualism. This has been extensively recognized by nondualists. Immortality has normally been understood to mean that we continue to exist when the present physical body has been destroyed. In conditions of existence in the past, and in any condition we can reasonably foresee now, the body one now has is very completely destroyed, as a functioning organism, very soon after we draw the last breath. Usually today it is reduced to ashes, and even if preserved in some mummified form, the chances of revivifying it to function as it does when we are alive, are too remote to be taken seriously. There is indeed a little more prospect today, owing to the advance of science, that the deterioration of living organisms could be arrested or reversed or that there might be some other 'life-prolonging episodes' or devices which would ensure our literal bodily continuity without end. But even if this were a prospect we could entertain with some confidence, it would be rather far removed from the expectations usually entertained by those who believe in immortality. The latter has been thought to be available to human beings past and present, to the millions whose bodies have suffered complete disintegration already as well as to the fortunate ones, assuming they are so, on whom endless bodily existence may be conferred some-

day by the advance of science. Indeed, the case for immortality
has hardly ever been made to rest on the avoidance of the reality of death; it concerns an expectation of something which
holds irrespective of the normal accepted facts of death and
decay, and for many, the attractiveness of the prospect turns,
in part at least, on our superseding the limitations as well as the
ills to which flesh is heir and embarking on other, presumably
richer, modes of existence.

Against this it may be urged that, in the Christian context at
least, what has been largely expected is that, notwithstanding
death and decay, there may still be a 'resurrection of the body'.
This, we are told, does not mean the 'resuscitation of corpses',
but it does then become difficult to know what it can mean.
Some just invoke here the omnipotence of God with whom 'all
things are possible'. But we still need to know in some measure
what is contemplated, and what reason there could be for supposing that God would in fact literally recompose our bodies. I
have, however, commented at more length on this issue in another recent symposium; [1] and have referred to the suggestion
that better scientific understanding of physical bodies can make
the present supposition more attractive. In the same context I
have also discussed the relevance, not very great it seems to me,
of the notion of an astral body and its intelligibility. I will therefore leave the point here with the general expression of agreement with the view that immortality must at least be understood to involve such independence of our present physical
existence as will make it intelligible to suppose that we continue
to exist and function notwithstanding the destruction of the
present body.

But suppose someone says: "I agree, but surely you will need
a body of some kind". I do not think I would concede this, at
least as an absolute requirement.[2] But if the point were conceded, it would still mean that my continued existence was independent of any particular body I might have at one stage.
The body is replaceable while I remain the same. This commits
us to dualism at least to the extent of making my own existence,

1. *Proceedings of the Aristotelian Society,* Supplementary Vol. 49 (1975).
2. See my *The Self and Immortality* (London and New York, 1973), chap. 9.

in essentials, independent of my having a particular body, and especially my present physical body which, I have no doubt, will come to its end with the end of my 'allotted span'.

On this score then there is nothing seriously in dispute between Shoemaker and myself, whether or not we would put our points in quite the same terms. But immediately beyond this point a gap begins to open. For I consider a dualist position to be an indispensable basis for belief in immortality in at least one markedly different way.

For me the dualist supposition is a requirement of any reasonable understanding of what it would be like to be immortal, or of what this notion *means*. On most of the widely held views of mind and body today, any kind of future existence is ruled out, and for this reason it is essential for anyone who wishes to defend the belief in immortality to counter the doctrines which plainly preclude it. I do not expect to do more than this, in the present context, in my defense of dualism. I only wish to keep the door open, to rule out the essential inconceivability of a future existence, in an immortal or more limited way. Nothing is claimed, on the present score, to make it certain, or even highly probable, that we shall survive the dissolution of our bodies. Other reasons must be invoked to accomplish this further aim. I am not concerned in this paper with what they are.

Shoemaker's attitude here appears to be different. He expects the case for dualism, especially in its stricter Cartesian form, as he labels it, to yield more positive results, indeed to establish nothing less than the essential indestructibility of the soul. Immortality is assured if the dualist case is made.

This is not because some of the obvious difficulties, for example, the indisputable causal dependence on the body in the present existence, are removed or have the sting taken out of them. Much more positively it is established that, in terms of what we find ourselves to be, we just cannot fail to be immortal.

Furthermore, the way this is understood is that, on a dualist view, we must be deemed to have a simple, indivisible nature, and nothing which is thought to have such a nature can ever be destroyed, on the grounds presumably that destruction must take the form of the dissolution of some entity into its component parts. This supposition, although it has never been central in discussions of the subject in the past, is not without an impressive ancestry. Plato has recourse to it, in the *Phaedo* and in the *Republic*, although he turns also to some other rather formal arguments such as the insistence that nothing is destroyed except by its own evil, the evil of the soul being injustice which is far from causing the death of the wicked. What is impressive in the case of Plato is the sustained conviction that the individual soul is immortal.

On the indivisibility argument, Plato would also find difficulty in his own sustained account of the tripartite division of the soul. The reply might be made that appetite and spirit on Plato's view come about through involvement with the body and do not belong to the true and essentially rational nature of the soul. But the famous myth in the *Phaedrus* at least ascribes both appetite and desire to the soul in its prenatal state. It is worth noting also that the discussion in the *Phaedo* finds the clue to the simplicity of the soul in its affinity with the Forms and this gives the former a somewhat different character from its invocation in later traditions.

The idea of the simplicity of the soul has lurked in the background of much subsequent Western thinking, but it has also been prevented from making fuller impact by anxiety not to impugn the essentially created character of all finite things. A soul that is, in virtue of its essential nature, not destructible would presumably have preexisted, and while this in some form would be acceptable to Plato, it would cause some embarrassment to later theism by coming close at least to elevating one kind of being into a state of existence in its own right over against a purported Author of all things.

To pursue the last point further on our own account, and in closer relation to Shoemaker's view, it is not at all clear to me why anything should be deemed impervious to destruction just by having an essentially simple nature. Can we take it for granted that nothing can come to an end except by dissolution into its constituent parts? This would confer inviolate, and thereby it would seem necessary, existence of any finite entity that has the appropriate simplicity. But we generally assume that necessity does not characterize any statement of finite existence. Indeed, the principle has sometimes been generalized to apply to all existence, as in J. N. Findlay's celebrated reversal of the Ontological Argument.[3] Generally it is conceded that necessary existence belongs solely to God and that it is so essential a feature of God, where the being of God is at all acknowledged, that it is impious to place it elsewhere. Less piously, I repeat the question, why should anything be thought essentially less destructible solely in virtue of the simple nature it is alleged to have?

That there is a sense in which the self does have a simple indivisible nature seems to me true, although the point needs to be presented very carefully indeed to avoid the difficulties instanced in discussions like that of Shoemaker. To the last point we shall return shortly. But in the meantime it seems evident to me, irrespective of any understanding we may have of our own natures, that we are in no way exceptions to what seems evident about other finite existences, namely that, in the last resort, we just find that certain things do exist. Granted, of course, the order of nature as in fact we find it, then we may claim that certain things are required. Our common speech reflects this as much as do scientific statements. "It must have rained", we say, "there must be another force at work somewhere, another planet drawing known ones from their anticipated orbit", but this holds only given the order of nature as we find it. There is no inherent ultimate necessity why the world should be as it is or why any particular entity should be; and anything we say in this respect in one finite context must apply in just the same way in all. There is nothing inviolable about simplicity, and if we do have some ultimately simple nature this does nothing at all to remove us from the class of things which, in the last analysis, we just find to be.

It may be that Shoemaker does not want to dispute what I say here, but is simply concerned to dispute the sort of grounds on which it seems to him the case for immortality is usually made, or has to be made. If he does take this line, then he seems to ignore the main course of the commendation of the

3. J. N. Findlay, *Mind*, 1948.

belief in immortality, at least in Western thought, where ideas of worth, of moral requirement or the known will of God for certain of his creatures and so forth hold the center of the stage. It is on these grounds, or in consequence of some alleged evidence of some measure of survival of death, rather than on a priori grounds, that most people, today and in the past, would wish to base a belief in immortality. Even if a priori grounds are invoked they are usually of a more wide-ranging kind than the insistence on alleged simple natures.

All the same, I agree, though on quite different grounds, that the maintenance of a dualist view is an indispensable part of any plausible case for immortality, and I also deem it an essential ingredient of a sound dualist view of persons that, in the last analysis, selfhood will be found to be ultimate and indivisible. This will become clearer if we now turn to the substance of Shoemaker's paper in the attempted refutation of dualism.

The case against dualism, as advanced by Shoemaker, involves the distinction he draws between two kinds of dualism, labeled for his purpose, without claiming historical accuracy, Cartesian Dualism and Non-Cartesian Dualism. The first he considers to be wholly untenable and the second is thought "not to be much help to believers in immortality". Both are said to be versions of 'Minimal Dualism'. In both the main forms, and thus in all Minimal Dualism, it is affirmed that there is an immaterial substance, a "continuant" which "can have different properties at different times" and such that our mental states must depend on those which the immaterial substance has. The states of the latter mediate all causal connections involving mental states between sensory "input" and behavioral "output", and we may exist without having a body as long as the immaterial substance exists and has the appropriate states. But, on Cartesian Dualism, the person *is* the immaterial substance, on the other view he is not. That is the crucial difference.

So, just as some philosophers say that a person may exist "as long as the brain exists" but without implying that persons *are* brains, Non-Cartesian Dualism holds that we have "a ghostly brain", the immaterial substance which is not however the person.

There are difficulties in this view which I shall try to bring out in due course. In the meantime let it first be noted that Shoemaker attaches very great importance to the notion of Non-Cartesian Dualism. The main weight of his arguments seems to rest, at the crucial points, on the availability to us of this alternative to Cartesian Dualism. The latter is not shown in this paper (though Shoemaker thinks it can be done) to be strictly incoherent. But we have no reason "to believe it", for all the considerations that might seem to require it are equally consistent with Non-Cartesian Dualism which has in addition attractions of a further sort, though not such as to induce Shoemaker to accept it. It seems then to follow that we can have no a priori argument for Cartesian Dualism, there can be no strict requirement of its being sound, for all thought directed to it leaves us with the rival version; and it seems thus to be shown that we are not bound to think of ourselves as simple immaterial substances which can thus be deemed, in virtue of what they are, to be incapable of destruction, in the only way deemed relevant, by dissolution into further components.

This seems to me the gist of Shoemaker's central thesis. Let us look at the details. The arguments turn much here on the questions of individuation and identity. This is in line with much that has recently been said by philosophers opposed to Cartesian views, even those who would not wish to give a behaviorist or a physicalist account of mental processes, for example, A. J. Ayer, P. F. Strawson and, very explicitly, Bernard Williams. What they say, in brief, is that, if it were not for the body, we could not be individuated, and Williams at least appears not unsympathetic, in that context, to the notion of a universal mind, at least as what we would have to think if we retained the notion of mental processes without bodies. The idea of a universal mind or some strictly shared, unindividuated consciousness has appealed to many religious thinkers and to psychologists from time to time—it is a widely held interpretation of mysticism. Many post-Hegelian idealists subscribed to it, and there might for that reason be some grounds for rebuking Shoemaker for not reckoning with this possibility—it is the approach that many who would defend the belief in immortality would be disposed to take. I do not myself, however, wish to make much of this point, partly because no one can deal with everything in one paper, and Shoemaker has his distinct target in Cartesian Dualism, but even more because there are few views which seem to me more mistaken than the notion of unindividuated finite minds, and I have done my own share of blowing upon it, in itself and in its ethical and religious consequences.

There must, then, I agree, be individuation. But how is this possible if the immaterial substances in question cannot, as the thought of them would seem to imply, "be individuated by spatial relations"? This problem, I must now add, does not worry me a great deal, and it never has. It has always seemed evident to me that everyone knows himself to be the being that he is in just being so. We identify ourselves to ourselves in that way, and not in the last resort on the basis of what we know about ourselves. The reaction to this is sometimes to retort that we seem to be running out of arguments, and we must surely make our case by argument. This is a trying situation for a philosopher to have to meet; quite clearly he does not want to seem unwilling to argue. But argument is not everything, we have also to reckon with what we just find to be the case, we cannot conjure all existence into being by argument and we cannot, as I hope does not sound portentous, argue against reality. There is a way of looking at what there is, and wisdom in philosophy has been thought, from Plato to Wittgenstein, to depend largely on knowing how to look. The bane of much philosophy, past and present, has been the supposition that we must provide arguments for everything, and Shoemaker himself seems to be in some measure a victim of this, as may perhaps become plainer later. Admittedly, famous dualists, Plato and Descartes, have been apt on occasion to fall back on very formal arguments little worthy of their proper attainments, and I suppose Descartes must have regarded the *Cogito* [4] as a strictly rationalist a priori argument; but the real strength of the *Cogito* lies elsewhere—the 'I think' refers to experience and

4. As also the Ontological Argument, although what remains is an initial insight into there having to be some necessary being.

what we find it to be. This does not commit us to dogmatism or an unthinking commitment to this or that view, or to the lack of taught thinking. It is just a caveat about the a priori and the wrong sort of exclusive reliance on argument. I shall not pursue this further, and I have indicated more fully elsewhere [5] how, without any quasi-empirical looking in on ourselves, we find ourselves to be the distinctive beings that we are in the fact of being so, and in the same way are aware of having the experiences we do have.

It is quite otherwise when we think of how we know, not ourselves but one another. I am not convinced that spatial media, or their like, are altogether essential for knowledge of other persons, and I have tried [6] to sketch how, taking telepathy as a possible partial clue, we might communicate in what I have called 'A world of thoughts alone'. But I readily admit that, in identifying other persons, normally at least in present conditions, we require observable evidence, though what we do establish is not itself observable. I shall not develop this further now, and must leave it with what I have said elsewhere, although a brief reference will have to be made to the same point below. But let us return to the way Shoemaker proceeds.

He does not think that the requirement of 'spatial relations' is altogether fatal even to Cartesian Dualism, although he notes that this has often been thought to be the case. But this is for very different reasons from those I might adduce.

He observes that we have to admit, and on the whole may do so without jeopardy to Cartesian Dualism, that immaterial substances can interact causally with material substances. That was certainly Descartes's intention and that of any dualist who claims to make sense of common experience. Shoemaker does indeed here touch upon the somewhat hoary objection of how minds having, ex hypothesi, "no spatial relationship such as contiguity" can affect material bodies and, in each case, one particular body—one recalls John Passmore observing [7] that

---

5. *The Elusive Mind* (London, 1969), chap. XI, and *The Self and Immortality*, chap. 5.
6. *The Self and Immortality*, chap. 9.
7. *Philosophical Reasoning* (London, 1961), chap. III.

minds do not push and bodies do not persuade. But he thinks we "must suppose that this difficulty can be overcome". The difficulty is not to my mind all that serious. It is indeed strange that minds do affect bodies, and vice versa, and peculiar, though generally fortunate, that one mind affects just one body. There seems to be no way in which we can account for this (and to postulate 'mysterious transactions' as Gilbert Ryle and others would require of their opponents is only to make matters worse). But here again we must not go against the facts because we have reached the limit of further explanation—no causal relation can be quite exhaustively explained. We must again take the world as we find it, and we do find that states of mind affect bodies (one particular body normally at least) and bodies minds. But granted this how do we proceed?

We come here to the crux of Shoemaker's thesis. If the difficulties in the supposition that immaterial substances can interact causally with material substances "can be overcome" (and if it cannot what do we say to the out-and-out materialist?), then we can establish relationships between substances of these two sorts, analogous to the spatial relationships which have their role in determining causal relationships between material substances and establishing their identity; and on the basis of these "quasi-spatial relationships" we can establish further "quasi-spatial relationships" between the immaterial substances themselves and, on this basis, determine their identity and continuity through time. This can furthermore apply to Cartesian Dualism and to Non-Cartesian Dualism, and it is for this reason, it seems, that the former cannot be rejected expressly by its failure to cope with the question of individuation. But in that case, how does Cartesian Dualism come to grief?

It comes to grief, as Shoemaker seems to hold, because of the availability to us, on the basis of what has just been outlined, of the notion of immaterial substances which can *have parts*. As he sums it up: "Finally, and this is, of course, the point of all this, if it is possible for immaterial substances (or things) to have parts or components; then there seems no reason to suppose that immaterial substances are not subject to destruction through the dissolution of their parts" (p. 272). There are further points in the elaboration of this to which I shall return. But first we should have the core, or central theme, of the argument clear. And the sum of it seems to be this. We might be tempted to object, as our first move, that the argument could cut in another way than the one intended by Shoemaker, that is, we might argue that, because Cartesian Dualism is available to us, we can reject Non-Cartesian Dualism. For all that has been shown that might be true. But I do not think this would quite take the force of Shoemaker's special contention here. What he seems to be holding is that, since Non-Cartesian Dualism is available, we cannot claim that immaterial substances as such are bound to be without parts and indestructible. And the presupposition of all this, in turn, seems to be that we need to establish in an a priori way the essential indestructibility of immaterial substance, and that by dissolution into parts. But how is this requirement itself established? Even within the ambit of Shoemaker's own procedures it could be urged that, as Cartesian Dualism has not been shown to be incoherent (and Shoemaker fully admits that) a person could, for all that has been shown, be a Cartesian substance in the present sense and so, ex hypothesi, indestructible.

In other words, why, on the argument as we have followed it hitherto, does anyone who hesitates to go along with Shoemaker have to show "that Cartesian Dualism is the only coherent form of dualism" (p. 272)? [8] If I have missed something vital here I shall be relieved to be shown what it is. It will not, of course, be enough to bring forward other reasons for rejecting, or having doubts about, Cartesian Dualism.

Let me now refer to other points of difficulty in the elaboration of Shoemaker's main thesis.

I would like first to reflect further on the way the notion of a person must be understood in the context of Shoemaker's notion of Non-Cartesian Dualism, and, in particular, to be clear

8. It could, I suppose, be argued, that the Cartesian Dualist has to hold that mental states are necessarily identical with those of an immaterial substance and that, in consequence, his position becomes untenable even if we can consider an alternative view. But the Cartesian Dualist would only hold his view on reflection on what he finds to be the case, not on some independent a priori ground.

how person and substance are taken to be related here. First of all, what would an immaterial substance, not itself the person, be in this case? Is it a Lockean 'something we know not what', and do we then just have to 'suppose' it? Or a Kantian 'thing in itself', and on which of the many versions of this? I do not by any means rule out the possibility that there may be types of existences of which we know nothing at present, as implied in the celebrated notion of 'infinite attributes'. We know only mental and physical reality, at least explicitly. The universe may have other things in it of which we have no conception. Is Shoemaker thinking along these or kindred lines? I doubt it. In that case, the immaterial substance, in the present context, must be some combination of mental states, on which more in a moment, and the quasi-spatial relationships indicated—or perhaps some combination of the latter alone (but where, in that case, would mental states come in?). Is the substance in the latter case to be defined exhaustively in terms of such combinations—if not what is left over? And where, in all this, does the person, which is not the substance, figure?

I suspect that the answer to the last question is that a person is a further combination of immaterial substances, and their relationships, and perhaps material substances. If so, it begins to be a far cry from what we normally think of persons. But it will certainly help to have this matter clarified. Moreover, when we are told that there could "(perhaps)" [9] be "atomic" immaterial substances, is this intended seriously, and where does it figure, if it does, in the account of persons and substances, if the latter at least require the quasi-spatial relationships for their identification?

The only clear example we are offered, to help us to determine how persons must be understood—or what constitutes a person—is not very helpful in fact. It is that of the Supreme Court on page 270. This is brought up in the context where it seems to be admitted that persons may be "simple and indivisible" although the relevant substances need not be so. One reaction to this would be to point out that, when people concern themselves with questions of immortality and survival of death,

9. Page 271.

it is persons that they have especially in mind—it is persons who are immortal, etc.—and if persons may after all turn out to be "simple and indivisible" they would qualify without more ado for Shoemaker—what is simple cannot be destroyed. But let us look more closely at the example itself.

The Supreme Court, it appears, is "in some important sense without parts and indivisible". This is, apparently, because it would continue to exist if all the members died or resigned at the same time. Now it certainly would be true that the Supreme Court, as part of the American Constitution, would continue in these sad circumstances, and it could function as before as soon as new members were appointed—and so indeed for any committee. A committee does not lapse when all its members leave. But what is it that remains? Surely a system of rules and procedures, for the appointment of members and their rights and duties—terms of reference, the rights of the chairman, etc. And while these are not manifold in the case in which the individual members are, they certainly involve some complexity and interrelations of parts. The Supreme Court is a fairly elaborate part of an elaborate constitution.

But in any case is this a proper model for our concept of a person? There are indeed doctrines of corporate personality, but when they are not explicitly taken to refer to legal or quasi-legal fictions, they seem to be misleading and, in fact, mischievous doctrines. Post-Hegelian idealists welcomed them, though in some cases with reluctance, and the sinister consequences of entertaining them were effectively exhibited by L. T. Hobhouse in his celebrated *The Metaphysical Theory of the State,* as relevant in its day as it is in ours. Hannah Arendt has taken up the same cause with vigor and eloquence in our time. This is a topic in itself, and having made it a central theme of some of my own writings, I must leave it there now. But the meeting of extremes in this way is not, perhaps, as unimportant a feature of current philosophy as some might suppose. When it appears in the work of highly professional and cautious thinkers like Shoemaker and Strawson [10] one wonders whether they appreciate whither their thoughts may be tending.

10. P. F. Strawson, *Individuals* (London, 1959), p. 113.

I should maintain by contrast that the person is the distinct individual, and to think of persons by analogy with abstract systems seems to put us gravely in danger of substituting hypostatized abstractions for individual beings. As a rule, in Western thought at least, it is of oneself as a particular being and not of some abstract constitution of one's individual existence, that one is thinking in relation to the prospect of immortality, whether that is attractive or not. The constitution of my own nature, or my 'values' as some have supposed, is repeatable, presumably ad infinitum and in diverse conditions. But will *I* live again?

Even in Oriental thought, the position, if properly scrutinized (as, alas, rarely happens) may not be as accommodating to Shoemaker's notions as some might be inclined to assume. But that is also a theme in itself.

Let me now add a brief word on mental states as they figure in Shoemaker's paper. Here we come closer to a materialist position than I thought previously he wished to go. The status of mental states is, we are told, the same as it would be if materialism were true, the view that whatever exists "is either a material substance or something whose existence consists in the existence of material substances, their states, and their relations to one another" (p. 273). But this does not apparently mean that mental states are just neurophysiological states of the brain. A person could in fact be in pain without having the neurophysiological states of my brain, or indeed of brains and bodies like ours at all when we are in pain. A mental state may have "sometimes one physical 'realization' and sometimes another". If this merely meant that the same mental state could conceivably be caused by different physical states, I would not dispute it. But it seems to mean more. There is no admission that the mental state is essentially (perhaps I could be allowed the word 'ontologically') other than its physical conditions. It is rather that we must adopt "a causal, or functional, analysis of mental concepts". The causal role of certain neurophysiological states could be taken over by others. Pain may thus be 'realized' in different sorts of physiological states. But just what is it that is being 'realized' What is being caused, what function is exercised—an exclusively physical or behavioral one? This seems most implausible.

Indeed, I must confess here to head-on collision with my cosymposiast. For while he could admit (and this makes him appear to concede a great deal more than he does) that pain could be "merely realized" in some immaterial attribute of an immaterial substance, in what may seem by now a rather unusual view of the latter, the pain could not be "*identical with* an immaterial attribute," for then it could not be 'realized in a physical attribute of a material substance.' Against this, which appears to be essential for Shoemaker's system, I should want to insist that pain, like all other mental states, is essentially an immaterial attribute and that a causal or functional definition does not begin to do justice to the facts. There are normally physical conditions of pain, and there is pain behavior. But I had hoped that it would be evident to philosophers by now that pain is neither of these, or their like. It is what I *feel*. I know it in experiencing it and in no other way. I could learn to recognize the physical accompaniments and the behavior but this would not tell me what pain was. I might also have pain without any awareness of conditions (a wound perhaps) which would normally induce it—or any disposition to behave in the way normally expected of people in pain. And so, even more obviously, of thoughts, the ones that go on while writing this paper or speaking to it. These are what I find them at the time to be, and that is essentially nonspatial reality. I have no independent proof of this, I can only reflect and invite you to reflect on what I find my experience to be like, and if this is not allowed, then I must protest against being put out of court before the only proper case can be stated.

The same goes for our knowledge of one another. Shoemaker reverts to the stock objection to a Cartesian account, namely that empirical evidence cannot tell us anything about a 'spiritual' or nonempirical substance. But why not? Shoemaker himself notes that if I saw "what looks like someone who is, with great ingenuity and resourcefulness, repairing a complicated machine" he would take it without question "to be a person having mental states". But if this is so obvious, is it not equally plain that the mental states, far from being merely causal or functional, are ongoing thoughts and purposings such as each of us would be aware of in the process of having them in his own case? Admittedly, in knowing other persons, we do not proceed through correlations of behavior and directly inspected states of mind of other beings, as that is ex hypothesi out of the question. But that, as Ryle and others have overlooked, is no bar to our finding the observable behavior explicable on the assumption of designs and purposes such as we have in our own inner life. It is sheer unwarranted dogma that empirical evidence can only establish empirical things.

This shows us what is wrong with the example of the Martian and the Venusians at the end of the paper. It is, of course, possible to be mistaken about one another, and we can never wholly eliminate that. With a different 'evolutionary history', etc., the same outward behavior may reflect a different state of mind, but this is something we could only discover if we had very elaborate evidence. In these peculiar circumstances we certainly could not know from the limited evidence of the present occasion that one of the creatures had not the thoughts and purposes we would normally ascribe to it. But in due course, from sufficiently comprehensive evidence, we would expect to discover this. And if for some reason we did not discover it, that would be just too bad, as in the case where we are, as often happens, at a loss in the case of identical twins. Such confusion, or failure of identity, is no bar to the confidence we otherwise have about identity and the ascription of mental states. But if the only course were to establish by some direct independent inspection a causal relation between physical and nonphysical states, the sort of quandaries that Shoemaker envisages would present insurmountable problems.

It may be urged at this point that I have not said much in a positive way myself about the possible simplicity of the self or subject and the relation of this to the obviously varied and changing mental states that we have. My reaction is that I find this a peculiarly difficult philosophical question, though in a very different way from Shoemaker. There seems to me to be a very unique or distinctive way in which everyone finds himself to be the being that he is, whether he reflects on that or not. We are also aware that certain states of mind are ours in the fact of having them. I do not, to keep to the relatively simple stock example of pain, infer that I am in pain—I do not have to tell myself, or note my bleeding finger or swollen limbs or hear my own cries. These are the ways in which I know that someone else is in pain, and if a coach were blacked out in an accident I might wonder which of my companions is in pain. I would not wonder about myself. I would know that I had the pain in having it, it is very much myself; I do not know first that there is a pain, and wonder about the ascription of it as in the case of other persons. I know it immediately as mine, and by this token, though not certain always in other cases who is in pain, I have no conception of a pain that is not in this immediate sense someone's pain. There could not be just a 'floating' pain. But to find adequate terms for this is peculiarly difficult—'belong', 'owned', etc., have associations with physical belonging (or with rights) which are quite out of place here, though we may have to be content with a cautious use of such metaphors. A hasty and oversimple use of terms in this sort of context is the bane of sound philosophy, and it is better to say nothing at all than be too hasty. There is, all the same, a peculiarly intimate sense in which a pain, or any other mental state—thoughts, purposing, etc.—is me or mine; and at the same time this is also not strictly correct.

It is not correct, not just because there is more to any of us than just being in this particular state, having this pain, etc., but also because I would be the being that I am, and know this, even if I did not have the actual states of mind I do have, or if all my experiences were different. The latter would make a difference in one sense to my identity, the sense in which I do not know who I am in loss of memory or split personality. But basic to all this is the sense of my being the one I find myself to be, an ultimate irreducible sense, in those or any other contingencies. Even if I should be born again, as on reincarnation theories, in some entirely different conditions, and with no knowledge of my present existence, I would have, in this new state, the same basic sense of being the being that I am in my present state, though ex hypothesi I could not know this, having no way, on our supposition, of knowing, by memory or other evidence, what had gone on previously.

There is in this way a simplicity and finality or ultimacy about personal identity to which no proper parallel is to be found elsewhere, though philosophers go astray, as many do today, by neglecting this and looking too closely for models or parallels in other cases of identity external to ourselves. At the same time our ongoing mental states are also, as was stressed, ourselves in a very distinct sense; and I am not at all happy about any way of presenting this situation. Perhaps there is not much more that we can say, but in granting the tension between similar, but not quite reconcilable, things we are forced to say, we may here be getting as deep as we can into the philosophical apprehension of the subject. I certainly want to say that the self is simple in the sense that it could not be or become another, however much the kind of experiences we may have may overlap or be shared. Nor is a person just the experiences he happens to have. At the same time, a self is not to be too sharply dissociated from the actual experiences or mental states it does have.

With this, and the awareness that much harder thought may have to be given to this subject to take it further than I have done, I return to the points I made at the start, namely that the most immediate relevance of the view of persons and identity which I advance to the question of immortality lies in the disassociation of the self, in its essential nature, from the bodily state which we have every reason to expect to be completely ended in due course. The issue of simplicity or finality does indeed relate very expressly to questions of absorption in some more complete or universal existence, which is how some think of immortality. But the alleged indestructibility of the simple has not, on my view, much significance at all. If it came within God's purpose that a tree should be conserved forever, I see no reason in logic, from the fact that a tree obviously has parts, why this could not be. But if I am identical with my body I cannot expect to be conserved in the absence of what seems altogether unlikely, namely the conservation as well of this seemingly mortal coil. But to dissociate a person, in essential being, from any material state is not to make the case positively for either survival or immortality; it is to remove an obstacle and make a start, but there is a long way to go beyond that.

15

Remarks

GODFREY VESEY

This symposium is on immortality, the endless existence of a person after what we call his 'death'. The symposiasts—Sydney Shoemaker of Cornell University and Hywel D. Lewis of King's College, London—agree about some things. They agree about bodily resurrection not being the answer. Shoemaker says of the belief in bodily resurrection that even if it cannot be faulted on logical or conceptual grounds, most people would agree that there are overwhelming empirical grounds for rejecting it. And Lewis says that the chances of resuscitating a corpse are too remote to be taken seriously.

I find this puzzling. The Christian belief in bodily resurrection is one of a number of religious beliefs, which include the belief that God is omnipotent. Believing in the omnipotence of God means thinking of everyday considerations as not having the ultimate importance which the nonreligious person attaches to them. It means thinking that with God everything is possible. What I find puzzling is that Lewis, who is a religious person, seems to regard the belief in resurrection as being on a par with nonreligious beliefs; that is, as being the object of the same sorts of evidence, for and against, as nonreligious beliefs. What I would have expected of a religious person is an expression of faith even in the face of evidence which the nonreligious person would regard as conclusive. Peter Geach, at the end of Chapter 2 of his book *God and the Soul*, writes: 'The traditional faith of Christianity, inherited from Judaism, is that at the end of this age Messiah will come and men rise from their graves to die no more. That faith is not going to be shaken by inquiries about bodies burned to ashes or eaten by beasts; those who

301

might well suffer just such death in martyrdom were those who were most confident of a glorious reward in the resurrection. One who shares that hope will hardly wish to take out an occultistic or philosophical insurance policy, to guarantee some sort of survival as an annuity, in case God's promise of resurrection should fail.' [1] I think the explanation must be that Lewis does not share that hope. He does not accept what Geach calls 'the traditional faith of Christianity' about immortality. And so he treats talk of resurrection as something to be dismissed on scientific grounds.

There is something else on which Lewis and Shoemaker agree. They agree in thinking that if bodily resurrection is not the answer then there can be immortality only if people are not what we ordinarily think of them as being. Antony Flew once remarked: 'People are what you meet. We do not meet only the sinewy containers in which other people are kept, and they do not encounter only the fleshy houses that we ourselves inhabit.' [2] The alternative to bodily resurrection as an account of immortality involves the denial of this common-sense notion of what a person is. It involves the idea that a person is essentially a nonbodily being—a being that is housed, for the duration of its natural life, in a body. In short, it involves some form of dualism, the doctrine that the people we meet are really compounds of bodies and 'souls' or 'minds'.

Now we come to where the symposiasts part company. Roughly, whereas Lewis is a Cartesian Dualist, and thinks he has an answer to such objections to Cartesian Dualism as that there are no criteria for the personal identity of a nonbodily survivor, Shoemaker is not a Cartesian Dualist. He agrees with Lewis that the only hope for immortality lies in some form of dualism, but he has doubts about Cartesian Dualism. He has another form of dualism to offer us, but it turns out that while it may provide for a limited span of afterlife, it does not guarantee the endless variety. So, in brief, while Lewis thinks that the endless existence of a person after his death is on the cards,

1. (London, 1969), p. 29.
2. "Immortality," in Paul Edwards, ed., *The Encyclopedia of Philosophy* (New York, 1967), IV, 142.

the cards being Cartesian ones, Shoemaker is more than skeptical. I should perhaps add that Lewis says no more than that immortality is on the cards. He does not say that Cartesian Dualism guarantees immortality. It is only an *enabling* doctrine. Shoemaker, on the other hand, treats Cartesian Dualism, if only we could accept it, as implying immortality.

I am not going to take you through the papers in detail. They are fairly straightforward as philosophical papers go, and Lewis usefully recapitulates a good many of the points raised by Shoemaker. I think it may be more helpful if I spell out the main difficulty in an attempt to give meaning to personal immortality in terms of the survival of a Cartesian soul-substance, and comment on Lewis's way of meeting the difficulty, insofar as I understand it.

Many philosophers use the term 'substance'. Aristotle distinguishes between 'primary substance', the individual man or horse, and 'secondary substance', the essence which makes the individual the kind of individual it is, for example, an equine individual. Descartes seems to want the term 'substance' to refer at one and the same time to a *thing* and to a *property*. A substance is 'a thing existing in such a manner that it has need of no other thing in order to exist'. So a substance is a thing. On the other hand his test of the distinction between substances is in terms of properties. If one can think of something as being conscious without thinking of it as being bodily then, God willing, there is a substance, mind, distinct from matter. I am not saying that Descartes is wrong. What I am saying is that I do not understand. I would understand if what he meant was that the property of being conscious is distinct from the property of being bodily. But he wants more than that. He wants 'this self (*moi*), that is to say the soul, by which I am what I am' to be distinct from the body, and so capable of being what it is 'even if the body were not there at all'.[3] The use of the personal pronoun 'I' is significant. He is concerned about *his* survival (and the survival of other 'I's), not the survival of consciousness as such, whatever that means. What I do not understand can be

3. *Descartes: Philosophical Writings*, ed. Elizabeth Anscombe and Peter Thomas Geach (London, 1954), p. 32.

put in the form of a question: Whence, on Descartes's account, comes the idea of souls, of there being different conscious things of which I am one? Consciousness as such does not make me the person I am, as distinct from other persons. There seems, in Descartes's account, to be no principle of individuation. A thing is not individuated by a property it shares with other things. A kind of thing, yes; but not a thing. (This, I think, may explain the attraction for Shoemaker of what he calls Non-Cartesian Dualism. There is a thing, a 'ghostly brain', of which consciousness is a property. But then there is the problem of explaining what a ghostly brain is.)

If people are 'what you meet' (to use Flew's expression) there is no problem. I can meaningfully ascribe things to myself as distinct from others. I am talking, you are not, and so on. It is what is meant by 'myself' when people are not 'what you meet' that is the problem.

One way of solving the problem would be with a piece of metaphysics in the grand style. For instance one may, with Fichte, pronounce the principle that 'The Ego posits originally and simply its own being', [4] a self-positing act about which Fichte later said: 'It requires each one to note what he necessarily does when he calls himself "I". It assumes that every one who really performs the required act, will find that he *affirms himself*, or, which may be clearer to many, that he is at the same time subject and object.' [5]

What Lewis says is that 'everyone knows himself to be the being that he is in just being so' and that 'we identify ourselves to ourselves in that way', that is, in a way that is quite different from the way we identify other people and they identify us. He says that he does not have an argument for this view; it is just something we find to be the case.

It is hard to understand, never mind criticize, a view for which no argument is advanced. At the risk of doing Lewis an injustice I shall take him to be saying something like what Fichte says, and comment on the assumption which Fichte says lies behind his principle about the Ego positing itself, the as-

4. *Werke,* F. Medicus, ed. (Leipzig, 1908–1912), I, 98.
5. Ibid., II, 441.

sumption about what a person 'necessarily does when he calls himself "I" '.

The point I want to make can be put quite simply. A person does *not* 'call himself "I" '. He uses the word 'I', certainly; but it is not a name. So the idea that a person is acquainted with something of which the word 'I' is a name, when he uses the word 'I', is wrong. Philosophers like Bertrand Russell [6] and J. McT. E. McTaggart [7] who had this idea made a mistake. The word 'I' is no more used to name a person than the word 'here' is used to name a place.

How is it, then, that so many philosophers have thought otherwise? What can explain their illusion of self-awareness? Let us pursue the analogy of 'I' with 'here'.

There is an informative use of 'here', as in 'I'm here' shouted to someone who can tell from what direction the sound has come, or 'Your passport's here' said to someone who can see the speaker looking in a drawer. Suppose that, *although I am quite lost*, I say *to myself* 'I know where I am, I'm here'. This use of 'here', although completely uninformative, may seem to be a significant, nonempty, use. It borrows a façade of meaning from the informative uses. Similarly, an empty, soliloquizing, use of 'I' may borrow a façade of meaning from the informative, interpersonal, uses.

Lewis, in his book *The Elusive Mind*, to which he refers in his paper, distinguishes two senses of 'identity'. I shall call them 'self-identity' and 'personal identity'. A person's 'personal identity' is what he does not known if he suffers from amnesia. But he still knows his self-identity, according to Lewis. Lewis holds that self-identity is primary, personal identity secondary. I maintain, on the contrary, that this is like saying that the empty use of 'here' is primary.[8] Saying what Lewis says, 'Everyone knows himself to be the being that he is in just being so', is like saying 'Everyone knows where he is, in that he can say "I'm here" and not be wrong'. If 'here' were the name of a place he

6. *The Problems of Philosophy* (London, 1912), p. 51.
7. *The Nature of Existence* (Cambridge, 1927), II, chap. 36, p. 63.
8. Godfrey Vesey, *Personal Identity: A Philosophical Analysis* (Ithaca, N.Y., 1977), p. 36.

really would know something. But it is not. No more is 'I' the name of a thing. Self-identification is an illusion, and so cannot give meaning to talk of personal immortality.

I am left with the conclusion that only bodily resurrection can do that. And bodily resurrection is a matter of faith, not of philosophy.

Postscript

SYDNEY SHOEMAKER

I shall not try to comment on more than a few of the points raised in Lewis's paper and Vesey's remarks.

Vesey speaks at one point of "the attraction for Shoemaker of what he calls Non-Cartesian Dualism" (p. 304). I hope that I made it clear in my paper that the "attraction" of this position for me is severely limited. The sole virtue I claim for Non-Cartesian Dualism is that it is the one version of dualism that seems to me not open to decisive logical objections. I have not the slightest inclination to think that it is true. The question of whether it is true I regard as a scientific rather than a philosophical question; and as best I can tell (as a sheer amateur on such matters) it is hardly more in the running as a scientific hypothesis than, say, the phlogiston theory of combustion. But if it *could* be, or *could have been*, true—if its truth is a logical possibility—then this seems to me of considerable philosophical interest. (For the sake of brevity I shall allow myself to speak in the following of such positions as "possible" or "impossible"; to say that a position like Non-Cartesian Dualism is possible will not mean that it may be true for all we know, but that it is logically possible that it should be, or should have been, true.)

One consequence of the possibility of Non-Cartesian Dualism is the impossibility of Cartesian Dualism. I make this point partly for the benefit of those broad-minded materialists who are fond of saying that while dualism is false, it could have been true, and so is not false as a matter of necessity. This can only be said of Non-Cartesian Dualism. Cartesian Dualism, unlike Non-Cartesian Dualism, is either necessarily true or necessarily false; so if it is not true it is not possible (i.e., its truth is not a logical possibility).

As Lewis points out, someone might try to argue from the (alleged) possibility of Cartesian Dualism to the impossibility of Non-Cartesian Dualism. Such an argument would be logically valid; for if Cartesian Dualism were possible, Non-Cartisian Dualism would not be. But where would it get its premise? Cartesian Dualism is possible only if it is true. And how could one argue for its truth? Quite apart from their other defects, the standard empirical and a priori arguments in favor of dualism are all such that they establish Cartesian Dualism only if it is the only possible form of dualism, and so only if Non-Cartesian Dualism is not one. But it would obviously be question-begging to assume the latter if the conclusion that Cartesian Dualism is true is to be used as a premise in an argument against the possibility of Non-Cartesian Dualism.

I think that Lewis suspects that I beg the question in the same way in arguing against Cartesian Dualism. But in order to claim that Non-Cartesian Dualism is possible I do not have to claim that it is true. And all that I have to maintain, in order to reject Cartesian dualism, is something even weaker than the claim that Non-Cartesian Dualism is possible—namely, that *if* it is conceivable there should be immaterial substances at all, and if *any* form of substance dualism is possible, then Non-Cartesian Dualism is possible. This seems to me plainly true, although I do not claim to have proven it in my paper.

As Lewis notices, I do not claim in my paper to have shown that Cartesian Dualism is incoherent or otherwise impossible, and claim only to have shown that there is no reason to suppose it true. To establish the stronger conclusion I would have had to show something which I had only enough space to hint at in my paper, namely that only on some version of the causal or functional theory of mental states—the view that mental states are to be defined in terms of their causal and other "topic neutral" relations to one another and to sensory input and behavioral output—is it possible to account for our knowledge of other minds, and that any such account is incompatible with Cartesian Dualism. I hoped to bring this out in my discussion of the case of the Venusian and the Martian, but I am afraid that I did not indicate clearly enough how I intended that case to be understood. Lewis assumes (reasonably enough from what I wrote) that it is only "the limited evidence of the present occasion" that would prevent us from concluding that one of these creatures lacks the mental states we would normally ascribe on the basis of the behavior it manifests, and that "in due course, from sufficiently comprehensive evidence we would expect to discover this" (p. 297). But the case I envisaged, which seems to me a possible one, is one in which this could not be discovered; it is one in which the different internal "makeups" (both material and immaterial) of the two creatures give them the same behavioral repertoires, and in which throughout their histories, and not just for some limited period of time, both exhibit the sorts of behavior we would normally take as establishing conclusively that something is a conscious, sentient, and intelligent being. Cartesian Dualism is committed to the possibility that in one or the other of these creatures, or in both, there are no mental states whatever, because the right sorts of immaterial states are lacking. Nor does there seem to be anything in this theory to imply that this is even unlikely. On such a theory, I believe, it is impossible that we should ever be justified in ascribing mental states on the basis of behavior; and a view that has this consequence seems to me plainly false. But to nail down the conclusion that Cartesian Dualism has this skeptical consequence I would have to show why the proponent of Cartesian Dualism cannot resort to the "argument from analogy" as an account of how we can have knowledge of other minds—and my allotted space did not permit me to argue this.[1]

Vesey says that I treat Cartesian Dualism as implying immortality. This is not quite right, although I can see why he says it. I do claim that arguments for dualism would have to support Cartesian Dualism in order to have any chance of showing persons to have a metaphysical immunity to destruction or dissolution from natural causes, e.g., in virtue of being "simple." This is because no such immunity is accorded them by Non-Car-

1. See, in this connection, my "The Problem of Other Minds," in Joel Feinberg, ed., *Reason and Responsibility*, 3d ed. (Encino, Calif., 1975), and my "Embodiment and Behavior," in Amelie Rorty, ed., *The Identities of Persons* (Berkeley and Los Angeles, 1976).

tesian Dualism. There is, to be sure, a prima facie plausibility in the idea that what is simple and without parts could not go out of existence (except by divine fiat). But my Supreme Court example was intended to show, among other things, that in one natural sense of "having/lacking parts" something which lacks parts (and so is in that sense "simple") can go out of existence. A better example, perhaps, is that used by Simmias in the *Phaedo,* namely the "attunement" of an instrument; there is no obvious sense in which the attunement has parts, yet plainly it ceases to exist if the instrument is broken. Of course, it will be part of Cartesian Dualism that the soul (self, person) is not only simple but also is not dependent for its existence on the existence of composite entities, in the way in which both the Supreme Court and the attunement of an instrument are dependent for their existence on such entities. Even so, I do not see how to deduce the immortality of the soul from the Cartesian Dualist's characterization of it, unless the former is simply incorporated into the latter as a part.

I should perhaps take this opportunity to assure Lewis that in introducing my perhaps ill-chosen Supreme Court example I was not proposing the Supreme Court as a proper model for our concept of a person, and was not flirting with mischievous doctrines of corporate personality. I was only trying to make the point that materialism is compatible with the existence of things which are in some sense without parts (and, by the way, that such things are not immune to annihilation), and so may be compatible with some versions of the thesis that persons are "simple."

While Lewis does not put much stock in metaphysical arguments for immortality based on the alleged simplicity of the self, he does claim that "the self is simple in the sense that it could not be or become another" (p. 299). But this seems to me either false or vacuous. It is false if it implies the denial of what would ordinarily be meant by saying that when I die and am cremated I will become a pile of ashes which will not be me. It is vacuous if it means that as long as a self exists it will be nothing other than itself. If the latter—being such that it cannot be other than itself—makes the self simple, nothing whatever could fail to be simple.

I am in basic agreement with what Vesey says against Lewis's view that "everyone knows himself to be the being that he is in just being so." But I fail to see how he gets from this to his conclusion that only bodily resurrection can "give meaning to talk of personal immortality." Nothing he says has any tendency to show that Non-Cartesian Dualism is meaningless or impossible; and if it is possible, then it is logically possible that there should be personal immortality without bodily resurrection. As far as intelligibility is concerned, immortality with resurrection and immortality without resurrection seem to me on a par. They are also on a par, I think, as far as plausibility is concerned.

Index

Contents

Library of Congress Cataloging in Publication Data
(For library cataloging purposes only)

Main entry under title:

Reason and religion.

  (Cornell paperbacks)
  Papers originated at a conference sponsored by the Royal Institute of
Philosophy and held at the University of Lancaster in 1975.
  Includes index.
  1. Religion—Philosophy—Congresses. 2. Good and evil—Congresses.
3. Immortality—Congresses. I. Brown, Stuart C. II. Royal Institute of
Philosophy.
BL51.R325   200'.1   77-3115
ISBN 0-8014-1025-8
ISBN 0-8014-9166-5 pbk.